WORD, IMAGE, AND THE NEW NEGRO

WORD, IMAGE,

REPRESENTATION AND IDENTITY

AND THE

IN THE HARLEM RENAISSANCE

NEW NEGRO

ANNE ELIZABETH CARROLL

INDIANA UNIVERSITY PRESS
Bloomington & Indianapolis

This book is a publication of
Indiana University Press
601 North Morton Street
Bloomington, IN 47404-3797 USA

http://iupress.indiana.edu
Telephone orders   800-842-6796
Fax orders   812-855-7931
Orders by e-mail   iuporder@indiana.edu

First paperback edition 2007
© 2005 by Anne Elizabeth Carroll
All rights reserved

Library of Congress Cataloging-in-Publication Data

Carroll, Anne Elizabeth, date
   Word, image, and the New Negro : representation and identity in the Harlem Renaissance / Anne Elizabeth Carroll.
     p. cm. — (Blacks in the diaspora)
   Includes bibliographical references and index.
   ISBN 978-0-253-34583-7 (cl. : alk. paper) ISBN 978-0-253-21919-0 (pbk.: alk. paper)
   1. Harlem Renaissance. 2. African Americans—Intellectual life—20th century. 3. African Americans—Race identity. 4. African American arts—History—20th century. 5. African Americans—New York (State)—New York—Intellectual life—20th century. 6. Harlem (New York, N.Y.)—Intellectual life—20th century. 7. New York (N.Y.)—Intellectual life—20th century. 8. African Americans in literature. 9. Ethnicity in literature. I. Title. II. Series.
   E185.6.C33 2005
   700'.89'9607307471—dc22
                                          2004015335

2   3   4   5   6   12   11   10   09   08   07

TO
MOM, DAD,
AND GRANDMA

CONTENTS

ILLUSTRATIONS

ACKNOWLEDGMENTS

I feel quite lucky to have attended the University of Maryland, College Park, for graduate school, where I began this study. I received wonderful support from many of the professors in the English Department. A number of them have extended their support through my years at Wichita State University. I am grateful for the continuing advice and support of Robert Levine and Elizabeth Bergmann Loizeaux and for helpful advice on the publishing process from Nicole King. Charles Caramello, who read drafts and drafts of this work, deserves special thanks for his patience and guidance. And Mary Helen Washington has been instrumental to my work on this project since I began. I deeply appreciate her generous gifts of time, feedback, and encouragement. They have been sustaining.

I would also like to thank the English Department and the Fairmount College of Liberal Arts at Wichita State University, particularly Dean William Bischoff and department chairs Margaret Dawe and Lawrence Davis. I am grateful for course releases in two semesters, a summer support grant from the college, and financial support from the department and the college. The staff of the Interlibrary Loan office at Ablah Library at Wichita State University also has my appreciation for its collective cheerfulness and unflagging willingness to provide me with the necessary materials, and I owe thanks to photographer Jim Meyer for his help in reproducing most of my illustrations. I also appreciate the time and efforts of Lacey Stratton and Sarah Rozzelle-Doom, who helped me with my quotations and my index.

I also wish to thank a number of scholars in African American literary and cultural studies who have offered support for my work: Houston Baker, George Hutchinson, Arnold Rampersad, and Cary Wintz. My respect for their work on the Harlem Renaissance—and the work of other scholars of the movement—is clear, I hope, in the endnotes of this book. I also want to thank Eric Sundquist and Cary Nelson, who read the manuscript and offered encouraging and helpful feedback.

A condensed version of my chapter on *The Crisis* appeared in *American Literature* (76.1 [March 2004]: 89–116). The anonymous readers for the journal and its editorial staff, particularly Frances Kerr and Priscilla Wald, offered insightful feedback and constructive criticism. I also published an essay on *Opportunity*—a combination of material that appears in chapters 2 and 3 here—in a special issue of *Soundings* on "The Future of the Harlem Renaissance" (80.4 [Winter 1997]: 607–40). The readers of the journal were kind enough to offer suggestions about an early draft of this piece that significantly helped me narrow my focus there and, in fact, in the project as a whole. My thanks to both journals for permission to reprint my essays here.

I also very much thank the members of the staff at Indiana University Press for their commitment to this work. Kendra Boileau, now at Rutgers University Press, guided this project through its early stages, and I appreciate her support and encouragement. Robert Sloan and Jane Quinet then took on the project, and they and other members of the staff at IUP have earned my gratitude for their support and enthusiasm. My thanks also to Cary Wintz and two anonymous readers of the press, who were remarkably generous with their time and expertise. The efforts of all have greatly helped me improve this work.

Finally, for listening to me talk through so much of this, I would like to thank my husband, John McConnell. I dedicate this book to my father, Dennis Carroll, and to the two women I am named for, my paternal grandmother, Betty Madden Work, and my mother, Margaret Ann Williams Carroll. I hope that this book does justice to the examples of dedication, courage, and persistence that they have provided.

WORD, IMAGE, AND THE NEW NEGRO

Introduction:
Texts, Ideas, and Identities

When I started this project at the University of Maryland, College Park, Professor Mary Helen Washington introduced me to *The New Negro,* an anthology edited by Alain Locke and published in 1925. As did many other African American intellectuals who participated in the Harlem Renaissance—or the New Negro movement, as they called it—Locke believed that a New Negro had emerged by the mid-1920s, an African American who by virtue of his accomplishments and spirit was far different from the Old Negro—or, more precisely, far different from African Americans as they had been represented in American popular culture. But too many Americans—particularly white Americans—were unaware of the realities of African Americans' lives. Locke conceived of his book, then, as a way to demonstrate them. As he wrote in his first sentence, "This volume aims to document the New Negro culturally and socially,—to register the transformations of the inner and outer life of the Negro in America that have so significantly taken place in the last few years" ("Foreword" ix).[1] The book, in short, was an effort by this African American editor and writer to intervene in the process of representation, to add to the available images of African Americans, and to publicize new ideas about African Americans.

Reading Locke's anthology for the first time, I was curious about how Locke attempted this project, what kinds of texts he used, and what he showed about African Americans. Those questions were surprisingly difficult to answer. My 1992 edition of *The New Negro* demonstrates that Locke used an impressive variety of texts to represent African Americans: essays, fiction, poetry, music, black-and-white drawings, and reproductions of art. But a few references to additional texts led me to a first edition of the book, where I also found stunning full-color portraits of Locke and other intellectual and creative leaders of the Harlem Renaissance. These seem essential to the book's project of representing the New Negro of the 1920s. They immediately engage the reader's attention like none of the other texts do, and they shape the reader's first impression of the New Negro. Furthermore, they add essential elements to the depiction of African Americans in the written texts, communicating information about African Americans that is not as clear elsewhere in the book. Without them, then, we miss important elements of Locke's portrayal.

I read a book like Locke's as an act of display, an act of holding up images of African Americans. My initial questions about who and what is shown and what kinds of texts are used can be supplemented with other questions: Who is creating this display? Who and what is left out? Are the arguments made in the texts complemented or complicated by the connotations of the kinds of texts used? How do the different kinds of texts, especially in differ-ent media, interact with one another? Do they complement one another, compete with one another, suggest opposing ideas?[2] As I continued to study the Harlem Renaissance, I found that these questions apply to many of its texts. The 1920s was a time when African Americans were able to create and publish texts to an unprecedented extent; it was a time, moreover, when they often combined many different kinds of texts in many different media. Pho-tographs, drawings, maps, charts, and graphic designs can be found in mag-azines such as *The Crisis, Opportunity,* and *The Messenger;* special issues fo-cusing on African Americans or the New Negro movement published in magazines like *World Tomorrow, Survey Graphic, Carolina Magazine,* and *Palms;* anthologies like *The New Negro* such as Charles S. Johnson's *Ebony and Topaz;* and books of poetry and fiction that were illustrated with cover art and drawings within the work, such as Countee Cullen's *Color,* Langston Hughes's *The Weary Blues,* James Weldon Johnson's *God's Trombones,* and Sterling Brown's *Southern Road.* These publications show that many partic-ipants in the Harlem Renaissance went out of their way to include visual texts with written texts. Editors, writers, and artists worked together to cre-ate multi-media portrayals of African Americans.

These collaborative efforts were not merely academic exercises, either. Many of the participants of the Harlem Renaissance believed that there was much at stake in these acts of representation. They hoped that texts like *The New Negro,* which demonstrated the accomplishments of African Americans and reflected the changes occurring in their lives, would alter how readers understood African Americans, and that this new understanding, in turn, would help undermine the racism that was still so painfully evident in America. In short, a text like *The New Negro* might carry out a kind of cul-tural work, might change readers' thinking and their actions. That possibil-ity raises the question of the effect of these texts. Did they succeed? Did they convince readers to respect African Americans? The easy answer, given the continued presence of racism, is that they failed. But these volumes were successful in other ways, and we can learn a great deal from them—about the Harlem Renaissance, about the relations between various kinds of texts, about the processes of representation.

Books such as *The New Negro* suggest a great deal about the Harlem Renaissance that is not so evident in other texts. First, the writers and artists of the Harlem Renaissance used many kinds of texts in different media to represent African Americans. Literary texts—the most often studied texts of the movement—constitute only one aspect of the struggle for representation during the movement. Second, these writers and artists were quite adept at and sophisticated about the processes of representation: they appropriated strategies from different disciplines and put them to work in creating images of African Americans. Furthermore, they identified a range of goals, each of which contributed to the overall process of changing public opinion about African Americans. Participants in the movement were not naive; they did not expect racism to disappear overnight. Instead, they launched an ongoing, ever-changing exploration of how texts might most effectively be used to undermine it. Finally, these texts reveal that their ideas about African Americans, too, were complex and dynamic. They developed sophisticated arguments about African American identity and came up with effective strategies for communicating those complicated ideas. In short, we find that participants in the Harlem Renaissance mastered a range of innovative strategies of representation and used them to successfully forward compelling images of African Americans.

Unfortunately, the full implications of the work of the Harlem Renaissance have yet to be appreciated by scholars of the movement, for these collaborative, illustrated magazines and anthologies, which are participants' most complicated efforts at representation, have largely been left out of assessments of the movement. A few of the books and magazines that include both written and visual elements have been discussed by scholars, but the relations among their various elements remain unexplored. Thus, for example, while the magazines of the Harlem Renaissance are recognized as being important supporters of and outlets for creative writers, the range of texts within them has not yet been analyzed, and while *The New Negro* is heralded as the defining anthology of the movement, only a few scholars have explored its inclusion of so many different kinds of texts. Other illustrated texts published during the Harlem Renaissance are only mentioned in passing. Unless we consider them, our judgments of the success of participants at representing African Americans are based on partial information.

My goal in this book is to return our attention to the collaborative illustrated volumes of the Harlem Renaissance and to use them as a basis for a reconsideration of the movement. I want us to rethink which texts we consider when we judge the movement, how we understand its goals, and how we measure its success. To urge us in that direction, I offer close readings of five illustrated volumes published during the 1910s and early 1920s. These include *The Crisis* and *Opportunity,* two magazines published by large organizations devoted to improving the treatment of African Americans; the March 1925 Harlem issue of the *Survey Graphic,* a magazine with a largely white readership; Locke's anthology; and *Fire!!,* an avant-garde arts journal launched by a group of young writers and artists in 1926. These serve as examples of the different kinds of illustrated volumes created by participants in the Harlem Renaissance. Each includes numerous depictions of African Americans in various media: each features some combination of visual texts —photographs, portraits, black-and-white drawings, and reproductions of paintings and sculptures—with written texts—news stories, essays, editorials, fiction, poetry, drama, transcriptions of music and folktales, biographical sketches, and bibliographies. These volumes thus offer particularly rich ground for exploring the question of how different kinds of texts work together to communicate information about African Americans. Furthermore, although each offers a relatively coherent collective portrait of African Americans, because each is collaborative—each includes contributions from many writers and artists—each presents a multitude of arguments about African Americans and a range of texts that put those ideas into practice. Each therefore hints at the complexity of the ideas about texts and identity that shaped the Harlem Renaissance. Taken together, finally, these five volumes demonstrate trends in representation and identity formation that developed through the decade preceding the Harlem Renaissance and the years when it was first emerging. They offer a narrative of changing ideas about African American identity and the role of different kinds of texts in demonstrating those ideas.

My analysis of these volumes is in no way exhaustive. These five volumes demonstrate important aspects of the Harlem Renaissance, particularly in terms of the ideas communicated about African Americans and the use of certain strategies of representation to send those messages. But I focus selectively even within these volumes, doing in-depth analyses of certain elements and arguments within them but merely hinting at others. There is much more, then, that could be said about these volumes. Furthermore, other magazines and anthologies published during these years also would reward similar analysis, as would newspapers published by African Americans during the 1910s and 1920s and illustrated books of fiction and poetry that were published in the later years of the Harlem Renaissance. This book, then, merely scratches the surface of the analyses that await scholars of the

Harlem Renaissance; I hope it will stimulate further study of these and other examples of its multi-media work.

The volumes I have chosen open a window onto the complex ideas about race and identity that confronted African Americans in the early twentieth century and reveal the various ways African American intellectuals responded to and engaged with those ideas. They demonstrate that participants in the Harlem Renaissance were wide ranging as they appropriated and adapted styles of writing and representation to the project of redefining African Americans. While they certainly did not eradicate racism, these volumes demonstrate that participants in the Harlem Renaissance did use remarkable combinations of written and visual texts to create compelling new images of African Americans and to offer vivid definitions of African American identity. These five volumes serve as examples that allow us to develop a more nuanced assessment of the success of the movement and its participants' efforts to use the processes of representation to define African Americans in complex, dynamic, and highly innovative ways.

I use as my starting point the launching of *The Crisis* in 1910, a moment significantly earlier than the events usually taken as marking the onset of the Harlem Renaissance. Many scholars of the movement link its beginning to the end of World War I, the return of black soldiers, and the racial violence that engulfed the U.S. in 1919. Others point to the publication in the early 1920s of books like James Weldon Johnson's *Book of American Negro Poetry*, Jean Toomer's *Cane*, and Jessie Fauset's *There Is Confusion* as signs of the emerging movement. I start more than a decade before the publication of these books to draw attention to the connection between the work of the Harlem Renaissance and African Americans' efforts to use texts to redefine themselves in the decades, even centuries, before the movement.

The collaborative illustrated volumes of the Harlem Renaissance fit into two important developments of the late nineteenth and early twentieth centuries: ideas about African American identity and the use of many different kinds of texts to communicate those ideas. The Harlem Renaissance is a crucial moment in African Americans' attempts to define themselves and to engage in broader discourses about racial identity, but that effort has roots in the years before the movement. In the eighteenth, nineteenth, and early twentieth centuries, American popular culture presented overwhelmingly negative ideas about African Americans. African Americans, as part of the rationale used to justify slavery, were defined as strikingly different from white Americans and as incapable of significant intellectual, economic, or moral advancement, and thus incapable of assimilation. Even worse, African Americans were believed by many to be threats to national social order, with racial violence—including lynching—defended as necessary to the maintenance of white Americans' security, and with the deportation of African Americans seen as possibly necessary for the assertion and development of American unity and culture. Even liberal white Americans, who believed that African Americans were capable of at least some progress and growth, generally assumed that African Americans were inferior to white Americans.[3]

These ideas were supported and reinforced by the representation of African Americans in many different kinds of texts, including novels, essays, and visual images. Apologists for slavery created literary and visual depictions of African Americans that defined them as inherently suited to slavery and in need of guidance and control by white Americans. This plantation school among novelists and artists of the nineteenth century was followed by works by postbellum novelists like Thomas Nelson Page, who used essays and books to depict what Page called a "new issue" Negro, an African American who was lazy, dishonest, and immoral.[4] Such representations of African Americans implicitly demonstrated them to be lacking in the Protestant or Puritan ethics and the innovativeness that were identified as characteristic of white Americans. Novels like those by Thomas Dixon sent even more vicious messages about African Americans. For example, his 1905 book *The Clansman* presented crime, disorder, miscegenation, and the rape of white women as the result of African Americans being given the vote in the South; civilization is restored only by the Ku Klux Klan. The negative representation of African Americans in such novels was reinforced by other kinds of written texts that circulated complementary ideas, such as sociological treatises like Lothrop Stoddard's *The Rising Tide of Color*, which predicted a looming race war. Newspapers and magazines frequently reported on "scientific" findings about African Americans that showed them as suffering from inferior anatomy and ancestry and being so significantly behind white Americans in intellectual development and so without a cultural past that they could make no contributions to American culture or society. Visual images reinforced such characterizations. Minstrel shows were extremely popular throughout the nineteenth century, and board games, dolls, lithographs, and sheet music also featured racist images of African Americans.[5]

The invention and popularization of photography in the nineteenth century and the development of movies at the turn of the century meant that new kinds of texts were available for the spread of racist imagery. Picture postcards became quite popular by the late nineteenth century, and many of these included racist depictions of African Americans—or photographs of the bodies of lynched African Americans.[6] The film version of *The Clans-man, The Birth of a Nation,* was released in 1915; it is perhaps the most infamous transfer of such assessments of African Americans into visual media. The same year, the Ku Klux Klan, which had gone out of existence in the early 1870s, was re-founded. It would be difficult if not impossible to prove that such an event was directly caused by the portrayal of African Americans in *The Birth of a Nation* or other texts, but certainly there were parallels between the treatment of African Americans and the messages sent about them in this and other texts. Protests against *The Birth of a Nation,* including many led by the National Association for the Advancement of Colored People (NAACP) and covered in *The Crisis,* testify to the degree to which African Americans living in those years believed in the danger of such images and took steps to counteract them. Protesters often attempted to stop the distribution or showing of the movie; in other words, they attempted to keep racist images of African Americans out of circulation (Lewis, *Du Bois* I: 506–509). They had only limited success, and W. E. B. Du Bois, for one, concluded, "Without doubt the increase of lynching in 1915 and later was directly encouraged by this film" (*Dusk of Dawn* 240).

But if negative images of African Americans could justify or even encourage racism and violence against African Americans, the reverse might also be true: alternative images of African Americans might have an ameliorating effect on racism and its manifestations. The belief in this possibility is evident in centuries of self-representation by African Americans. African American writers, artists, and editors have long used written and visual texts to counteract derogatory assumptions about African Americans, perhaps since 1619, when black slaves first "set out to redefine—against already received racist stereotypes—who and what a black person was, and how unlike the racist stereotype the black original indeed actually could be" (Gates, "The Trope" 131). For African American writers, including a portrait of themselves turned a book into an opportunity to use both written and visual texts to represent themselves. One example is Phillis Wheatley's *Poems on Various Subjects,* published in London in 1773 and apparently the first book published by an African American writer (Gates and McKay 164). Wheatley was effectively put on trial in front of eighteen prominent white male citizens of Boston and required to prove that she was capable of writing these poems; in the letter that appears as a preface to her book, the men declare their belief that she was literate and that the poems were her work. Across from the title page is a portrait that contributes to that argument: it depicts Wheatley, seated at a desk with pen and paper, eyes raised in contemplation (see fig. I.1). It complements the letter with a visual assertion of Wheatley's writing ability.[7]

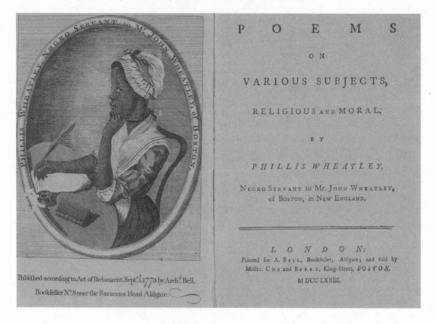

Fig. I.1. Frontispiece portrait of Phillis Wheatley and the title page of her book of poetry published in 1773. *Reproduced from her* Collected Works, *ed. Shields, n.pag.*

Visual portraits like this one of Wheatley also appeared in many slave narratives, often signed by the narrator. They are so common that James Olney has identified their inclusion as one of the "early" and "firmly established" conventions governing the genre (152). They serve an important role in depicting the narrator, particularly when signed: they serve as testimony both of the existence and the literacy of that narrator (Olney 155). This point is reemphasized by variations of the phrase "written by himself," commonly included as part of the title (Olney 152). Such representations of African Americans as intelligent and literate vividly contradict assumptions that African Americans were ignorant and uneducable. Frederick Douglass's 1845 *Narrative* is an example that demonstrates the importance of the visual as well as the written text. It was published, according to promotional materials, with "a finely executed and admirable likeness of the author" (Douglass, *Autobiographies* 1078–79). A 1960 reproduction of the *Narrative* includes such a portrait, perhaps the original, which shows Douglass in the formal attire stylish during the period, posed with a serious and intelligent expression on his face. Below the portrait is Douglass's signature (see fig. I.2).[8] The portrait and signature show Douglass to be a sophisticated, literate individual, and they reinforce the assertion of the subtitle that the *Narrative*

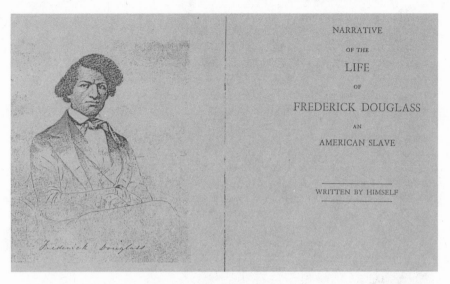

NARRATIVE

OF THE

LIFE

OF

FREDERICK DOUGLASS

AN

AMERICAN SLAVE

WRITTEN BY HIMSELF

Fig. I.2. Portrait of Frederick Douglass with the title page of his *Narrative*. This portrait probably was published with the *Narrative* in 1845. *Reproduced from the* Narrative, *ed. Quarles, n.pag.*

was "written by himself." This point is reemphasized in Douglass's final paragraph, in which he reiterates his hope that his book will hasten the end of slavery. Douglass pledges himself anew to this cause, and "subscribe[s]" himself, leaving his name as the final words of the book.

After his escape from slavery, as Douglass took on the roles of journalist, editor, and publisher, he continued to use texts to define and assert himself and to redefine African Americans as a whole. His hope, as he made clear in comments about the role of the black press, was that such texts might bring about important changes in public opinion about African Americans:

> The grand thing to be done . . . was to change the estimation in which the colored people of the U.St. were held; to remove the prejudice which depreciated and expressed them; to prove them worthy of a higher consideration; to disprove their alleged inferiority, and demonstrate their capacity for a more exalted civilization than salary and prejudice had assigned to them. (Qtd. in Wolseley 35)

Douglass carried out such efforts to redefine African Americans through his lifetime, and he was only one of many African Americans who launched periodicals full of images of and arguments about African Americans.[9] Such efforts started as early as the launching of *Freedom's Journal* in 1827, but the numbers of African American papers and magazines rose greatly in the mid-

I Sell the Shadow to Support the Substance.

SOJOURNER TRUTH.

Fig. I.3. A *carte-de-visite* of Sojourner Truth. *Reproduced from Painter,* Sojourner Truth: A Life, a Symbol, *n.pag.*

to-late nineteenth century and the early twentieth century. Although many of them were short-lived, by 1905 Du Bois could claim that thousands of small papers had been founded by African Americans ("A Proposed Negro Journal" 78).

The speaker and activist Sojourner Truth used a different kind of text to circulate images of herself in the 1860s. Truth, whose words were distributed through newspaper accounts of her speeches, carefully controlled photographs of herself, using visual images, historian Nell Painter asserts, "to embody and to empower herself, to present the images of herself that *she* wanted remembered" ("Representing Truth" 462). An image that Painter identifies as one of Truth's favorites was taken in 1864; it shows Truth wearing eyeglasses and holding knitting, seated next to a table with a book and a vase of flowers (see fig. I.3). The props are symbols, Painter argues, "of leisure and feminine gentility," motherliness, seriousness, and intelligence, and her well-tailored clothing establishes her status (483–85). Truth's control of such images demonstrates her appropriation of the growing popularity of portrait photography but also the development of *cartes de visite,* small visiting cards that were inexpensive and very popular by the 1860s (482). By the turn of the century, African American editors began to use new printing technology to include illustrations in magazines like *Colored American* and *Voice of the Negro*—and, as Henry Louis Gates, Jr., has shown, they used the written and visual texts in these magazines to redefine African Americans ("The Trope" 138–46). The inclusion of line drawings and portraits in these publications corresponds to the rise in the number and popularity of illustrations in periodicals in the mid-to-late nineteenth century. The development and improvement of halftone techniques in the 1880s made it possible and more common to reproduce photographs and written text on the same page. Though many periodicals stayed with the old look of pages filled with only type, the more innovative papers and magazines included increasing numbers of drawings and photographs.[10] Periodicals published by African Americans were among this group.

Visual texts were common in books, too, during these years, and African Americans also used this medium to present images of themselves. Gift books and illustrated editions of novels were increasingly popular in the late nineteenth century—so much so that the end of the century is often referred to as the golden age of book illustration in the United States (Harthan 241–44). A book like *A New Negro for a New Century* is an example of African Americans' participation in this trend. Edited by Booker T. Washington and published in 1900, this book includes written contributions that retell the history of African American soldiers and American slavery, report on recent developments in the women's club movement, and describe the advances of African Americans in education and industry. It is also, as the title page proclaims, "magnificently illustrated," including portraits of sixty prominent African American men and women, beginning with the stately image of Washington that appears as the book's frontispiece (see fig. I.4). Its visual and written texts, Gates asserts, were "clearly intended to 'turn' the new century's image of the black away from stereotypes scattered throughout plantation fictions, blackface minstrelsy, vaudeville, racist pseudoscience, and vulgar Social Darwinism" ("The Trope" 136–37). It did so by demonstrating, through words and visual texts, the changes that had occurred among African Americans since Emancipation.

Such changes were dramatic. The movement of hundreds of thousands of African Americans from Southern rural to Northern urban areas during the Great Migration and the experiences of many African Americans as soldiers and workers during World War I fed into a sense that, by the 1920s, African Americans as a group were changing the nature of their existence,

Fig. I.4. Booker T. Washington's portrait, the frontispiece of his *A New Negro for a New Century*.

achieving significant accomplishments, and demonstrating their abilities in ways that exceeded what they had done before. But the discrimination and racism that they faced from many white Americans seemed to be holding steady—if not increasing. This led to redoubled efforts to create more and better publications, for many African Americans assumed that white Americans would change their ideas about African Americans and their treatment of them once they were made aware of the accomplishments and the progress of the race. But the changes among African Americans also led to a growing appreciation of the importance of black readers—and the need to convince them, too, of who and what African Americans could be. As Gates argues about *A New Negro for a New Century,* "As much as transforming a white racist image of the black, then, [the book's] intention was to restructure the *race's* image of *itself*" ("The Trope" 140). Showcasing the achievements and potential of African Americans, in short, was a way to redefine African American identity for the benefit of black readers and for the education of white readers.

The multi-media work of the Harlem Renaissance, then, fits into a long tradition of efforts by African Americans to use many different kinds of texts to provide images of themselves, and the optimism in the 1920s about the potential effect of those images similarly has a long history. But the idea that texts might influence public opinion has opened up the Harlem Renaissance to a good deal of criticism. In fact, until recently, the tendency among scholars of the Harlem Renaissance was to argue that the movement was a failure. Critiques of the movement began even while it was under way in the 1920s, when iconoclasts like Wallace Thurman argued, in numerous essays and reviews, that it was ridiculous to expect literature to change the perceptions of white racists. But by the 1970s, the desire to seek out and study important moments in black history fed into a number of important assessments of the movement, including Nathan Huggins's *Harlem Renaissance* and David Levering Lewis's *When Harlem Was in Vogue.* These seminal works provided the historical information that would become the basis for later studies of the Harlem Renaissance. And yet Huggins and Lewis both promoted the assessment that the movement failed, particularly in its social goals. Lewis, for example, concluded that the social goals of the contributors to *The New Negro* were "irresponsibly delusional" (117); they also were, he asserted, characteristic of the movement as a whole, which he judged an elitist and ultimately unsuccessful response to racism in the United States. Other critics concluded that the movement failed for different reasons. Some argued that participants had not been innovative enough in their creative efforts or that they had failed to significantly intervene in the processes of representation. bell hooks, for instance, commenting not on the Harlem Renaissance in particular but more broadly about African Americans' "struggle to gain control over how we are represented," concluded that there have been "few, if any, revolutionary interventions in the area of race and representation" (1–2). Presumably, then, the work of the 1920s did not have the impact for which its creators hoped.

But a new note was sounded in 1987 by Houston A. Baker, Jr. Instead of assuming the Harlem Renaissance failed, he insisted, scholars needed to look for ways it succeeded. For example, Baker argued that *The New Negro* was "an intensely successful act of national self-definition" and demonstrated "a broadening and enlargement of the field of traditional Afro-American discursive possibilities" (72, 73). If we reassess such texts, Baker implied, we might find that they had "profoundly beneficial effects for areas of Afro-American discourse that we have only recently begun to explore in depth" (12). To support that argument, Baker considered the visual as well as the written texts in *The New Negro* and the other texts he analyzed; he considered the arguments asserted by writers in the context of the photographs, drawings, and graphic images with which they were published. His focus on a range of texts, however, has not been repeated by many scholars. While the 1980s and 1990s saw the publication of a multitude of important new studies of the Harlem Renaissance, much of this work focuses almost exclusively on the literature of the period. While this new scholarship contributes important reassessments of texts and recovers texts and authors who had been lost, it remains for critics to assess the connections participants forged between the arts in order to measure their potential to represent African Americans.[11]

But steps in this direction are being taken in a few collections of primary work from the Harlem Renaissance and critical studies that place the literary output of the movement in the context of other kinds of creative work done in the early decades of the twentieth century. Donald Petesch, for example, in *A Spy in the Enemy's Country* pairs his analyses of African American writers with discussions of images of blacks in popular culture. Studies like Lewis's *When Harlem Was in Vogue,* Steven Watson's *The Harlem Renaissance,* and Cary Wintz's *Black Culture and the Harlem Renaissance* also provide insights into the relationships among writers, artists, musicians, actors, editors, and so on. More recent work that demonstrates the range of texts important to the Harlem Renaissance includes anthologies like *Call and Response: The Riverside Anthology of the African American Literary Tradition,* which sets written texts alongside samples of African American oral and musical traditions. The section of the anthology on the Harlem Renaissance includes a number of different kinds of music and oral texts as well as essays and creative literature. *Rhapsodies in Black: Art of the Harlem Renaissance* takes an even broader multi-media approach to the Harlem Renaissance. This book is a catalog of material from the movement that was exhibited in England and the United States in 1997 and 1998. The exhibit included movies, music, paintings, photographs, graphic designs, and sculpture as well as books published in the 1920s, and the catalog includes a number of essays that discuss each of these kinds of texts. This breadth of focus, as Richard Powell argues, allows us to move beyond the tendency to think of the Harlem Renaissance as an overwhelmingly literary and musical movement and to appreciate it as a movement that involved many cultural forms (16–17). Such works point toward the multi-media dimensions of the Harlem Renaissance, and Powell's argument hints that our understanding of the movement may change if we consider not just its literature but also the many other kinds of texts produced. My goal in this book, then, is to move us a step in that direction.

I begin, in my first chapter, with the strategies of representation and the arguments about African Americans presented in *The Crisis* in the 1910s. This monthly magazine, edited by Du Bois and published by the recently formed NAACP, demonstrates techniques of representation that were found in a number of the periodicals of the time: it includes sharp, vivid, and angry protests of the treatment of African Americans as well as evidence of African Americans' accomplishments and potential. *The Crisis* combines these in important ways, and it uses visual and written texts in each. For example, editorials denouncing the lynching of African Americans and extensive reports about such violence are often illustrated with gruesome photographs of the mutilated bodies of African Americans. But these protest texts have drawbacks, particularly that they can continue or even reinforce the dehumanization of their subjects. *The Crisis* offsets these drawbacks by countering its coverage of lynchings and violence against African Americans with features that highlight African Americans' achievements in business, education, and politics, as well as their promise for future accomplishments. "Men of the Month" columns and special issues on education and children provide the clearest examples of such laudatory coverage. The most compelling images in *The Crisis* occur when these affirmations are juxtaposed with coverage of lynchings; the resulting composite texts demonstrate the success and potential of African Americans despite the racism and violence still directed against them, and they thus convincingly assert the need for dramatic changes in the treatment of African Americans. The cognitive dissonance created by such juxtapositions is crucial to the impact of the magazine: combining these texts allows *The Crisis* to launch a vicious critique of the treatment of African Americans in America but also to assert African Americans' ability to overcome such treatment, and it motivates readers to act.

The strategy of combining written and visual texts into composites remained a crucial aspect of the collaborative illustrated volumes produced in the 1920s. But the stunning juxtapositions in *The Crisis* in the 1910s fade out in the following decade. Though some of the publications of the 1920s—like *The Messenger* or Marcus Garvey's *Negro World*—maintained the anger, even outrage, that was obvious in *The Crisis* in the 1910s, many of the publications of the Harlem Renaissance took a different tone. By the 1920s, many of the participants in the movement—including Du Bois—moved away from protest. Some offered instead texts that were constructed to appear objective rather than opinionated. My second chapter focuses on one example of such an approach: Charles Johnson's use of expository studies and news texts focusing on African Americans in *Opportunity*. When Johnson and the National Urban League (NUL) began to publish this monthly magazine in 1923, they left out the fiery protests that characterized *The Crisis* in the previous decade. They emphasized *Opportunity*'s role in providing more apparently realistic and objective texts, such as expository essays and documentary photographs, to provide readers with information about and understanding of African Americans. These texts follow the conventions of the emerging fields of sociology and social work, and these enable contributors to *Opportunity* to provide information that challenges stereotypes about African Americans. But these texts implicitly position their African American subjects as passive, as victims who need the help of the magazine's readers. It is important, then, that the creators of *Opportunity* complemented its studies with news stories and photographs that identify African Americans as active contributors to American society and culture. The combination of essays and news stories is crucial to the magazine's ability to challenge stereotypes and to offer positive definitions of African American identity.

By the mid-to-late 1920s, both *The Crisis* and *Opportunity* devoted more and more attention to the role of the arts in providing new images of African Americans. Each magazine included numerous essays asserting the usefulness of the arts in demonstrating the characteristics of African Americans, correcting misunderstandings of or distorted ideas about African Americans, demonstrating African Americans' contributions to national and global culture, and adding emotional insight to the intellectual understanding offered by other kinds of texts. Furthermore, each magazine published significant numbers of poems, short stories, plays, drawings, and graphic designs. This attention to the arts and the discussion of the potential of the arts to offer new ideas about African Americans is often discussed by scholars of the Harlem Renaissance. It is less often recognized that in these publications, contributors emphasized that the potential of the arts is greatest when different kinds of art work together. As I show in my third chapter, this understanding is evident in discussions of the arts in *The Crisis* and *Opportunity*, which range in focus from musicals to literature to film. Furthermore, the complementary nature of the arts is evoked in features that combine different kinds of texts. These composite texts prove highly adept at demonstrating the complexity of African American identity.

Similar combinations of written and visual texts can be found in a number of single-volume collaborative illustrated works—special issues of magazines, anthologies, opening issues of literary journals—that were published in the mid-to-late 1920s. *The Crisis* and *Opportunity*, as periodicals, record ongoing experiments with texts and developments of ideas about African Americans' status in America. In contrast, each of the single-volume works offers a definitive, collective portrait of African Americans. These volumes are more explicitly focused on asserting a collective identity for African Americans than are the two magazines, and these single-volume works demonstrate the importance of national identity, racial identity, and other aspects of identity in defining African Americans. The Harlem issue of the *Survey Graphic,* the focus of my fourth chapter, was one of a number of special issues of magazines published by white Americans and read primarily by white Americans; it was the first such issue in which African Americans were able to represent themselves. But the issue also included some of the trademarks of the publication, such as its ethnographic nature. Its visual texts, photographs and two series of portraits by Winold Reiss, depict African Americans as exotic objects of study, mute before the spectator. But the writers who contributed to the issue, including editor Alain Locke, argued passionately that African Americans were important contributors to American culture. A struggle over the representation of African Americans emerges explicitly from these pages, then; at stake is their identity as Americans or as others, as outsiders to American society and culture. In the end, the issue succeeds in destabilizing the categories of "American" and "other": the two portrait series in particular define Americanization as a process, and they show that it bridges the distinctions between the elite and the folk, between men and women, and between the viewer and the viewed. They assert a narrative of progress that implies a link between the subjects of this exhibit, the creators of these texts, and the readers of the issue. By preventing its readers from establishing a distance between themselves and those they read about or look at, the issue is able to challenge the us/them mentality that was a crucial element of racism and a component of definitions of American identity in the 1920s.

When Alain Locke expanded the contents of the *Survey Graphic* issue into *The New Negro*, the anthology he published in late 1925 and the focus of my fifth chapter, he refocused the volume's attention from the American identity of African Americans to the unity of African Americans as a race, particularly through his assertions of the development of race pride and race consciousness. He used art to demonstrate both, and the most distinctive texts in the anthology are written and visual texts that assert African Americans' connection to an African past and the development of an African American folk culture. But *The New Negro* also includes a range of other texts with other emphases, many of which undermine or even contradict its representation of African Americans as a unified group of people. In the end, the format of this book as an anthology means it contains a cacophony of voices, and the book simultaneously asserts and undermines a simple definition of African American identity. Its complications and contradictions finally identify any construction of African American identity as only one possible interpretation. The tensions in *The New Negro* around the concept of race contribute to its success at representing African Americans: the complexities of the book allow for an assertion of collective identity that remains open ended and dynamic rather than locking its subjects into stasis.

Locke dedicated *The New Negro* to "the younger generation," but those younger artists and writers responded to his volume with a very different portrait of African Americans: they launched publication of an avant-garde literary and arts journal in 1926, and they used strategies of representation modeled by white American avant-gardes to distance themselves from their elders. In *Fire!!*, as I show in my sixth chapter, they used creative literature, visual art, and polemics against prescriptive arguments about art to draw attention to aspects of identity that had escaped attention in other volumes, particularly sexuality and ideology. Even the subtitle of their magazine, which identified it as "dedicated to younger Negro artists," emphasized the importance of race but also of age and artistry as crucial aspects of their collective identity. The aesthetics, contents, and tone of individual texts within its first issue mark the publication as linked to the avant-garde, yet race is clearly an important issue for contributors. Furthermore, within that first issue, different texts show that the importance of each aspect of identity varies according to the circumstances facing an individual. *Fire!!* thus asserts an anti-essentialist construction of African American identity that highlights the multiple factors that define any one individual.

Ending this study with *Fire!!* leaves us at the mid-point of the Harlem Renaissance. The following years turned out to be the most productive of the movement, the time when the most books were published, particularly novels. These works display a range of focus that is fitting for the complexity glimpsed in these collaborative illustrated volumes. It seems, then, that the early years of the movement—those focused on in this study—provided a platform off of which followers leapt in many, many directions. In my conclusion, I consider briefly the work published in the later years of the Harlem Renaissance, reflecting on the opening up of discourse about African Americans seen in these texts.

A final word needs to be said about my methodology: this is a study that does not focus on the process by which these volumes were created. It would be fascinating to investigate who put what texts where, or why they decided to include certain texts rather than others. However, there is little published information available that would shed light on such questions. To answer them, then, would require a different kind of archival work than what I do here: it would require an exploration of primary materials by those involved—combing through letters, diaries, personal notes, and so on. Such work may yield significant insights into the process of creation of these works. My focus, though, is on the finished volumes. I analyze these as they were first published, asking not how they got that way, but, given that they included such a range of texts, what their implications are and what we can learn from them.

The implications of this study extend well beyond the Harlem Renaissance. The mix of texts in these volumes helps us understand how texts work and in what combinations they are able to redefine a group of people. These volumes serve as examples of what happens when a group of people—in this case, African Americans—undertake an effort to redefine themselves, and they offer us the opportunity to analyze what gets shown and how. We can determine which aspects of the texts add to their impact and which aspects undermine their ability to change readers' understandings of African American identity. Both to the degree that the texts of the Harlem Renaissance failed and to the degree that they succeeded, we can use them to ask important questions about the process of defining an identity for a group of people and about using texts to communicate that new definition to readers. These insights identify the Harlem Renaissance as an important precursor moment to contemporary explorations of concepts of identity and the use of texts in asserting those concepts. The insights gleaned from these volumes, then, can be applied to efforts to define groups of people in more recent decades. Reconsidering the Harlem Renaissance can lead us to a more thorough understanding of the challenges and potentials of representation and identity formation. The participants in the Harlem Renaissance, with their sophisticated, complicated, and largely successful work of representation and identity formation, provide us with models we can use to shape our own efforts, decades later, to use texts to communicate ideas and define identities.

1

Protest and Affirmation: Composite Texts in *The Crisis*

The Crisis *magazine, as the monthly publication of the NAACP;* the product of editor, intellectual, and political and social leader W. E. B. Du Bois; and a supporter of the development of literature and arts by African Americans, particularly in the 1920s, was one of the most important periodicals of the Harlem Renaissance. But its work in offering information about African Americans actually began in the decade leading up to the movement. Starting with its first issue in November 1910, *The Crisis* was a source of thousands of texts that depicted African Americans and their experiences. Many of these texts are positive in nature and draw attention to African Americans' accomplishments. But others focus on the mistreatment of African Americans, demonstrating the extent and consequences of American racism. Both protest and affirmative texts in the magazine include visual elements: individual pages of *The Crisis* are composite texts that pair written copy and headlines with photographs, drawings, maps, and graphs. These combinations make its protests against the treatment of African Americans and affirmations of their achievements and potential particularly convincing and compelling.

Also significant to the impact of *The Crisis*, though, is the juxtaposition of these protests and affirmations. Many features that demonstrate the accomplishments of individual African Americans are positioned alongside those that record and decry American racism. The resulting pages have an incongruence that is characteristic of montages or collages, and art and film theory about these forms suggests that the discord among their elements heightens their effect. These striking combinations of diverse texts and images are particularly common in the magazine's first decade; the disjunctions in *The Crisis* of those years make its critique of American racism and its affirmation of African Americans' achievements especially compelling. Returning our attention to *The Crisis* as it was originally published during those years and analyzing the relations among its various texts deepens our appreciation of the importance of its multi-media format and its layout. Studying the mix of texts on its pages, furthermore, makes it clear that, when we turn our attention to the collaborative illustrated volumes published during the next decade, we will similarly need to pay attention to the relations among the many kinds of texts on their pages.[1]

The combinations of different kinds of texts in the pages of *The Crisis,* however, have not been reflected in scholarship on the magazine. While scholars have paid a fair amount of attention to *The Crisis* in the 1920s, particularly its role in drawing attention to the arts in the 1920s and in promoting the Harlem Renaissance, analyses of the magazine in the 1910s have been more limited.[2] Such studies are aided by a number of anthologies of the essays Du Bois published in *The Crisis,* such as the relevant volumes of *The Complete Published Works of W.E.B. Du Bois,* edited by Herbert Aptheker.[3] Because original copies of the magazine are difficult to come by, such collections and analyses of its contents are extremely helpful to scholars. But they fail to reflect the combinations of texts in *The Crisis* in two ways. First, many of the studies and reprints of protests from *The Crisis* do not set them in the context of the magazine's extensive attention to the achievements of African Americans. Second, much of the scholarship on *The Crisis* focuses almost exclusively on its written texts. This work includes few, if any, illustrations from the magazine, and it rarely refers to the numerous portraits, news photographs, and drawings that were included in each issue.[4] Most scholarship on the magazine, therefore, has failed to address the fact that *The Crisis* included both protest and affirmation and both written and visual texts.

The importance of each of these kinds of texts to *The Crisis* is made clear, first, by a consideration of the goals originally articulated for the magazine by Du Bois and the mission of the NAACP. Du Bois had wanted to edit a monthly magazine that would be primarily aimed at African American readers for some time before he launched *The Crisis.* He had surveyed the black press in 1905 and had found no publication that filled what he called a "great need" for a "high class journal to circulate among the intelligent Negroes." Writing to a potential financial supporter, he made the purpose of his ideal magazine clear: it would tell African Americans "of the deeds of themselves & their neighbors, interpret the news of the world to them & inspire them toward definite ideals." He acknowledged that there were "many small weekly papers & one or two monthlies" published for African American readers but argued that none accomplished these goals.[5] Du Bois was confident that he could do better. With "a knowledge of modern publishing methods" and "a knowledge of the Negro people," he was sure that an editor could publish a long-lived and widely circulated magazine ("A Proposed Negro Journal" 79).

Though this appeal for money was unsuccessful, Du Bois launched two magazines within the next few years. Both, however, were short lived and suffered from a lack of funds and readers: the *Moon Illustrated Weekly* lasted from 1905 to 1906, and *Horizon: A Journal of the Color Line* lasted from 1907 to 1910.[6] Du Bois got a third chance when the NAACP hired him as director of research and publicity in 1910. Originally, the organization did not plan to publish a monthly magazine, and there was, in fact, significant resistance to the idea, particularly because of the potential expense involved. The board of directors finally agreed to let Du Bois start *The Crisis,* with the qualification that it would provide only a fifty-dollar monthly line of credit toward its cost.[7] Though disagreements between Du Bois and the board were ongoing, particularly over the magazine's editorials, his position with the NAACP gave Du Bois a salary, office space, and a large number of potential readers among the organization's members.[8]

The disagreements between Du Bois and the board notwithstanding, *The Crisis* generally does reflect the goals of the NAACP. The organization was founded in part as a response to the absence of protests of the murder of African Americans in Springfield, Illinois, in August 1908. Riots had resulted in two lynchings, six fatal shootings, and more than eighty injuries (Lewis, *Du Bois* I: 388). William English Walling, a socialist reformer, lamented after the violence that there was no large organization that would stand up against such treatment of African Americans. With the encouragement of Mary White Ovington and a few other white reformers, Walling started the group that would become the NAACP to serve that purpose (Lewis, *Du Bois* I: 387–89). They carefully included both blacks and whites in planning sessions and on the board of directors; the organization, then, and the readership for its magazine were interracial.[9]

The organization's aim of protesting American racism is reflected in its magazine, beginning with a number of editorials that define the mission of both. The purpose of the NAACP, according to one, was to supply and nurture "earnest, active opposition" to the increase of racism by "doing away with the excuses for prejudice ... showing the unreasonableness of prejudice ... [and] exposing the evils of race prejudice" ("Editorial: N.A.A.C.P." 16). The role of *The Crisis* in that effort, another editorial made clear, would be to "set forth those facts and arguments which show the danger of race prejudice, particularly as manifested to-day toward colored people" ("Editorial: The Crisis" 10). That editorial also explained, though, that the magazine would include more than protest. It also would "record important happenings and movements in the world which bear on the great problem of inter-racial relations, and especially those which affect the Negro-American"; in addition, it would include reviews of "books, articles, and important expressions of opinion in the white and colored press on the race problem"; short articles; and an editorial page that would "stand for the rights of men" ("Editorial: The Crisis" 10). It would serve, then, as a forum for recording and discussing events and ideas about race and the treatment of African Americans. Not mentioned but very much a part of every issue were texts that recorded African Americans' accomplishments. In fact, it is perhaps the affirmative texts in *The Crisis* that were most successful at undermining excuses for prejudice and showing its unreasonableness; they challenged racism by establishing and defining the character traits of African Americans, refuting the stereotypes that underlay assumptions about African Americans. Both protests and affirmations, then, were part of the magazine's response to the depiction and treatment of African Americans.

Illustrations, too, were common in the pages of *The Crisis*. Pictures were highly valued contributions to the magazine, and they were actively sought. An advertisement for *The Crisis* in its fourth issue noted, "It is especially desired to increase the number and quality of the illustrations so as to make the magazine a pictorial history of the Color Line."[10] Starting in September 1913, the importance of "Pictures" was indicated by the fact that they were listed as the first item in the table of contents for most issues through 1921. Years later, Du Bois attributed the success of *The Crisis* in part to its inclusion of affirmative visual images. "Pictures of colored people were an innovation," he wrote in 1951. Those that showed African Americans in a positive light were particularly crucial, Du Bois explained, because "at that time it was the rule of most white papers never to publish a picture of a colored person except as a criminal."[11] The photographs in *The Crisis*, then, were important antidotes to images of African Americans published in the mainstream press.

In his reflections on the success of the magazine, Du Bois also mentioned the news the magazine carried and the "blazing editorials which continually got us into hot water with friends and foes" ("Editing *The Crisis*" xxix). Du Bois's assessment suggests that its protests and affirmations, both in written and visual form, were important to the impact of the magazine. Its inclusion of so many kinds of texts also sets it in line with emerging trends in newspaper and magazine publishing in the late nineteenth and early twentieth centuries. For instance, when Du Bois described the "Negro journal" he wanted to establish in 1905, he explained that the publication would be "on the order of *Harper's Weekly* or *Colliers* [sic]" ("A Proposed Negro Journal" 78). Both included news, editorials, creative literature, and discussions of politics; in addition, both were heavily illustrated, with comics, political cartoons, portraits, maps, and photographs accompanying the written texts.[12] Du Bois's proposed journal, he wrote, would include a similar mix of texts: it would be a "literary digest of fact and opinion," would include news about black people in the United States and elsewhere, and would feature "[i]llustrations attempting to portray Negro life on its beautiful and interesting side" ("A Proposed Negro Journal" 78). The difference between established magazines and Du Bois's would be their attention—or lack thereof—to African Americans and to the color line. Far too many "mainstream" periodicals of the time were racist and derogatory in their depictions of African Americans, as was shown in numerous examples in *The Crisis*.[13] A few white periodicals devoted occasional attention to the achievements of African Americans and protested lynchings and acts of racism and violence against African Americans, but such coverage was the exception rather than the norm.[14] The mix of visual and written texts in *The Crisis*, then, can also be found in other periodicals of the early twentieth century, but Du Bois filled a gap in their coverage when he used this mixed-media format to depict the experiences of African Americans.

The coverage in *The Crisis* of racism and violence against African Americans also parallels the rise of investigative journalism—also known as muckraking—in the late nineteenth and early twentieth centuries. Muckraking's exposés of wrongdoing in various aspects of American society, such as politics, labor relations, and health care, were important elements in the two magazines Du Bois mentioned: *Harper's Weekly* and *Collier's* both featured muckraking journalism, such as investigations of the corrupt Tammany Hall politicians in the 1870s (Aucoin 211; Rounds 221). It would have made sense for muckrakers to focus their attention on the injustices of American racism, but most did not. In fact, at least one of the leading publishers of investigative journalism, *McClure's*, was quite open to racist contributions and quite closed to responses from African Americans.[15] In 1907, after the magazine had run a particularly offensive essay by Thomas Nelson Page, Du Bois proposed that he write a piece that would respond to this kind of "anti-Negro propaganda." The editors of *McClure's* first denied him the opportunity, saying that they did not want "to open our pages to a controversy." After Du Bois insisted that the magazine needed to show "some elementary justice toward us," the publisher invited him to submit an article, but it was later rejected.[16] Du Bois must have been particularly frustrated by the fact that even this magazine, devoted as it was to revealing other kinds of social iniquities, refused to challenge public opinion about African Americans or even allow African Americans to respond to negative arguments about themselves.

In contrast, Du Bois would have found precedents for the protest elements of *The Crisis* in other black periodicals. The protests in *The Crisis* fit, for example, in the tradition of abolitionist journalism established in nineteenth-century newspapers like *The North Star, The Liberator,* and *Freedom's Journal* (Lewis, *Du Bois* I: 410–11). In the decades after Emancipation, periodicals edited by African Americans continued to protest the treatment of African Americans, pushing for the granting of civil rights to African Americans and critiquing the destruction of property owned by African Americans, acts of violence against African Americans, and the rise of the Ku Klux Klan. But African American publishers paid a price for issuing such protests and demands: they often faced threats of violence and attempts to suppress the publication or distribution of their periodicals. Elements of protest largely dropped out of the black press in the last decades of the nineteenth century and the early years of the twentieth century, with a few important exceptions such as Ida B. Wells's *Free Speech and Headlight* and William Trotter's *Boston Guardian*.[17] Another exception was *Voice of the Negro,* which Du Bois identified as a precursor to *The Crisis* and called "the greatest magazine which the colored people had had" before it ceased publication in 1907 ("The Colored Magazine in America" 33–34). The weekly newspaper the *Chicago Defender* would become an important publisher of protest, but it had not yet reached its peak when Du Bois launched *The Crisis*.[18] There was a need, then, for more coverage of the wrongs done to African Americans; to Du Bois, the black press had a responsibility to report and protest such treatment.

Du Bois often was critical of periodicals he found too accommodationist, including those influenced by Booker T. Washington.[19] Moreover, periodicals in Washington's camp were unlikely to include news about the NAACP, which Washington initially opposed.[20] Such publications provided examples of the kinds of affirmative images Du Bois wanted to include, though, for many of them drew attention to the achievements of African Americans. *Colored American Magazine,* for example, included literature, black history, and biographies, as well as a column devoted to "Famous Men of the Negro Race" and one on "Famous Women of the Negro Race" (Johnson and Johnson 5). Numerous other periodicals of the time worked at redefining African Americans, and illustrations played important roles in many. *Voice of the Negro,* for instance, included both written and visual texts, and it showcased African Americans' achievements as well as protesting their mistreatment.[21] *The Crisis,* then, became an important complement to existing publications, in terms of its protest and its role in publicizing the NAACP's activities; it also built on traditions in other black periodicals of using visual and written texts to redefine African American identity.

However, *The Crisis* is notable not just for its inclusion of these different kinds of texts but also for their arrangement on its pages. The relation between *The Crisis* and other periodicals in terms of its layout, though, is difficult to assess. Visual and written texts were often paired in *The Crisis*: portraits of successful individuals appeared with descriptions of their accomplishments, and photographs, maps, and charts demonstrating the extent and effects of racism accompany reports and news stories. The layout of these protest and affirmative features also is significant. The "Men of the Month" column, for example, might come after a list of acts of violence toward African Americans; it might be followed by an NAACP report on a lynching, itself followed by descriptions and portraits of African American college graduates. It is not clear whether juxtapositions like these are unique or are typical of other publications of the period. As is the case with *The Crisis*, little of the scholarship on these publications includes discussion of their use of illustrations or of their layout.[22] It also is difficult to tell to what extent Du Bois valued the magazine's layout: he rarely, if ever, mentioned it in his comments about the magazine.[23] In fact, it is difficult to determine whether he or someone else was responsible for laying out the texts in each issue. It is tempting to give Du Bois credit, particularly since he controlled so much of the content of the magazine, but he traveled a great deal during his years as editor of *The Crisis*, so he would not have been in New York City to arrange many of the issues. The appearance of the magazine, however, remains constant. Perhaps, then, one of the other staff members had partial or even primary responsibility for its page design. But they, too, rarely discussed the layout of the magazine; perhaps they did not see it as important.[24]

Furthermore, it is possible that mixing protests and affirmations was simply an unintended consequence of the layout process. Similar juxtapositions of contrasting texts have been noted in other periodicals well before the founding of *The Crisis*. The literary critic Walter Bagehot, for example, in 1858 argued that the coexistence of incongruent elements was typical of newspapers and of the cities they covered. In a city, as in a paper, Bagehot explained, "Everything is there, and everything is disconnected. There is every kind of person in some houses; but there is no more connection between the houses than between the neighbours in the lists of 'births, marriages, and deaths.' As we change from the broad leader to the squalid police-report, we pass a corner and we are in a changed world."[25] Newspapers and magazines often group similar stories into departments or columns; the kinds of contrast Bagehot noted, then, occur between those columns. In fact, this is in many cases what happens in *The Crisis*, when, for example, the affirmations in a "Men of the Month" column butt up against the reports of violence in an NAACP account.

But in *The Crisis,* the juxtaposition of protest and affirmation creates particularly pronounced effects. Furthermore, in the early twentieth century, artists—often inspired by the juxtapositions in newspapers, in fact—began to reproduce such effects in their work, with results that suggest that the mix of texts in *The Crisis* is worth attention. For example, Pablo Picasso and Georges Braque began to include pieces of newsprint in their paintings in the years before World War I, and many of the Cubist and Dadaist painters followed their lead after the war (Golding 65–71). In the 1920s and 1930s, Russian filmmaker Sergei Eisenstein began to practice a similar technique: as he edited his films, he spliced together individual shots with no transitional material, creating disjunctions in the finished text. Composite texts like Picasso's usually are referred to as collages; Eisenstein used the term montage for his. Artists working in other media practice similar techniques, juxtaposing pieces of existing texts to create their own composite texts. A writer who creates a collage might include allusions, quotations, and non-verbal elements; one who makes a montage might juxtapose brief scenes or images without apparent order or connection.[26] A visual artist might produce a collage by cutting, arranging, and pasting pieces of paper in either two or three dimensions, while forming a montage would involve arranging existing pictures into a composition, always in only two dimensions.[27]

Theories about the effects of the juxtapositions in such texts illuminate the importance of the discord on the pages of *The Crisis.* For example, montages and collages are often discussed as creating tension because the individual texts do not seem related and in fact often seem at odds. Readers or viewers have to struggle to make sense of the disparate elements, and thus they must fully engage with the composite text. Eisenstein, for example, argued that because the relations among the individual shots in his films are often perplexing or unclear, the viewer of these cinematic montages must mentally assemble them. By forcing such involvement, Eisenstein asserted, the juxtapositions in his films create an "inner creative excitement" in the viewer that gives the text "a maximum degree of affectiveness" ("Word and Image" 32–35). A similar effect occurs with montage in other media: it "allows, even forces, the reader of the visual or verbal text to synthesize meaning from its disparate pieces" (Wettlaufer 516). As a result, reading is turned into "a participatory, subjective experience" that presents "a more forceful lesson because it is *experienced* rather than merely understood; meaning is produced, rather than consumed by the reader, ready-made" (Wettlaufer 523).

It is possible, as well, that the discomfort created by a juxtaposition of disparate items motivates a reader toward action. Walter Benjamin's opinion, for example, was that texts that allow readers to remain comfortable are conservative in effect because they turn readers into "uncritical spectators and voiceless tokens"; in contrast, texts that "constantly administer shocks to the audience" incite readers to respond (Koepnick 60, 72–73). When readers in the 1910s flipped through the pages of *The Crisis,* they could not have known what to expect. They may have been reading the accounts of African Americans' achievements with pleasure, only to be suddenly confronted with an account of a lynching. Benjamin's argument suggests that that reading experience would have pushed readers toward action. Furthermore, the shocks of the juxtapositions may have encouraged readers to change their thinking about African Americans. Artists who created collages, for example, often viewed the abrupt juxtapositions between individual elements "as a means of undermining conventional associations and shocking the viewer or reader into a perception of a new reality—social, political and psychological, as well as aesthetic" (Raaberg, par. 5). The properties of a collage or montage in *The Crisis,* then, might force readers who had internalized racist ideas about African Americans to rethink their assumptions.

Finally, these juxtapositions prove particularly helpful in depicting African Americans' experiences and achievements in the 1910s. First, the juxtapositions in *The Crisis* formally echo the discontinuities and shocks that were inherent in the treatment of African Americans in the 1910s. If the conflict between texts in a montage suggests a break with order, "the presence of powerful and violent oppositions at work" (Tambling 46), the juxtapositions in *The Crisis* mirror the eruption of violence against African Americans in the early decades of the twentieth century. The effect is fitting. Picasso described the juxtaposition of elements in his collages as creating a "strangeness" that matched his sense that the world "was becoming very strange and not exactly reassuring" (qtd. in Golding 66). The same description could be applied to the treatment of African Americans—with great understatement—and the juxtapositions of protest and affirmation in *The Crisis* communicate a similar sense that something is horribly wrong. In addition, the juxtapositions in *The Crisis* allowed its creators to suggest meanings without explicitly spelling them out. As Eisenstein wrote of shots in a film, each shot might suggest a particular meaning, but the juxtaposition of two shots results in more than "a simple sum of one shot plus another shot" ("Word and Image" 7). In other words, in any montage, two juxtaposed elements create what Eisenstein called "a third something" (9). This third something is the message not spelled out explicitly in any of the individual component texts but suggested by their juxtaposition (10). By creating juxtapositions, an artist provides "guideposts by which the reader arrives at the artist's meaning without the artist having *said* what is really *meant*" (Wettlaufer 516). For *The Crisis* in the 1910s, that third something was its harsh critique of American racism—and, in a time when any overt criticism of racism made *The Crisis* subject to intense scrutiny and persecution from the United States government, particularly the Justice Department and the post office,[28] the ability to suggest rather than spell out this critique was crucial.

Theories about the effects of juxtaposition in composite texts thus suggest that if we are to fully measure the potential of *The Crisis* to redefine African American identity and to protest racism, we need to analyze the mix of texts within it and to assess the relations among those texts. If we do so, we find that its juxtapositions, which forced readers to experience racism and confront the injustice of life on the color line, enhanced its ability to raise readers' awareness of and frustration with African Americans' treatment in the United States—and thus to motivate them to act.

Before we begin our analysis of the juxtaposition of protest and affirmation in the magazine, we need to assess the potential impact of each on its own. What we find is that the effect of protest and affirmative features is enhanced by the layout of *The Crisis*. The pairing of written and visual texts in each makes its depictions of the treatment and achievements of African Americans particularly persuasive. However, each also has limitations, and these are most effectively overcome when protests and affirmations are paired.

Protest texts served crucial roles in demonstrating the extent and impact of racism in early twentieth-century America—in short, in documenting the mistreatment of African Americans and its consequences. The protest texts in *The Crisis* took many forms, and they reveal the lawlessness, ruthlessness, and injustice of violence and discrimination against African Americans. Accounts of acts of racism and discrimination in housing, employment, education, and other areas provide a record of racist acts against African Americans. These were included in a number of the magazine's regular columns, and they were made persuasive in various ways. For example, the "Along the Color Line" column included unadorned reportage of who did what to whom, why, when, where, and how. The writers of these news items refrained from editorializing; they simply recorded what happened and left readers to interpret the events. For skeptical readers, the lack of commentary in these reports lends credibility to the magazine, establishing it as a reliable source of information.[29] *The Crisis* also often paired its own coverage with news stories published in other periodicals. Again, a skeptical reader might have been able to dismiss a news item in *The Crisis* as potentially biased or exaggerated, but the reports from other published sources corroborate these accounts—particularly when reprinted from Southern white periodicals, which would not have been expected to share the outlook of *The Crisis*. In addition, reports written by NAACP "agents" often were published with photographs that demonstrate that the writers were not exaggerating their accounts. One example that demonstrates the latter two techniques is the coverage of the riots in East St. Louis in July 1917. The August 1917 issue of *The Crisis* included reprints of reports that had first appeared in other papers, and the following month, the magazine published a twenty-page NAACP report, complete with photographs that depict burning buildings, injured people, and residents displaced from their homes. These photographs demonstrate the validity of the writer's claims about the human and financial toll of the violence, as do the accounts from the previous month.[30]

The credibility of *The Crisis* thus established, its creators then could add editorials that made sure readers understood its reports and news items in particular ways. Many of the editorials in *The Crisis* appealed to American ideals and decried acts of racism as violations of those ideals, and they often dripped with bitterness and anger. The appeals to readers' values and emotions and the writers' expressions of their own outrage in editorials complement the effect of the more objective texts. Again, the response to the violence in East St. Louis serves as an example: one editorial in the September 1917 issue called the violence a "pogrom" and described the "pools of blood through which we must march" if justice is to be served ("Editorial: East St. Louis" 215–16). A second insisted that ending the kind of mob violence the riots demonstrated was especially important given the looming war: "May no blood-smeared garments bind our feet when we rise to make the world safe for democracy" ("Editorial: Awake America" 216). While the reports work on readers' intellectual understanding of the events, such editorials evoke readers' emotional responses.

The protest function of *The Crisis* thus is enhanced by its inclusion of news, editorials, and illustrations. No topic illustrates this better than lynching. Accounts of lynchings and attempted lynchings were regular features in its pages, whether in the columns "Along the Color Line" and "The Burden" or in the reports from the NAACP. "The Burden" often opened with a chart showing how many lynchings had occurred in previous months or years, and it sometimes included maps showing the states in which lynchings had happened. These visual texts identified lynchings not as isolated events but as examples of a widespread pattern. Longer reports of individual lynchings immersed readers in the details of such acts. Particularly gruesome lynchings were given extended coverage in supplements to the regular issues, and these often included photographs of the bodies of the victims. In many cases, the horror of the lynchings was magnified by the dispassionate tone in which the events were reported. But in other cases, writers spelled out what readers' responses should be. At times, editorials denouncing lynchings spilled into full-fledged calls to action, as though the magnitude of these crimes against humanity could not be contained by the reports.

These many different kinds of texts about lynching were included in *The Crisis* from its opening issues. The first mention of lynching occurred in the premiere issue of *The Crisis*, with a brief critique of the murder of two naturalized Italian immigrants ("Editorial" [Two Italians] 11). In July 1911, the objective reporting style of *The Crisis* was put into play in the "Along the Color Line" column, which included under "Crime" brief accounts of the murders of twelve African Americans in seven different events. These accounts are factual only: for example, the first merely reported that "[s]ix Negroes suspected of complicity in the murder of a prominent citizen were taken from the jail in Lake City, Florida, on May 21, carried to the suburbs of the city, tied to trees, and riddled with bullets" ("Along the Color Line: Crime" 99). More details were given in the NAACP report in the same issue, but the brevity of the notice here means that the reader immediately proceeds to the other items. The accounts of the additional six lynchings follow one another relentlessly. The final blow is a brief mention of President Taft's refusal to push for a federal law against lynching (99–100). Placing this item on the heels of these accounts makes his refusal seem particularly heartless, even though no judgment is voiced by the writer. In contrast to these objective notices, an editorial published the next month demonstrates Du Bois's compelling use of emotional appeals. The editorial decried lynching as evidence of a growing disrespect for the law and for the value of human life. Du Bois argued that such acts of violence result in "mob and murder" and "barbarism and cruelty," and he demanded that his readers respond: "Come, Americans who love America, is it not time to rub our eyes and awake and act?" ("Editorial: Lynching" 159).

Elsewhere, written and visual texts were combined in ways that enhance their impact. The first such example is a striking drawing by John Henry Adams, reproduced in the January 1911 issue as a two-page spread. This "cartoon" depicts a woman collapsed over a newspaper that reports on the lynching of a black man (see fig. 1.1). A photograph of a man, presumably the victim, sits on the table; the woman may be his wife, mother, or sister, or she may be a friend. The caption of the cartoon identifies lynching as "the national pastime" and notes, "Seventy-five per cent. of the Negroes lynched have not even been accused of rape" (Adams 19).

The drawing offers a powerful argument against lynching. It can be quickly comprehended and it has a strong emotional impact on the reader. The woman's grief is immediately apparent; the illustration successfully draws attention to the emotional toll of lynching on the family or friends of

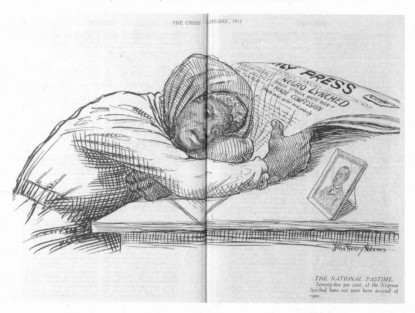

Fig. 1.1. "The National Pastime," a cartoon by John Henry Adams. The Crisis (*Jan. 1911*): *18–19.*

its victims, who must mourn the death of their friend or loved one. Read more carefully, the cartoon also offers a number of additional arguments against lynching. First, the caption, by pointing out that most victims were not even accused of rape, throws into question the usual rationale for lynching: that it was necessary to protect white women from the sexual assaults of black men. The headline of the paper reveals the error of this logic, for it identifies only "Brute Struck White Man" as the reason behind the lynching. There is no claim for sexual assault. Furthermore, the drawing hints at the violation of American ideals inherent in such a murder: the second headline of the paper reads, "American People Love Justice and Fair Play," a claim in tension with the identification of lynching as the national pastime. Finally, the photograph of the man presents him as anything but a brute: he is well dressed, with a dignified facial expression. The contrast between this image of him and the characterization of him as a brute in the headline casts doubt onto the accuracy of the report. The reader wonders, then, what else is wrong in the logic behind the lynching.

In effect, the drawing throws into question the justification of lynching and the assumptions made about the nature of its victims, and it demonstrates its consequences, in terms of national ideals and in terms of its human toll. The fact that these points are presented visually gives them an

Fig. 1.2. Illustrations for "NAACP: Holmes on Lynching." The Crisis *(Jan. 1912): 110.*

immediate impact, for readers can comprehend this visual text at a glance, more readily than they can process written texts.[31] But the caption extends the implication of the visual image, as do the written elements within the drawing, the headlines on the paper. This drawing, then, is an early example of the ways visual and written texts work together to communicate particular arguments about their subjects.

Another illustrated text published a year later demonstrates the ability of visual texts to increase the persuasiveness of written texts. John Haynes Holmes, a Unitarian minister and one of the founding members of the NAACP, delivered a denunciation of lynching at a meeting at the Ethical Culture Hall in New York City in November 1911; *The Crisis* printed his remarks in the January 1912 issue. Holmes argued that lynching revealed "the lawlessness of the American people" and that it was a disgraceful, evil crime. To demonstrate its dehumanizing effect, he described a photograph of the victim of a lynching in Oklahoma, emphasizing the similarities between it and a photograph of huntsmen returning with their kill. "In both cases," Holmes argued, "the huntsmen are proud that they have shot an animal, and therefore they stand before the camera in order that the evidence of the story may be sure" ("NAACP: Holmes on Lynching" 109). Accompanying Holmes's words is the reproduction of a postcard he received showing just such a scene. The front shows a crowd of men gathered, just as he described, around the victim's body (see fig. 1.2). Most look toward the camera. They do not hide their faces but, in fact, seem to want to be sure their presence is documented. The defiance, belligerence, and satisfaction apparent in their expressions make this photograph a perfect example of Holmes's assertions about the behavior of lynch mobs. Especially shocking is the message typed on the back of the card: "This is the way we do them down here. . . . Will put you on our regular mailing list. Expect one a month on the average."[32] For any readers who might have doubted Holmes's description, the reproduction of both the front and back of the card in *The Crisis* is indisputable evidence that his characterizations were accurate.

But printing such images and written protests of lynchings forced Du Bois to address questions of what the magazine should include. In the issue that followed the reprinting of the postcard as well as a photograph of another lynching, Du Bois defended the presence of these images: they were "a gruesome thing to publish, and yet—could the tale have been told otherwise? Can the nation otherwise awaken to the enormity of this beastly crime of crimes, this rape of law and decency?" ("Editorial: The Gall of Bitterness" 153). Du Bois acknowledged the brutality of these images and the strong revulsion they evoked, but he saw those aspects of the images as necessary. However, the reproduction of the card and other photographs of lynching victims has even more troubling implications. *The Crisis* used the bodies of lynched African Americans to stir up opposition to lynching, but in doing so it also continued the process of dehumanization that lynching enacted. Lynching photographs reduced African Americans' bodies to symbols; by showing only their corpses, they implied that the only important factor about their lives was how they ended.

This point is demonstrated in a supplement to the July 1916 issue that includes a written account of a lynching that occurred in Waco, Texas, along with photographs of the event and the victim. Jesse Washington, a young black man, was accused of assaulting and then murdering the white woman for whom he worked. He was tried, found guilty, and brutally murdered by a mob that included many of the prominent citizens of the town. The supplement includes the details of the events, as compiled by a "special agent" for the NAACP; it reports that Washington was stripped, mutilated, stabbed repeatedly, dragged through town, hung from a tree, and burned. His torso was dragged through town a second time after he died, and parts of his body were taken as souvenirs by members of the crowd of thousands ("The Waco

THE WACO HORROR

THE TORTURE (Note the "Frenzied" Mob)

that woman?' He answered, 'No.' 'If it had been a colored boy and a colored woman? No.' 'We would not have stopped the niggers doing anything they wanted to.' 'Do you think they would?' 'No.' 'Then, they prove their superior civilization.' Then he began to tell me how he knew all about the niggers and we northerners do not. He said that as an old southerner he knew perfectly well how to handle the colored population. He told me how he was raised with them, had a colored mammy, nursed at her breast, etc.

"There is a bunch of people in Waco who are dying to see someone go forward and make a protest, but no one in Waco would do it. Ex-Mayor Mackaye and Colonel Hamilton both said, 'We do not know what to do. We are not organized to do it. It is a case of race and politics.'

"I put out a lot of wires for a lawyer to take up the case, but no human

being in Waco would take it up. I wrote to a friend in Austin and one in Houston, and the Austin friend telegraphed me that he would send me word as soon as he had found someone. I had a letter from the Houston friend who gave me the names of three lawyers, but am not sure whether they would take up a case of this kind. All have their doubts of ever getting the case into court.

"I did not dare ask much about lawyers.

"As a result of the lynching a Sunday School Convention which was to have met there, with 15,000 delegates, has been stopped.

"W. A. Brazelton, the foreman of the Jury, was very outspoken against the whole affair and blames the officials for it. He felt that as foreman of the Jury he could not lead in a protest but *thought* some protest ought to be made.

"Mr. Ainsworth, one of the newspaper men, seemed the

Fig. 1.3. Illustrations for "The Waco Horror." The Crisis *(July 1916): Supplement:* 6–7.

Horror" 2–6). The photographs that accompany the report offer visual evidence of the brutality of the murder. They show Washington's charred torso hanging from the tree, the onlookers visible behind it, many of them smiling and even tipping their hats (see fig. 1.3). But the state of Washington's corpse is even more shocking than the crowd's reaction. Washington has been so brutalized that all of his limbs have broken off; what remains hardly looks human. It is difficult to imagine that, hours before these photographs were taken, this body belonged to a living person.[33]

Although the NAACP writer included a few details about Washington's life, the photographs objectified him and used his body to serve the efforts of *The Crisis* to oppose lynching. Even after his death, that is, Washington had no privacy; his body was displayed once again. He was, as the title of a recent collection of lynching photographs suggests, "without sanctuary."[34] Certainly the photographs as they were used here have a very different purpose and intention than they would if they were reproduced as postcards or souvenirs for proud participants of the events. Perhaps Washington would have wanted people to see these images, to know what was done to him, to have the evidence of his body serve the purpose of protesting lynching. But, of course, it was the creators of *The Crisis* who made the decision to include these photographs, not Washington.

The problematic dynamics of these photographs were increased by the fact that *The Crisis* republished one of them in July 1917. This issue includes a supplement on the lynching of Ell Persons in Memphis; it also reprints an account of the murder that had been published in the Harvard *Crimson*. Above that account is one of the photographs that appeared in the supplement covering Washington's murder ("The Looking Glass: Memphis" 134). If the photograph in the 1916 supplement is of Washington's body, the reproduction of it in the 1917 issue is a troubling incident of the magazine using Washington's body for its own purposes, to stir up revulsion for such crimes. Again, perhaps Washington would have wanted his death to serve such a purpose, but even so, the reproduction of this photograph turns his body into a symbol. In addition, it undermines the usefulness of photographs, if part of their impact depends on readers interpreting them as accurate, objective records.[35] The reproduction of this photograph, for a reader who realized that the editors slipped it into *The Crisis* a second time, demonstrates the degree to which apparently objective photographs can be manipulated according to the needs and interests of the person who presents them. The reader is left to wonder, then, if the photograph even shows what it seemed to show in the July 1916 supplement. Is this really Jesse Washington's body? The fact that a reader may ask that question indicates that the value of the photograph as evidence of the crime has been undermined.

As long as the reader did not recognize this photograph as previously published, its appearance in the 1917 issue adds to the impact of the arguments there. But the fact that its effect can be thrown into question illuminates one aspect of the difficulties of using lynching photography in a way that supports the goals of *The Crisis*. For such photographs to have the strongest impact possible, the magazine had to use them very carefully. Furthermore, their usefulness is offset, at least to some extent, by the fact that they communicate only limited information about their subjects and that they potentially continue the violation of these individuals' rights and dignity. Such photographs can support arguments about the nature of lynching, but what they show about the identity of African Americans is less clear —or more problematic, for these protest photographs can reveal only what has been done to African Americans.

In other words, while such images show the horrors of lynching, they do little to counteract the common assumptions about lynching victims. Du Bois was perhaps aware of this dilemma: he argued, in the same editorial in which he defended the need to reproduce the photographs of lynching victims, that the all-too-common attitude about race relations was that "all was well or if aught was wrong the wrong was with the colored man." Even worse, depictions of African Americans too often implied that "the shortcomings of black men are stupendous, if not fatal." Lynching photographs—and other protest texts—did little to what Du Bois here called a "debauch of defamation."[36] They could show that acts of racism and violence were horrid and evil, but they did not offer compelling redefinitions of African American identity.

The inability to indicate much to readers about the people who had been murdered or mistreated is true for many of the protest texts in *The Crisis*. In effect, protesting the racism in American society put *The Crisis* into a double bind: to persuasively demonstrate the horrible treatment of African Americans, it had to demonstrate their dehumanization and their disempowerment, and that demonstration, in turn, risked perpetuating that status. It was only with the addition of affirmative texts that the magazine was able to protest American racism but still empower African Americans.

Perhaps it is no surprise, then, that affirmative texts appeared in every issue of *The Crisis;* the magazine never included protest without affirmation, and the extensive coverage in *The Crisis* of the accomplishments of African Americans provided a constant counterpoint to its protest texts. Against the dehumanization perpetuated in the magazine's coverage of racism, violence,

MEN OF THE MONTH

A FLORIST.

PEYTON M. DeWITT, of Bridgewater, Pa., is rated by Bradstreet at $40,000. Mr. DeWitt is one of the most successful horticulturalists in the country and has worked up in his trade from gardener's assistant to the proprietor of a large business which has put several new varieties of flowers on the market. He was born in Georgia just before the outbreak of the Civil War, and came with his mother and her three other children to Bristol, Pa. At the age of 8 he was a mule driver on the canal and then became a gardener.

In the summer of 1880 came the first undertaking—a partnership with his brother in a small house, 12x50, at Bristol. After

DR. GEORGE W. BUCKNER.

seven years of successful effort he became the sole proprietor of a large establishment at Torresdale. For the past fifteen years the plant has been beautifully located at Bridgewater upon a tract of thirty acres. The plant comprises, roughly, eight greenhouses, each having a depth of 150 feet and a breadth of twenty feet, covered by 20,000 feet of glass; a central hot-water plant under pressure, fed by two boilers of twenty-five and forty horse power, respectively; a water tank of 15,000 gallons capacity and other necessary equipment.

A regular force of six men is employed, including a very capable foreman, who has been in Mr. DeWitt's service for eighteen years.

PEYTON M. DeWITT.

Fig. 1.4. A typical "Men of the Month" page. The Crisis *(Nov. 1913): 325.*

and murder, *The Crisis* featured African Americans who had achieved success in sports, politics, business, education, or the arts. In effect, this coverage established a collective identity for African Americans based on the achievements of notable individuals. Here, too, different kinds of texts were combined into composites that enhance the persuasiveness of the magazine's contents.

The Crisis featured many kinds of affirmative texts, and these display a number of strategies for defining African American identity. Photographs and news stories, for example, were combined in nearly every issue in coverage of African Americans' activities in institutions like the YMCA, their participation in conventions, and their work in fraternities and other associations. Regular columns like "Men of the Month" presented written descriptions and photographic portraits of successful individuals. Typically the "Men of the Month" column was about four pages long, featured between five and eight individuals, and printed their portraits in prominent positions alongside the written copy (see fig. 1.4).[37] The portraits depict individuals who are dignified and sophisticated, while the written descriptions testify to their dedication, persistence, and success in their chosen fields of endeavor. These written and visual texts work together to provide compelling evidence against stereotypes of African Americans as incapable of progress and achievement. Furthermore, the fact that *The Crisis* never had any shortage of such individuals to present—month after month, it was packed with descriptions and photographs—asserted their representativeness. These individuals, their numbers implied, were typical rather than exceptional.

In special issues, written and visual texts were combined to depict certain groups of African Americans. Such issues were devoted to athletes, soldiers, and residents of selected cities, and these defined particular character traits as typical of African Americans. One characteristic of African Americans that *The Crisis* emphasized was their financial success, especially as it was manifested in real estate. For example, the magazine drew a great deal of attention to the accumulation of wealth and property by African Americans in special issues devoted to individual cities or areas of the country, such as the Pacific Northwest or Seattle.[38] The first such feature, in the August 1913 issue, included a story about "Colored California" that focused on the African American communities in a number of cities in the state. Du Bois conceded that Los Angeles was "not Paradise," given how sharply the color line was drawn there.[39] But he also emphasized the positive characteristics of the African Americans who lived in the city, using the homes owned by them as proof; they are, he explained, "pushing and energetic. They are without doubt the most beautifully housed group of colored people in the United States" ("Colored California" 193). The photographs of the homes of four prominent African American families living in Los Angeles demonstrate that point. Two other photographs show a tailor shop and a "business block" owned by African Americans. The significance of property owned by African Americans is even more clearly asserted in the photographs included in the October 1920 issue, the "Homes Number." On a two-page spread, a photograph of a rural cottage, identified as "The Old Cabin," faces a photograph of "The New Mansion," a home owned by an African American man in Memphis, Tennessee (see fig. 1.5). The juxtaposition of these two photographs, and the identification of these as "old" and "new" homes, positions the homes as material, physical evidence of the progress of African Americans. This progress is further demonstrated in photographs that appear later in the issue, of the interiors and exteriors of twelve other homes owned by African Americans.

The Crisis also drew extensive attention to the achievements of African Americans in education and to the promise of African American children. Special issues on African American graduates from high schools and colleges appeared nearly every July in the 1910s. These issues are filled with lists and photographs of African American graduates, many of them wearing their regalia. The representation of the graduates in the first education issue, in July 1912, set the pattern that the other education issues followed: the written description of their achievements is framed by their photographs, which run across the top and bottom of many of the pages (see fig. 1.6). The editorial commentary emphasizes the significance of the graduates' accomplishments and their promise as future citizens. In special children's issues, which appeared nearly every October starting in 1912, The Crisis published photographs of children sent in by readers, with as many as 70 to 100 photographs per issue.[40] Editorials spelled out particular arguments about what these children demonstrate. For example, in an essay called "Our Baby Pictures" in October 1914, Du Bois emphasized that the physical attractiveness of these children disproved arguments that African Americans were physically degenerate (298). His argument is illustrated by photographs of African American children, scattered across the pages of the essay.

The affirmative news stories and features in The Crisis thus offer important arguments about the characteristics, achievements, and potential of African Americans, and these are particularly persuasive because of their presentation in both written and visual texts. In effect, what emerges from these texts is a group portrait of African Americans. The magazine's portrayal of these representative individuals showed the race to be educated, financially successful, and capable of significant achievements in business and the professions. Its presentation of these members of the elite—the Talented Tenth, as Du Bois called them—demonstrated the degree to which African

THE OLD CABIN

THE NEW MANSION: RESIDENCE OF J. W. SANFORD, MEMPHIS, TENN.

Fig. 1.5. "The Old Cabin" and "The New Mansion." *The Crisis (Oct. 1920): 264–65.*

THE YEAR IN COLORED COLLEGES   135

T. G. DOUGLASS, Lane   MISS S. E. HAMILTON, Talladega   E. O. BERRY, Lincoln

its place is a widespread belief that there is no "demand" for such persons, and that they are unable to earn a living.

There have been, in the years 1823-1912, over 5,000 Negroes graduated from college. Returns for a thousand living graduates indicate the following occupations:

Teachers 54%
Preachers 20%
Physicians 07%
Lawyers 04%
Business and other occupations.15%

As teachers the college-bred Negroes have made the Negro industrial school possible. Tuskegee is directed by them in nearly all positions of importance, from the wife of the principal (Fisk, '89) down. At Hampton, Calhoun, Kowaliga, and a score of other schools, the colored college man has given invaluable service. As leaders in social uplift the Negro collegians have been especially valuable. Why, then, are they the object of so much criticism and innuendo? Apparently because white Americans fear them. We do not fear Negro criminals—rather we encourage them. We do not fear ignorance—we invite it. But trained knowledge and efficiency in this subject race is instinctively dreaded by a large number of people. President Taft said yesterday at Hampton: "Although education along scientific lines is useful, vocational education for the Negro is better, for the present at least;" but "vocation" is a large word. What vocations does the President have in mind? The vocation of citizen, voter, molder of public opinion? Probably not. He is thinking with the Memphis News-Scimitar, which says:

"Higher education fads find no place in the curriculum of the Memphis High School for Negroes. The whole policy is to train the Negro youths of both sexes in occupations which the South has accorded almost entirely to the race."

In other words, the principal vocation in

E. W. LATSON, Atlanta Baptist   MISS A. L. BOTHWELL, Atlanta   G. F. DAVID, Wilberforce

Fig. 1.6. Illustrations for "The Year in Colored Colleges." The Crisis (July 1912): 134–35.

Americans did not fit stereotypes that defined them as incapable of progress or achievement.[41] Furthermore, through these individuals, the magazine offered role models to African American readers; it showed ideals to which black readers could aspire. Of course, there are limits to this portrait. It shows little of the other 90 percent of African Americans, and its implications about gender roles are significant. It is primarily—though not exclusively—men who are depicted in the "Men of the Month" column; while women appear among the graduates in special issues, they are more commonly depicted, anonymously, on the covers, in glamour photographs and drawings.[42] Though there are exceptions, then, men most often are used to show the business and financial success of African Americans, while women demonstrate their beauty and social achievements. In the context of the 1910s, though, these images were quite progressive in their depiction of African Americans, and they enable *The Crisis* to fulfill the goals Du Bois had articulated in 1905, of offering both news and inspiration.

But Du Bois clearly believed that there was a danger in affirmative texts if they were the only kind offered: too much focus on the achievements of African Americans might divert attention from the need to challenge the racism and violence practiced against them. In the April 1911 issue, for example, Du Bois asserted that to focus only on progress, without also recognizing continuing acts of racism and discrimination, would be telling only half the truth and would be a "dangerous injustice"; he concluded that "it is a dangerous falsehood to overlook the tireless and daily assaults of enemies of humanity" ("Editorial: The Truth" 21–22). In June 1911 he reasserted the argument and described the beliefs that guided his editorship of *The Crisis:* "Awful as race prejudice, lawlessness and ignorance are, we can fight them if we frankly face them and dare name them and tell the truth; but if we continually dodge and cloud the issue, and say the half truth because the whole truth stings and shames; if we do this, we invite catastrophe" ("Editorial: Starvation and Prejudice" 64). Du Bois's repeated emphasis on the "danger," even "catastrophe," invited by a failure to protest racism forcefully asserts the need to complement affirmation with protest: the former without the latter would not give a complete picture of African Americans' lives.

While the presence of both protest and affirmation in *The Crisis* thus is crucial, the combinations of the two kinds of texts heightened their impact even further; together, the two demonstrated that African Americans' success was earned in spite of racist injustice and violence. Juxtapositions of protest and affirmation were frequent; texts that reported on lynching and

THE BURDEN

ANOTHER SOUTHERN IDYL.

CHAPTER I.

HE received a high-school education and taught school.

CHAPTER II.

He got married and here is the family:

CHAPTER III.

He took the civil-service examination and entered the postal service, being the first colored carrier.

CHAPTER IV.

He received a letter from the "Superior Race," who were his "Best Friends," smeared with blood and reading:

"April 12, 1902.

"To * * *, Negro Postman

"*you had better not* be Seen carrying or delivering mail in * * * after to-day 12th day of April. *Don't forget.*

"If you should your life will pay the penalty. A word to the wise is sufficient.

"We are yours for trouble."

CHAPTER V.

He received a second letter to the "Nigger Mail Carrier":

"Your days are numbered, *leave,* LEAVE, LEAVE. DEATH, DEATH."

CHAPTER VI.

He writes us: "I am still in the service!" Which is what we call pluck.

⁂

CHARLESTON, S. C.

FOR the past years Charleston has been considered queen of the Southern cities as far as privileges granted colored people were concerned. But at last she has fallen in with the other places over which we used to triumph. For years the "Jim Crow" trolley car has been in effect all over the South except in Charleston. But at last our enemies have succeeded in getting it here. To-day it is the same here as in other towns—white people have two-thirds of the car, while we have but the two rear seats, yet we pay the same fare as our white brothers. The privileges granted us at the theatre were excellent. Now the same conditions as elsewhere prevail here; only a limited number of tickets are sold to us, and then if we are overanxious to see the show we pay double what our white brothers pay.

There are hospitals, sanitariums, libraries, etc., for the whites, from which they debar us, and when we apply for permits to erect buildings we are often denied. I don't know what we are going to do; something ought and must be done. Just think of the number of teachers employed in our public schools, of which there are three, and only two colored teachers are employed. If we are "Jim Crowed" on cars, in theatres, churches, stores, then why not in schools? Give us colored

Fig. 1.7. "The Burden: Another Southern Idyl." The Crisis *(March 1913): 246.*

violence against African Americans were often placed next to, above, or facing reports of accomplishments and achievements. For example, the "Men of the Month" column usually ran immediately following the column "Along the Color Line." While the latter included notes about the achievements of African Americans, it often ended with a list of crimes against African Americans, including lynchings. In the November 1913 issue, for instance, "Along the Color Line" began with accounts of accomplishments by African Americans in a range of fields, and it ended five pages later with a list of African Americans who had been lynched during the previous month, had barely escaped lynching, or had otherwise been the victims of violence or the threat of violence. The "Men of the Month" column immediately followed, creating a two-page spread that juxtaposes, on the left-hand page, a list of victims of violence and, on the right-hand page, the photographs and descriptions of the accomplishments of the successful individuals. The resulting layout suggests that acts of violence happen in the midst of—and despite—such accomplishments.[43]

Other such composite texts remind readers that violence against African Americans cannot be used to interpolate the characteristics of the race as a whole. Furthermore, the layout of these two types of features show that few assumptions can be made about individuals who were threatened with violence or were victims of violence. For example, in the March 1913 issue, the column "The Burden" included a photograph of an attractive, apparently financially successful family. The man, woman, and child are well dressed, and their posture and facial expressions demonstrate dignity and poise (see fig. 1.7). But the written copy informs readers that they had been subjected to threats of violence and even death. The man, identified as the first African American postal carrier in his town, had received anonymous notes demanding that he leave his position and, in fact, the city. If he did not, the letters warned, "your life will pay the penalty" ("The Burden: Another Southern Idyl" 246). The man reported to *The Crisis,* however, that "I am still in the service!" This mail carrier belonged in the "Men of the Month" column; the fact that his story appeared in "The Burden," with its accounts of lynchings and other acts of violence and racism against African Americans, demonstrates that his success did little to protect him from danger.

That point is further emphasized in a story about Anthony Crawford that appeared in the December 1916 issue. The written text explains that Crawford, a farmer who lived in Abbeville, South Carolina, "had raised a family of sixteen children, was reputed to be worth $20,000, and had always been a law abiding, self-respecting citizen" ("Anthony Crawford" 67). The photograph of Crawford furthers this impression: he is well dressed in a suit

ANTHONY CRAWFORD

A NTHONY CRAW-
FORD, a colored farmer, of Abbeville, S. C., owned 427 acres of the best cotton land in the county. He had raised a family of sixteen children, was reputed to be worth $20,000, and had always been a law abiding, self-respecting citizen. On October 21, he came to Abbeville, and went to the store of W. D. Barksdale, to sell a load of cotton seed. The two men quarrelled about the price, although no blow was struck by either one. Crawford was arrested by a local policeman and a crowd of idlers from the square, pictured below, rushed to give him a whipping for his "impudence." He promptly knocked down the ringleader with a hammer. The mob set upon him and nearly killed him. He was thrown wounded into jail. A few hours later, fearing that the sheriff would remove him secretly, the mob dragged his wounded body forth, jumped on it, and mutilated it, and finally hanged and shot it. They then warned his family to leave the county by November 15.

A full account of this lynching as investigated by Roy Nash, Secretary of the N. A. A. C. P., will appear shortly.

PUBLIC SQUARE, ABBEVILLE.
67

Fig. 1.8. "Anthony Crawford." The Crisis *(Dec. 1916): 67.*

and tie and looks with dignity at the reader, a hint of a smile on his face (see fig. 1.8). A photograph of a public square in Abbeville is reproduced at the bottom of the page; the reader might expect, then, to find that Crawford was a successful businessman, with the town square being the place of his accomplishments. But the rest of the written copy tells a different story. After a quarrel with a white man, Crawford was arrested, nearly killed, thrown in jail, kidnapped from the jail, mutilated, and finally hung and shot. The square, it turns out, is not the site of business success for Crawford but the place where the mob gathered to torture and then murder him.

The presentation of the stories about Anthony Crawford and the mail carrier is crucial to their impact. Both men could appear, by virtue of their accomplishments, in the "Men of the Month" column, and the layout of their stories is similar to the layout of that column, with its dominant portrait photographs of individuals and its written descriptions of their accomplishments. Having seen so many of those columns in these and other issues, a reader might assume, upon glancing at these pages, that the written copy would include accounts of the individuals' achievements. The fact that that expectation is not met registers the disruption produced by racism.

Many of the education issues and the children's issues create similar discomfort for the reader through disturbing juxtapositions. In the first education issue, for example, the prose that runs alongside the portraits of the graduates identifies them as representatives of a future in which the mistreatment of African Americans would be less possible: "As a matter of fact here are a group of healthy, bright-eyed, clear-brained young folk of Negro descent, who are going to make the cheating, lynching and oppression of black folk more difficult in the future than in the past!" ("The Year in Colored Colleges" 134). The horror of such treatment in the present, though, is detailed in the columns "Along the Color Line" and "The Burden." The disparity between African Americans' achievements and their treatment is especially vivid in the July 1916 issue, when the education number includes the supplement on the lynching of Jesse Washington. On the editorial page, a piece on "Our Graduates" is sandwiched between two other editorials. One draws attention to the supplement and an advertisement for the NAACP and its fight against lynching; the other justifies the use of the gruesome photographs of Washington's charred body. In this case, the account of accomplishments is sandwiched between two reminders of violence against African Americans. The issue itself includes the same kind of portraits of graduates shown in other education issues as well as a cover photograph of five anonymous graduates. The two men are wearing suits, the women dresses, and all are holding their diplomas and gazing with dignity and pride at the viewer (see fig. 1.9). In the table of contents, the photograph is enti-

EDUCATION NUMBER WITH WACO, TEXAS, SUPPLEMENT

The CRISIS

Vol. 12—No. 3   JULY, 1916   Whole No. 69

ONE DOLLAR A YEAR   TEN CENTS A COPY

Fig. 1.9. "Up from Georgia." The Crisis *(July 1916): cover.*

tled, in a perhaps ironic retort to Booker T. Washington's educational philosophy, "Up from Georgia." The photographs in the supplement provide a
shocking contrast to this cover image: the dignity of these educated graduates and the horror of the charred human remains offer a stunning visual
testament to the irrationality of racism and violence.

The same kind of juxtaposition occurs in many children's issues. For all
the promise that the future held for African American children, Du Bois also
acknowledged that they were subject to violence and discrimination. In the
first children's issue, he argued in an editorial that African American adults'
first impulse should be to shield children from the offenses that they were all
too likely to face ("Editorial: Of the Shielding Arm" 287–88). Two years later,
in the 1914 children's issue, he pointed out that these children are "beautiful,
bright, and wholesome. There is no reason in the world why in any civilized
human society they should not easily, gracefully, and effectively take their
place and do their work, receiving the respect due to decent human beings"
("Our Baby Pictures" 299). However, as he mentioned, "they will be looked
upon as 'problems'" (299) and, if current methods of "race proscription and
restriction" continued, their opportunities and their potential would be denied (300). His argument is made manifest by the placement of photographs
of children alongside reports of segregation, racial friction, and lynching in
the "Opinion" section of the issue: the photographs frame the editorials on
these topics, running above and below the written text (see fig. 1.10). The
layout draws attention to the injustice of the possibility that the lives of these
innocent children would be circumscribed by the racism discussed in the
written texts.

Certain children's issues include even more startling juxtapositions. In
October 1916, for example, a photograph of a young girl appears over the
NAACP column, the main article of which is an account entitled "Another
Lynching" (see fig. 1.11). Readers might expect this photograph to operate
like the photographs in "Men of the Month," with the written copy discussing the girl's achievements or at least her representative identity as the
embodiment of the hope for the future of the race; instead, the picture is
horribly incompatible with the written text, which describes deadly violence
against African Americans living near Gainesville, Florida. A man named
Boisy Long was accused of stealing hogs; after he killed the local sheriff and
escaped, his wife and four neighbors were lynched. He was eventually captured and was in jail at the time of the publication of the story. He and his
wife had four or five children; another of the women lynched had two children and was pregnant; one of the men killed also had a family (M. A. H.
275–76). The girl in the picture is not named; presumably, she is not one
of these children whose parents were killed. But the juxtaposition of her

PENNSYLVANIA   TENNESSEE   FLORIDA

MUST BE LESS TALK OF RACIAL FRICTION

Booker T. Washington Advises Negroes Not to Fight Segregation Laws

Muskogee, Okla., Aug. 19.—Booker T. Washington, of Tuskegee, Ala., to-night told delegates to the annual convention of the National Negro Business League, in session here, that there must be less talk of racial friction and more attention to the acquiring of intelligence and wealth if the Negro race is to progress.

"Quit thinking of the parts of the cities you can't live in, but begin to beautify that part in which you can live," he advised in discussing segregation laws recently enacted in several cities.

LYNCHING

"MINOR DISCRIMINATIONS" *Leslie's Weekly*, which has never been top-heavy with brains, has this delicious advice in an editorial on "The Negroes' Future":

"Let not the Negro imagine because of lynchings and minor discriminations here and there that every man's hand is raised against him. The Negro must help himself. He must win a place for himself. Whenever he does this he possesses self-respect and receives also the respect of others."

"Minor Discriminations" is excellent, and it must be gratifying to the 2,692 Negroes who have been publicly lynched and burned in the last 29 years to know that they are receiving the "respect" of others.

Meantime, the London (Eng.) *Spectator* insists that President Wilson's first and largest duty is to stop the disgrace of lynching. Answering the criticism of a correspondent it says:

"We, of course, knew as well as he does that the Constitution gives no power to the President or to Congress to apply our proposals to districts where lynchings have taken place. Therefore we suggested that the President should take the lead in inaugurating legislation, including, of course, the necessary amendment of the Constitution. We shall, of course, be told that such an amendment is absolutely hopeless. To which we

TENNESSEE   DISTRICT OF COLUMBIA   OHIO

Fig. 1.10. Illustrations from a children's issue. The Crisis *(Oct. 1914): 278–79.*

National Association for the Advancement of Colored People

THE LYNCHING FUND

A S we go to press the Ten .Thousand Dollar Anti-lynching Fund has reached the sum of $10,177.50 in cash and pledges. We Congratulate America.

ANOTHER LYNCHING
By M. A. H.

G AINESVILLE, a charming town about eighty miles southwest of Jacksonville, Fla., has a population of about 11,000. It is in a turpentine country, but the immediate neighborhood is chiefly devoted to truck and cotton farming. The University of Florida, with its beautiful buildings, is on the outskirts of the town.

Newberry is eighteen miles west by the driving road. It is entirely different in character. It is a railroad station; its total population is recorded at 1,000, but that seems a high figure, and two-thirds of the inhabitants are Negroes. Newberry was built when the phosphate fields were being worked in the close vicinity. These phosphate fields have been closed for several years and since then farming and trading have been the chief occupations.

The town is a desolate place of shanties and small houses, and has the reputation of lawlessness. There is not one good building in the place and many of the houses are vacant. The sun beats down on the roofs and there is almost no shade. The white men live chiefly by small stores. The colored people hire out to farmers, etc. Many of the colored women go out to service in other cities.

The driving road between Gainesville and Newberry is more of the Gainesville character. Most of the land is under cultivation. Four or five large farms lie along the road, but most of them are small farms. Roads branch off from the main road leading to other farms. The chief products are cotton, corn, some sugar cane, peanuts, pecans, melons, cucumbers, and other garden truck. A large number of the farmers are Negroes. They own their own land, to a large extent, and are prosperous.

Jonesville is a blacksmith shop and a store with adjacent farms five miles from Newberry and thirteen miles from Gainesville. The rioting was along the road between Jonesville and Newberry. The white men were all either from Newberry or the neighborhood.

The trouble arose over hogs. In the last few years hog raising has become profitable here. A Gainesville firm buys the farmers' hogs and ships them to a large packing concern in Georgia. Many of the farmers have hogs which roam at large in the road and in the woods. They are supposed to be branded, but they are not always and there is constant trouble about them.

Some of the white farmers accused Boisy Long and another colored man of stealing hogs. The latter man was arrested on a warrant and is now in jail.

The story is that the sheriff went to serve a warrant on Boisy Long at two o'clock on the morning of August 18, which seemed an extraordinary thing to do—to go out on a lonely road to arrest a man at this hour. The reason given is that he got the warrant in Jacksonville and came out on the train at 12:30 at night to Gainesville, where he took an automobile. Why he should be

275

Fig. 1.11. The opening page of M. A. H.'s "NAACP: Another Lynching." *The Crisis (Oct. 1916): 275.*

photograph with this account, particularly because she is anonymous and her image appears above the copy, suggests this possibility: a reader whose imagination is engaged by the combination of texts might wonder if perhaps the girl's father or mother were one of the victims. That reader also might ponder the future: If this treatment of African Americans were to continue, would the girl's future husband, or even her son, become a victim? Does a future of grief, loss, and violence await her? Imagining such possibilities reinforces the urgency of the need to act immediately to fight racism.

Such juxtapositions thus have the potential to engage the imaginations —and outrage—of readers. Pairing protest and affirmation in the 1910s must have heightened readers' frustration but also given them a sense of urgency. The continuing violence in the midst of growing achievements is impossible to justify; the layout of *The Crisis* draws attention to this disparity between African Americans' accomplishments and their treatment, and, ideally, it ignites in the reader a drive toward action and change.

In protest and affirmative features, then, combinations of written and visual texts enhance the ability of *The Crisis* to undermine racism and redefine African American identity. Furthermore, the juxtaposition of these texts and the implications of the resulting disjunctions enhance the impact of the magazine as a whole. If we are to fully appreciate its efforts to bring about social change, then, we must consider its multi-media format and its layout. By extension, the importance of the composite texts in *The Crisis* in the 1910s suggests the need for a thorough analysis of the use of a range of texts in the magazines and books published the following decade, as the Harlem Renaissance really got under way. But the focus and tone of many publications would shift as the Harlem Renaissance developed. By the late 1910s, *The Crisis* was joined by a number of other periodicals that featured harsh critiques of American racism, including Marcus Garvey's *Negro World* and *The Messenger,* edited by Chandler Owen and A. Philip Randolph. These publications gave voice to African Americans' frustration with continued racism— and increasing violence—carried out against them. World War I seemed a reason for optimism, at least for some. Du Bois, for example, hoped that the war would be a turning point in the treatment of African Americans. Believing that the service of African American soldiers to their country would be an effective tool against racism, he urged African Americans to set aside their grievances against white Americans and enlist in the nation's battle in his famous July 1918 "Close Ranks" editorial. But the optimism reflected here proved unfounded: African Americans' enlistment and service did not earn them respect or even fair treatment, either during or after the war. Du Bois himself became painfully aware of how entrenched American racism was in the battle over the commissioning of black officers, the treatment of black soldiers and the slandering of their conduct, and then in his discovery of a document circulated by the U.S. military to the French, demanding that the French stop treating African American soldiers so well (Lewis, *Du Bois* I: 553–74). Faced with this continued abuse, Du Bois called African Americans to battle a second time in May 1919, in this case to fight "against the forces of hell in our own land" ("Editorial: Returning Soldiers" 14). He listed the ways America treated its black citizens: "It *lynches*. . . . It encourages *ignorance*. . . . It *steals* from us. . . . It *insults* us." He called for a militant resistance and response to this treatment, in the name of American ideals: "We *return*. We return *from fighting*. We return *fighting*. Make way for democracy!" (14). But instead of democracy, racial intolerance rose, as did lynchings, and riots flared in Charleston, South Carolina, Washington, D.C., Chicago, and more than twenty other cities.[44] James Weldon Johnson characterized the period as one when "even the stoutest-hearted Negroes felt terror and dismay" at the violence being carried out against African Americans (qtd. in De Jongh 7).

But within a couple of years, the frustration of the post-war disillusion began to give way to optimism. Certainly there still was much to protest, but the movement of hundreds of thousands of African Americans to the urban North during the Great Migration swelled the population of vibrant African American communities, including Harlem. The concentration of African Americans in such areas led to shifting ideas about African American identity. Furthermore, the publication of a number of books by African American writers in the early 1920s was cause for celebration. That, coupled with the growing presence of films by African Americans and their presence on stage as musicians and actors, led to new ideas about how texts might most effectively be used to shape public opinion. Although *The Crisis* continued to include protests of acts of violence against African Americans in the early 1920s, its tone mellowed and its attention to the arts increased. By the mid-1920s, the stunning juxtapositions of protest and affirmation had largely disappeared from its pages.

However, the mix of visual and written texts in *The Crisis* continued through the 1920s, and it also was present in other publications of the period. As they did in *The Crisis* in the 1910s, the mixes of texts in these magazines, anthologies, and books allowed their creators to offer complicated, dynamic representations of African Americans' experiences and ideas. Realizing the significance of the juxtapositions of written and visual texts in *The Crisis* in the 1910s, then, draws our attention to other composite texts produced by African Americans, and it suggests that we need to analyze these texts in their full complexity if we are to appreciate their potential to engage in the representation of African Americans. But beginning a study of the illustrated texts of the Harlem Renaissance with *The Crisis* in its first decade also reveals how much would change by the peak of the Harlem Renaissance, in terms of ideas about African American identity and about the use of texts to contribute to social change.

2

Objectivity and Social Change: Essays and News Stories in *Opportunity*

If the riots in Springfield, Illinois, in 1908 were one of the catalysts that led to the launching of *The Crisis*, the riots in Chicago eleven years later prompted a different kind of magazine and a different understanding of how texts might promote social change. By the end of the Chicago riots of 1919, 23 African Americans and 15 white Americans were dead, 537 people were wounded, and more than 1,000 were homeless (Lewis, *When Harlem Was in Vogue* 20). Significantly, periodicals that included protest and agitation were seen as heightening the intensity of the conflict. In the aftermath of the violence, a committee that studied its causes concluded that the newspapers in the city had fanned animosity between black and white residents to dangerous levels. The Chicago Commission on Race Relations called on the media to step back from these practices and to instead serve as a source of information that might help ease tension between black and white Americans and encourage interracial cooperation. One magazine that answered that call was *Opportunity.* Founded by the NUL in 1923, shaped by the NUL's emphasis on uplift and integration, and edited by sociologist Charles Spurgeon Johnson—one of the leading members of the Chicago Commission— *Opportunity* contains little of the fiery protest found in the 1910s in *The Crisis.* Instead, its contents include less inflammatory texts, such as expository essays, documentary photographs, and news stories and photographs.

In *Opportunity,* these texts serve the same purpose of redefining African American identity as did texts in *The Crisis.* But the texts in *Opportunity* in its early years fit into different conventions of representation. Its pages reflect the emphasis on facts and objectivity that Johnson learned in the Sociology Department at the University of Chicago and that was embraced by the NUL, and its contributors used rhetorical techniques common in sociology at the time to persuasively present their findings about African Americans' experiences and identity. But the magazine complements these objective and informative strategies of representation with appeals for action more common in the emerging field of social work. Furthermore, the written texts in *Opportunity* often are paired with documentary photographs—as are many essays in sociology and social work—and *Opportunity* used these combinations of photography and reports to draw its readers' attention to the aspects of African Americans' lives that needed improvement and to encourage its audience to join reform efforts.

But these kinds of illustrated essays also have potential drawbacks, particularly because they often imply that their subjects are powerless to change their own lives. This disadvantage is countered in *Opportunity* by essays that demonstrate African Americans' positive contributions to American industries, education, and public service as well as news stories and photographs that highlight the success of individual African Americans. These news texts are much like the affirmative texts so common in *The Crisis* in the 1910s, but they broaden the portrait of African Americans offered by Du Bois's magazine. Where *The Crisis* showcases primarily the achievements of the Talented Tenth, *Opportunity* shows more of the other 90 percent. Furthermore, while the primary purpose of *Opportunity*'s studies and news stories about African Americans' achievements is perhaps to define African Americans as capable of integration and accomplishments, they also assert that American society would benefit if African Americans were granted greater opportunities. *Opportunity,* then, includes a different mix of texts than did *The Crisis,* offers a different collective portrait of African Americans, and demonstrates that the changing identity of African Americans necessitated changes in American society and the functioning of American institutions.

Though *Opportunity* was carefully non-inflammatory, and though it emphasized the ability of African Americans to successfully fit into and contribute to American industries and social institutions, it also acknowledged the continuing racism and discrimination that was practiced against African Americans. Its contributors' awareness of American injustice perhaps fed into the shift in its content within a few years of its founding. Johnson came to see the arts as particularly important in the struggle against racism and oppression, and by 1925, expository texts had a less important role in *Opportunity* than literature and the arts. But in its first years, *Opportunity* used strategies of representation common in sociology and social work to provide persuasive information about African Americans. Mixed with news stories and photographs that emphasize the achievements of individual African Americans, these texts effectively redefine African American identity and prove to be important parts of efforts to improve African Americans' treatment.

Opportunity and Johnson's accomplishments as its editor have received far less scholarly attention than Du Bois and *The Crisis*, although there have been some efforts to record the history of the NUL, the development of its monthly magazine, and the work of its editor. Many of these focus on Johnson's and *Opportunity*'s roles during the Harlem Renaissance as a supporter and an outlet for the work of young writers and artists.[1] In its attention to the arts, it was not alone; as we shall see, other African American periodicals of the 1920s also drew attention to work by African American artists working in many different media. But its inclusion of expository essays like those found in the fields of sociology and social work makes *Opportunity* unusual among African American periodicals of the 1920s. None of the other big African American publications—neither magazines like *The Crisis* or *The Messenger* nor newspapers like the *Chicago Defender*—included many of these texts. *Opportunity*'s use of studies, news stories, and photographs provides a distinctive record of important developments in the ways texts were used to challenge derogatory ideas about African Americans and redefine African American identity.

The NUL's efforts to bring about social change began more than a decade before it began publishing *Opportunity*. The organization was created by the consolidation of three social work organizations in 1911. Its overall goal was to eliminate racial and class discrimination, but its specific focus was on carrying out research on migration and urban conditions, training social workers and others in leadership positions, and improving employment opportunities for African Americans (Weiss 42–43). Its economic focus and its research agenda complemented the aim and methods of the more legislatively and politically focused NAACP.[2] As the efforts of the NUL spread to include public health, recreation, housing, education, and other aspects of African Americans' lives, it often emphasized that it simply wanted to secure fair and reasonable facilities and opportunities for African Americans. Its slogan was "Not Alms, but Opportunity," a phrase that was reproduced on the cover of many of the issues of *Opportunity* published in 1923 and 1924. Like the NAACP, the NUL was a decidedly interracial organization: both "believed that both races should work together on an equal footing to secure common ends" (Weiss 58). Both had black and white members and leaders.

The NUL's primary mission when it was founded focused on conducting research and distributing information. Much of its work in the 1910s and early 1920s was in carrying out studies of the health, work habits, employment and housing opportunities, and education of African Americans. These studies did not necessarily advocate for change; they were meant simply to provide information about the challenges facing African Americans, which then could be used by social service institutions to meet their social and economic needs (Weiss 217). In order to be kept up to date on these studies, NUL executives demanded "some regular information bulletin," so the organization in 1921 established the bimonthly *Urban League Bulletin* to summarize the studies and their findings. In October 1922, the NUL decided to expand the newsletter into a larger, more formal publication (Parris and Brooks 170–71). Its readers might include professional sociologists and social workers. As we shall see, changes in the magazine's content by the mid-1920s allowed it to appeal toward an even broader audience, but even then it never had anywhere near the circulation of *The Crisis* at its peak.[3]

The first monthly issue of *Opportunity* appeared in January 1923, with Johnson as its editor. Johnson, by that time, had gained "a national reputation in the field of race relations" (Gilpin 219). After serving in World War I, he attended graduate school at the University of Chicago and began to study and then work with sociologist Robert E. Park. Johnson was head of the Department of Research and Investigation for the Chicago Urban League when the riots broke out in 1919. Two months after the five days of violence and destruction, Illinois governor Frank Lowden appointed a panel of six white and six black civic leaders, businessmen, and politicians to study the violence and determine, as much as possible, its causes. Johnson was made the associate executive secretary of this Chicago Commission on Race Relations, and he had a major and well-respected role in the conception, collection, and analysis of the necessary research.[4] Although he did not head the commission, he wrote much of the study and is acknowledged to have been its guiding force (Gilpin 218–19; Robbins 4, 34–36; Lewis, *When Harlem Was in Vogue* 47). When that work was done, he moved to New York City in 1921 to begin work as the NUL's national director of research and investigation and, two years later, became the editor of its magazine.

It is difficult to pin down exactly how much Johnson is responsible for the content of the magazine. Most discussions of it, the NUL, and Johnson's career speak about the production of the magazine only in broad terms. Furthermore, unpublished records, according to NUL historian Nancy Weiss, cast little light on the creation of the issues.[5] It is not clear, then, who determined the content, wrote the editorials, or arranged the texts in the magazine.[6] But it seems safe to assume that Johnson played a key role in at least the first two, for *Opportunity*'s focus and tone match his interests. For example, the magazine's contents are in keeping with the conclusion that Johnson —with other members of the Chicago Commission on Race Relations—

drew in *The Negro in Chicago*. The study's relevance to the magazine is explicitly signaled by the fact that the first issue includes a discussion of the group's 672-page report. V. D. Johnson, the writer of the review, emphasized the commission's conclusions that the Chicago riot had been "only a 'symptom of serious and profound disorders lying beneath the surface of race relations,'" and that "neither the Negroes nor the whites were in a good mood toward each other at the time of the riot" (27). This was, in large part, a result of the press: the commission found that the *Chicago Defender* had stirred up the bitterness of its black readers against whites, and that the *Chicago Tribune* had "served hatred for the Negro with the breakfasts of Chicago's white population" (27).[7] The commission also concluded that ignorance fueled that hatred: it found that white Americans knew very little about black Americans, and their perceptions of African Americans were largely shaped by images "that cause the Negro to appear only as a criminal or a fool" (27). The commission advised that if similar violence was to be avoided in the future, better understanding and attitudes between black and white Americans were necessary, and it argued that the press had to play a major role in promoting those changes. *Opportunity* would serve exactly that purpose.

Two essays in the July 1923 issue further demonstrate the relevance of the Chicago study to *Opportunity*. These are transcripts of speeches delivered at the National Conference of Social Work in May by Johnson and Graham Romeyn Taylor, the white man who had served as the executive secretary of the Chicago Commission. The two writers again summarized the findings of the commission, laying out its conclusions about the importance of information to the improvement of race relations and the role of the media in shaping public opinion. Taylor, for example, cited the commission's discovery that there were an incredibly small number of articles in white papers in Chicago about the achievements of African Americans, but many devoted to riots and crime involving African Americans (198). The effect, he asserted, was that white Chicago residents were misled into believing that African Americans were much more violent than was the case. Understanding the link between news coverage and public opinion would allow people to break the pattern. He pointed out, "At the core . . . of our consideration of race relations, are the mental attitudes of the people of one race towards those of the other. We must study what is in the minds of people, how it came there, and how the distorted conceptions, upon which opinion and action are so frequently based, may be modified" (197). That modification is, essentially, the goal of *Opportunity*.

Johnson's essay demonstrates how facts and information can challenge assumptions and change actions. After asserting that the problem of tension between blacks and whites stemmed from the assumption that stereotypes were true, Johnson spent much of his essay debunking a number of beliefs about African Americans. He used extensive facts, statistics, and quotes from authorities to disprove "three cardinal beliefs" about African Americans: that they were mentally inferior, immoral, and criminal ("Public Opinion and The Negro" 202). He offered statistics, quotes, and examples to disprove each of these claims. His essay, then, is an extensive challenge to these common myths and beliefs about African Americans; only through such a process of acknowledging and challenging ideas about African Americans, he concluded, can "many of our inhibitions to normal, rational and ethical conduct" be removed (206). The process he outlined and demonstrated here, of challenging stereotypes with facts so that behaviors would change, was used by many of the contributors to *Opportunity*.

The magazine most obviously put this strategy into play in its studies and reports. Essays in the very first issue, for example, included "The Diary of a Child Placing Agent," reports on two experiments with "Negro Labor in the Industries," two discussions of social work, an article on zoning, and an account of efforts to control tuberculosis. Such essays were mainstays in every issue of the magazine during its first years. Each issue also included editorials, reviews of fiction and non-fiction books somehow related to race relations, and, with greater frequency in the mid-to-late 1920s, fiction, poetry, and drama, as well as reviews of the arts. In April 1923, the journal also began to include brief notices about events relevant to race relations in columns titled "The Bulletin Board" or "Pot-Pourri." These columns, like the affirmative features in *The Crisis*, provided written descriptions of the accomplishments of individual African Americans and photographs of the individuals in question. The rousing and angry protest texts common in *The Crisis*, though, were almost never found in *Opportunity*. When the latter did note acts of discrimination and violence, its coverage was muted.

The style, focus, and conventions of *Opportunity*'s expository essays link it to the field of sociology. Auguste Comte had named the field in the mid-nineteenth century; its early American practitioners were primarily concerned with identifying the causes and explanations of human behavior (Faris 3–6). Early on, sociology was seen as "an ethical discipline," one in which the scientist "had a distinctive role to play in the improvement of society" (Bulmer 35). The methods and ameliorative goals of the field could easily be applied to African Americans and race relations. Du Bois, for example, had begun his career in the 1890s as a sociologist. His intention in his early work was "to study the facts, any and all facts, concerning the American Negro and his plight" (*Dusk of Dawn* 51). For *The Philadelphia Negro*, which he published in 1899, he conducted hundreds of interviews and compiled extensive data in order to create a portrait of the city's African American residents and to describe their experiences. Du Bois did not merely present information: he also interpreted it, building his study to powerful arguments about what needed to be done to empower African Americans and counteract the unemployment, poverty, and family breakdown that plagued the black community (Bracey, Meier, and Rudwick 7). Despite his own efforts to use sociological studies to push for change, he came to feel that such work did not offer a sufficient response to the violence carried out against African Americans, particularly because he grew to see sociology as centered on the collection of facts rather than on the use of this information to advocate reform (qtd. in Green and Driver 35). The ongoing murders of black men moved him to turn his efforts to propaganda and protest; he came to believe that "one could not be a calm, cool, and detached scientist while Negroes were lynched, murdered, and starved."[8]

Johnson, in response to the violence in Chicago in 1919, came to the opposite conclusion. The findings of the Chicago Commission that inflammatory texts made violence more likely and more severe—both by and against African Americans—made objectivity and detachment appealing to him, and those had become important features of sociology by the late 1910s, when Johnson was at the University of Chicago. He found an important mentor in Park.[9] One of Park's primary interests was race relations, and he carried out numerous studies of interactions between different ethnic and racial groups.[10] He was a strong believer in the importance of facts and objectivity, and he applied this criterion to his work with African Americans. For example, Park was associated with Booker T. Washington and Tuskegee for a decade before he went to Chicago. One of his projects, with Monroe Work and Emmett Scott, was co-founding the *Negro Yearbook* Publishing Company in 1910. The annual yearbooks included facts and statistics about African Americans and became important sources of information for both the NAACP and the NUL (Hutchinson 53). Park also was the first president of the Chicago Urban League, where Johnson worked in 1917–1918, and he advised Johnson as the latter worked on studies of the migration of African Americans from the South to the North and on the investigations in Chicago (Bulmer 75–76). Finally, Park had worked as a journalist for nearly ten years, and he was interested in the ways public opinion was shaped by the media, including newspapers but also other forms of publicity (Hutchinson 52, 56). The topics covered in *Opportunity*, then, parallel those of interest to this important early sociologist.[11]

Furthermore, many of the techniques used in the magazine to collect and present information about African Americans follow methods advocated by Park. Park's research often involved collecting personal life histories from his subjects, either through interviews or questionnaires (Matthews 162–63). Johnson did the same, for example, when he studied the Great Migration, in part by analyzing thousands of letters from migrants and their families, and he contributed essays to *Opportunity* that drew on this research. Park valued such case studies because they shed light on the formation of individuals' ideas; he was not a fan of statistics, which he felt "did not allow for the subjective sense of identity" and offered only limited insights (Matthews 179–80). *Opportunity*'s essays often include statistics, but these are just as often complemented by portrayals of individuals, which introduce readers to people who would have been affected by the conditions the statistics indicate. The magazine's inclusion of photographs and illustrations, furthermore, matches Park's belief that visual texts—"maps, charts, graphic representation"—were important in "the presentation and interpretation of the findings" (qtd. in Bulmer 72). Finally, Park believed that sociological studies would contribute to social change. Sociology, he felt, could illuminate how and why attitudes developed; by doing so, it might help people develop "a more detailed and complex understanding of themselves and their situation" (Matthews 187). Sociological research might ease the kind of tension seen in Chicago: Park felt it could enhance a person's "'acquaintance with' his fellows, particularly those of other races and life styles, so that they would become less strange to him, more 'real' or individuated, and therefore less threatening" (Matthews 192). As we shall see, this optimism about the possibility of changing attitudes through sociological research permeated *Opportunity* in the mid-1920s.

But the magazine also moved beyond the sociological methods taught in Chicago's sociology department, particularly on the question of objectivity. Park and other professors in the department played a key role in shifting the field away from social improvement and reform and toward neutrality. These scholars wanted to establish sociology as a scientific discipline; as such, it would have "no room for an ameliorative approach" (Bulmer 69). For Park, the objectivity of the researcher was crucial; he insisted on the need for sociologists to be "determinedly detached, apolitical" (Matthews 183). Johnson's sociological research followed this dictum: his work was so dispassionate that a friend of his wrote that his "colored friends scold[ed] him for being a calm student rather than a rabid reformer" (qtd. in Bracey, Meier, and Rudwick 15). But *Opportunity* represents a step away from this neutrality: although its writers generally remain calm, many implicitly identify solutions to the problems they identify. In that sense, *Opportunity*, though it has clear ties to Park's style of sociology, also can be linked to the field of social work and the reform efforts associated with it.[12] These were more explicitly aimed at bringing about change than was sociology. The mandate of the new profession of social work, for example, was to "relieve social pressures by combining direct help to the poor with legislative corrections or 'reform' of injustices such as child labor."[13] One branch of social work that is particularly relevant to *Opportunity* is the social survey movement, which peaked in popularity in the 1910s and 1920s. Social surveys were meant to identify problems and suggest ways to bring about change (Bulmer 67). One of the most famous studies was the Pittsburgh Survey, directed by Paul Kellogg from 1909 to 1914. Kellogg meant the project to aid in the identification of "what is ugly, wrong, and unhealthy and unjust in social conditions" in the city so that a "fuller life" might be made possible (qtd. in Stange 50). It had social change as its goal: "the survey tried to persuade all citizens, but chiefly those with economic and social power, to act on behalf of 'community'" (Trachtenberg 196). While it shared sociology's potential to identify problems and how they came about, then, it also lobbied for ways to change them. The NUL carried out many such surveys, and their methods are typical. The organization's researchers collected information through questionnaires and interviews; they also often consulted existing statistics. They tabulated and analyzed data and usually included recommendations for ameliorative action (Weiss 218).

Opportunity thus can be read, in many ways, as an extended, ongoing survey of black America. Like the Pittsburgh Survey, it includes studies of the industrial workforce and of the relations between workers and managers but also of neighborhoods, schools, and economic and political systems. Its inclusion of visual texts, too, parallels the presentation of information in surveys. Kellogg, for example, insisted on the necessity of maps, charts, diagrams, and photographs (Stange 51). For the Pittsburgh Survey, he hired the photographer Lewis Hine, whose work for the survey focused mostly on the city's laborers. These included children, and child labor became one of Hine's primary subjects between 1907 and 1917. His photographs of children working in coal mines, factories, and textile mills were crucial to efforts to reform child labor practices (Rosenblum 377–78; Trachtenberg 198–201). Hine's images also were influential in establishing the conventions of documentary photography and its role in reform efforts. His photographs have a spontaneous feel to them: his subjects, though they sometimes look at the camera, are generally captured while at work. Hine's photographs, then, show people bent over machines, carrying tools, and so on. The apparent spontaneity of the images adds to their impact, for it encourages viewers to read them as accurate records of working conditions. When his photographs were used by reform organizations, they often were paired with captions, headlines, and written texts in exhibits, reports, magazine and newspaper articles, posters, and leaflets (Trachtenberg 198–99). In these forms, visual and written texts work together to present information in compelling composites that might push their audiences to act.

As we shall see, the creators of *Opportunity* used similar techniques in the layout of its pages. The fact that they drew both from the conventions of sociology and social work also is significant to the impact of the magazine. In fact, it walks a fine line between the two fields, including elements of each but maintaining a middle ground that allowed it to appeal both to sociologists and to social workers and to advance its own goals. On one hand, the magazine was much more restrained than texts produced as part of reform movements. These could be quite emotional in their appeals; they are perhaps too close to protest and agitation to fit with the recommendations of the Chicago Commission on Race Relations.[14] Furthermore, if *Opportunity* became too much like these texts, it might have lost the respect of sociologists like Park who distinguished their research from social work. Park, in particular, was "disdainful of 'do-gooders'" and was critical of the ways social workers blurred the line between science and social intervention (Bulmer 68). On the other hand, the careful neutrality demanded by sociologists probably would have been too conservative for the magazine. Stepping beyond that neutrality allowed *Opportunity* to appeal to readers who might have been able to effect change because of their positions, such as employers and philanthropists who could financially support the necessary reforms. But by emphasizing its objectivity and its research methods, it would have satisfied readers in the two fields, both of which were struggling to professionalize in the early 1920s. The magazine's careful balance between objectivity and activism, in short, established its credibility as an accurate and dependable guide to action.

In other words, the conventions followed in *Opportunity*'s written studies and documentary photographs helped the magazine convincingly document existing problems and conditions that needed to be changed. By drawing the attention of sociologists and social workers to the obstacles faced by African Americans, *Opportunity* played an important role in the 1920s. Too often, these problems were neglected by both fields. Park's interest in race relations is an example of the relevance of sociology to African Americans, but sociologists like Du Bois, who made African Americans their primary focus, were kept on the periphery of the field (Ladner xxi; Bulmer 66; Bracey, Meier, and Rudwick 7–9). Social workers and progressive reform movements most often focused on class conflict, labor relations, and political and economic legislation (Painter, *Standing at Armageddon* 216, 220–21); the conditions affecting African Americans only occasionally drew their attention. In addition to combining the strategies of these two fields, then, *Opportunity* also expanded their focus.

But the conventions of these fields would not have allowed the magazine to fully enough challenge assumptions about African Americans. First, to the degree that sociological and social work studies suggest that the people who would be most able to effect change would be the readers rather than the subjects of the studies, they disempower their subjects. Second, such texts can have a dehumanizing effect. The information they communicate is about the conditions, not the people depicted, as Trachtenberg suggests about Hine's photographs (180). Hine's subjects are rarely identified by name; the age of child laborers often is the only information given about them. In effect, then, the human beings shown in such texts almost become props, instruments whose presence allows for greater understanding of the situation. In that sense, the work of photographers like Hine can be seen as "ultimately diminish[ing] the social and political presence of the very working people who were its subjects, encouraging their treatment as unimportant details in schemes administered by established business, commercial, and political interests" (Stange 65). Finally, the texts in *Opportunity* that focus on obstacles faced by African Americans do little to challenge the assumption that African Americans were wards of the state who needed to be cared for or problems who needed to be solved. For these three reasons, it is crucial that *Opportunity* complemented these texts with others that depicted African Americans in very different ways: studies and news stories about the achievements of African Americans and their contributions to American industries, education, politics, society, and culture. These texts might have inspired *Opportunity*'s African American readers toward collective effort and greater achievement. But these texts would have been important for readers of any race who had been exposed to the ubiquitous texts representing African Americans only as problems. *Opportunity*'s studies of African Americans' achievements in industries and its affirmative news stories identify African Americans as agents of change whose work contributes to the improvement of American society and institutions.

Opportunity's inclusion of these texts makes it different from sociological studies and social work. They might also have helped it broaden its readership: like the affirmative texts in *The Crisis,* the news texts in *Opportunity* might have drawn in African American readers who wanted to find positive images of themselves. The magazine's mix of texts, then, helps it meet its dual audiences and purposes: to reach a popular and professional audience, to engage black and white readers, and to show problems with existing conditions but also African Americans' ability to overcome current obstacles and become valued contributors to American society. The combinations of sociological and social work texts with news stories and photographs, then, were crucial to the magazine's ability to challenge assumptions about African Americans and to fashion a compelling, convincing, and empowering redefinition of African American identity.

Analyzing sample texts from *Opportunity* allows us to explore its contributors' success at using the conventions of sociology and social work for their own ends. For example, one of the insights gleaned from the fields of sociology and social work is that the persuasiveness of information depends in part on the credibility of the presenting organization. Contributors to *Opportunity* used a number of editorials and essays in the magazine's first issues to identify it and its parent organization. In 1923, for instance, in "'Cooperation' and 'Opportunity,'" NUL executive secretary Eugene Kinckle Jones explained to readers the goals of the NUL and its devotion to revealing facts and information. The organization, he pointed out, "has sought to make its contribution towards elevating the Negro in the social scale, the motive being to make it easier for the Negro to assimilate the cultural advantages of American civilization and to aid more Negroes of capacity and talent to emerge from the mass of their fellows of less promise" (4). Crucial in those efforts, he emphasized, were the NUL's attempts to "make available to white people information on the Negro that would tend to clear up many of the mooted questions about the Negro" (4). The NUL and *Opportunity*, he insisted, were committed to presenting dependable information about African Americans: the magazine's contributors would "try to set down interestingly but without sugar-coating or generalization the findings of careful scientific surveys and the facts gathered from research, undertaken not to prove preconceived notions but to lay bare Negro life as it is" (5). In offering this definition of the magazine's goals and methods, Jones asserted its credibility, a key step in enhancing the persuasive potential of the news and studies it contained.

A number of the contributors to the magazine emphasized the magazine's and the organization's neutrality and credibility over the next two years, and they also insisted that another of its priorities was avoiding inflaming tensions. In the February 1923 issue, the writer of "Why We Are" warned of the dangers of not recognizing the changes that African Americans had undergone in the past few years: "The pernicious influence of ignorance and misinformation has provoked disastrous consequences" (3). But the writer also emphasized that *Opportunity* would provide information that would change that situation in a carefully measured way:

> The policy of "Opportunity" will be definitely constructive. It will aim to present, objectively, facts of Negro life. It hopes, thru an analysis of these social questions to provide a basis of understanding; encourage interracial co-opera-

tion in the working out of these problems, especially those surrounding the emergence of the Negro into a new industrial field and the consequent reorganization of habit and skill. (3)[15]

Two years later, the writer of "We Begin a New Year" also emphasized the magazine's ability to present information in a way that did not arouse passions. Looking back on *Opportunity*'s content, the writer asserted that the magazine's "policy has been one of intelligent discussion rather than fireworks; of calm analysis rather than tears" (2). Making a resolution for the year to come, the writer identified *Opportunity*'s goals: "to create more light with no more heat than is necessary for warmth" (2). The repetition of this emphasis on exposing and illuminating, but not inflaming, reveals the continuing focus of *Opportunity* on providing information, rather than stirring up emotions, and it reassures readers that the magazine will help ease tension—even when its focus might be on problems.

But this emphasis on objectivity and cool presentation of facts did not mean that *Opportunity* accepted conditions as they were. The magazine, in fact, defined itself as using objective information to promote social change. For example, in "Why We Are" the writer emphasized that the magazine's "frank and unbiased presentation of facts and views" was meant to make it "a dependable guide to action" (3). Such a claim moves the magazine more toward social work and underlines the fact that many of *Opportunity*'s contributors suggested ways to ameliorate situations. The coupling of such recommendations with *Opportunity*'s emphasis on objectivity identifies its writers as professionals whose conclusions were based on evidence found in factual studies.

The careful objectivity of *Opportunity*'s writers can be seen even when it exposed acts of racism and discrimination. Like *The Crisis, Opportunity* recorded the occurrence of such events. But in keeping with the Chicago Commission's recommendations, *Opportunity* drew attention away from the victims. Rather than decrying the effects of the violence, contributors to the magazine investigated its causes. Doing so allowed it to debunk the rationalization that mob violence was necessary to control African Americans. *Opportunity*'s writers showed that it was a manifestation of anti-American attitudes, and they firmly attached blame to white Americans, not black Americans.

The difference between *Opportunity*'s coverage of such acts and the protest texts common in *The Crisis* in the 1910s is clear in two essays published in *Opportunity*'s September 1923 issue that analyze the ideas and practices of the Ku Klux Klan. In a total switch from Du Bois's coverage of lynching and mob violence, the two essays and the accompanying photographs in *Opportunity* keep readers' attention away from the effects on

African Americans. Robert Bagnall and Guy B. Johnson, the writers of the essays, focused their attention on the Klan's attitudes. Both writers, as they did so, made it clear that African Americans were not alone as targets of the prejudice of the Klan. Bagnall's main argument was that the ideas of the Klan reflected feelings of inferiority on the part of white Americans and a perceived need "to prevent the rise of Jews, Catholics, foreigners, and Negroes" (265). He used quotes from the Klan's own publications to support that point. He also emphasized that "Klan spirit" was manifested well beyond the Klan, in the racist and discriminatory actions of congressmen and representatives as well as local school boards. As he offered examples of white Americans' racism against African Americans, he set it in line with religious and xenophobic persecution; rather than singling out the treatment of African Americans, he also mentioned examples of violence against suspected communists, antisemitism, and anti-immigrant hostilities. He closed with the argument that these actions, and the spirit behind them, were "the manifestation of a group mentally sick" and "the fevered expression of a sick world that must be healed, if it is not to die" (267). Bagnall persuasively demonstrated that violence against African Americans was not, as some called it, "a Negro problem" but part of a larger discriminatory attitude that needed to be changed if the health of the nation was to be restored. His essay is remarkably restrained in its tone: he clearly expressed his disapproval of the Klan, but his emotions and attitude are revealed in his choice of adjectives, rather than in fiery calls for response or in impassioned protests. Implicitly, then, his restraint identifies him as a calm, cool analyst who has studied the facts and then drawn his conclusions.

The same is true of Guy Johnson. In his essay, he focused more exclusively on the Klan's ideas about African Americans and its treatment of African Americans. In part, his essay challenges an assertion by the Klan that it was not a racist organization. Johnson quoted extensively from statements made by Klan members and material published by the Klan to establish the principles it espoused, thus persuasively demonstrating its racist attitudes toward African Americans. He also cited newspaper accounts of a number of specific acts of violence threatened or committed by the Klan, using these to establish the danger of the organization. Having proved the nature of the Klan's beliefs, he closed by emphasizing the necessity of challenging those ideas:

> Do not social attitudes of hatred and prejudice affect the social heritage of the next generation more surely than do mere acts of violence? In other words, violence presupposes a suspicious, intolerant attitude. Lynching, whipping, and other forms of mistreatment are merely outward expressions of a potential antipathy which is infinitely more dangerous than they are. (270)

Johnson's downplaying of the importance of Klan violence is a bit surprising, particularly in light of the images included in *The Crisis*. But it allowed Johnson to avoid stirring up frustration on the part of his African American readers, which fits with his conclusion that the real danger of the Klan was that it would drive the races farther apart, *"when their salvation depends upon their co-operation"* (270). Furthermore, it allowed him to make a stronger case about the importance of changing beliefs; if the way people think changed, he asserted, their actions would follow.

Significantly, these two essays on the Klan are illustrated by photographs that show meetings of Klan members rather than violence against African Americans (see fig. 2.1 for Bagnall's opening page). These images of mobs of Klan members certainly have a stunning effect, particularly given how many of them are in each photograph. Furthermore, the photographs depict Klan meetings in different locations; seen together, then, they demonstrate the spread of the Klan through different cities and states. But it is significant that these photographs do not show the bodies of African Americans mutilated by the Klan or by other racists. First, unlike the photographs of the corpses of African Americans seen in *The Crisis* in the 1910s, these images avoid depicting African Americans as the victims of violence. Second, they evoke a less visceral response. Though still disturbing, they do not have nearly the impact of protest photographs in *The Crisis*. Third, making Klan members the subjects of the photographs helps Bagnall and Johnson identify this aspect of "the race problem" with white Americans, not black Americans. In other words, the photographs imply that if readers wanted to join the effort to prevent the spread of violent actions or ideas by the Klan, they needed to focus their efforts on the white perpetrators of such actions and ideas, not on African Americans. In that sense, these illustrated essays intervene in important ways in typical discussions of mob violence as provoked by the behavior of African Americans or as a necessary form of vigilante justice.

These two essays are followed, later in the issue, by an essay by Charles S. Johnson on the migration of African Americans from South to North. Like Bagnall's and Guy Johnson's essays, Charles Johnson's essay challenges ideas connected to the Klan. But the real argument of "How Much is the Migration a Flight from Persecution?" is that the move of black Americans from the South to the North was not, in fact, a flight from the persecution discussed in the articles about the Klan. Johnson presented data, including facts about the rise and fall of the population of African Americans and white Americans in certain areas, to assert that mistreatment in the South was not always what motivated migration: his studies revealed that the number of lynchings that occurred in a particular area did not necessarily correspond to falling populations of African Americans. This information thus contra-

OPPORTUNITY 265

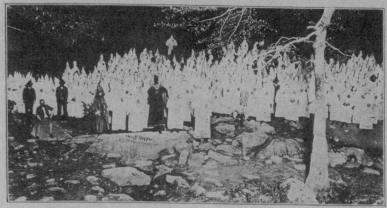

Knights of the Ku Klux Klan Assembled on Stone Mt., Georgia

The Spirit of the Ku Klux Klan

By Robert W. Bagnall

I

Beginning with silly pranks of young men, there developed in this country during the days of Reconstruction a murder-band, which killed and maimed 50,000 people before the government disbanded it. This was the old Ku Klux Klan and its namesake and successor is worthy of it. Barbaric in form, with silly jargon for a ritual, with masks and shrouds, dreadful oaths, and weird ceremonies, it yet makes its appeal to a number of men who have been regarded as decent and sensible.

Appealing to all pet prejudices, it has spread in unsuspected circles in the North, South, East and West. It makes its members censors of morals, judge, jury and executioners. It especially seeks to prevent the rise of Jews, Catholics, foreigners and Negroes. Its weapon is terrorism and its method—flogging, branding, mutilating, and killing. Its victims make a formidable list, and in many regions it overrides all law and order. Witness Oklahoma and Louisiana. Yet it terms itself patriotic and one hundred per cent American.

Certainly such patriotism is that of which Samuel Johnson spoke,—"the refuge of fools and scoundrels." It seeks to control government—municipal, state and national, and is no neglible factor in the politics of many places.

II

The Ku Klux Klan is an astonishing phenomenon. What is its explanation? Is it the savage in man seeking expression in mystery, weird symbolism, and regalia? Is it the brute in man which, made safe by masks, strikes at its enemies? Is it the base prejudices finding in this organization a focal point? Is it the prudence of scoundrels, who realize they are far safer within a censoring organization where they can do the censoring? Is it the American whites' inferiority complex in the face of foreigners, Jews, and Negroes? All of these enter, I believe, into the explanation of the phenomenon of the Klan, and in addition, there is something more —a desire to bolster up a waning sense of superiority.

What does it object to in those it opposes? The Klan is against Jews, for it claims that Jews seek to control the finances of the world. It feels that American whites who are non-Jews cannot cope with them in this project,—are their inferiors in financial ability, and, therefore, force and terrorism must be invoked against them. The Klan is against foreigners, for they say these would change our institutions. This presupposes that our institutions are perfect and cannot be improved. It also presupposes that they cannot stand the contest with the newer ideas. Again a sense of inferiority. The Klan is against Catholics because with a strange bigotry it imagines that they seek to suborn the government to their religion. The silliness of this needs no comment. The Klan is against Negroes, hereditarily so, because "this is the white man's country", and the Negro is disposed not "to remain in his place." Here again, we see a sense of inferiority and fear, seeking an explanation in empty myths; the myth that this is only the white man's country, and it follows that the Negro or any other American has or can be made to have a static, caste place.

III

The result of the Klan's teaching is always racial intolerance, religious bigotry, jingoism, obsoletism, lawlessness and violence. If these things are good, then the Klan is good; if they are evil, then the Klan is evil.

Fig. 2.1. The opening page of Robert W. Bagnall's "The Spirit of the Ku Klux Klan." Opportunity *(Sept. 1923): 265.*

dicted the assumption that lynchings led to migration. Instead of fleeing persecution, he emphasized, "It is indeed more likely that Negroes, like all others with a spark of ambition and self-interest, have been deserting soil which cannot yield returns in proportion to their population increase" (272). Johnson then insisted on the difficulty of farming in the South: tenant farmers, he argued, were being reduced "to a state of unrelieved and helpless peasantry" (274). The migration of African Americans to the urban North, then, reflected the attempts of the migrants to find places where they could live more productive and successful lives.[16]

Johnson also explained the importance of challenging assumptions about why African Americans were leaving the South. The danger of the belief that migrants were simply fleeing persecution, he emphasized, was that blaming the move solely on persecution in the South was "apt to obscure what seem to be even more vital issues and more substantial elements of Negro character" (272). Errors in judgments of the character of the migrants, in turn, would have made their adjustment to life in the North more difficult. If their flight was from persecution, Johnson explained, that "excites little sympathy either from the practical employer or the northern white population among whom these Negroes will hereafter live. Every man who runs is not a good worker and from the point of view of the Negroes who have come, they cannot sustain themselves long on sympathy" (274). The perception of African American migrants as victims of mistreatment, in other words, contributed little to their ability to make a living in the North. On the other hand, the argument that African Americans who moved from South to North did so in pursuit of greater opportunities posited them as industrious, motivated individuals, with character traits that probably would have been favorable to employers, among others. That understanding of the Great Migration replaces the misperception that migrating African Americans were victims with the idea that they were making a decision and a move to better their lives. This shift in perception, in theory, would correspond to a shift from sympathy to respect for African American migrants on the part of Johnson's readers. His mention of employers also emphasizes that this change in thinking could correspond to a growing realization of migrants' potential contributions to the American workforce.

This argument demonstrates the relevance of strategies of representation common in sociology and social work to race relations and the definition of African American identity in the 1920s. Explaining why a phenomenon like the Great Migration was happening, Johnson showed, helped reshape ideas about African Americans. But the presentation of this essay demonstrates that sociological methods had both benefits and drawbacks for the representation of African Americans. Johnson's written argument is paired with a documentary photograph. The photograph, taken by C. M. Battey, a well-known photographer by the early 1920s, covers about two-thirds of the two-page opening spread of the article and is completely surrounded by the written text (see fig. 2.2). The headline and copy run across the top of the photograph, and the copy continues down the left column, across the bottom of the page, and down the right column. The photograph depicts an impoverished farm scene. In the left foreground, a barefoot woman sits on a stool and a young boy stands, partially hidden, behind her; on the right a man, his pants patched, stands in front of his chair. Behind him, boards from the roof of a barn are propped up tenuously. The weather-beaten barn and a smaller building appear in the background. The dirt of the yard is covered only with sparse grass. The poverty depicted by this photograph suggests the hardships of farming in the South. It also implies a lack of working-age people in the area; although a younger man sits in the right background of the photograph, he occupies only a small space and is out of focus; the older man and woman and the child dominate the shot. A caption set below the photograph emphasizes the poverty of the scene: "'COMPEN-SATION' / Theirs is to labor and have such pay, / As just keeps life, from day to day." The caption works with the photograph to draw the reader's attention to the poverty that is visible in the photograph; it guides the reader in his or her interpretation of the scene.

This depiction of living conditions in the South plays an important role in supporting the argument Johnson made in his essay. With its clear portrayal of the poverty of this scene, the photograph demonstrates the situation Johnson described. A reader who interprets this photograph as an objective record of conditions in the South would see it as evidence that Johnson's claims had merit. Like the facts and figures he presented, the photograph becomes a piece of data that helped Johnson make his point. Because it fits the conventions of documentary photography, it is especially likely to be taken by its viewers as realistic and thus believable. The essay and photograph, then, work together to convince *Opportunity*'s readers that conditions in the South were bad enough to inspire migration to the North; in turn, this information has the potential to change readers' perceptions of African Americans toward views that would support the inclusion of African Americans in established American workplaces.

However, this illustrated essay also disempowers black Southerners because of the conventions it follows. As is typical of sociological or social work texts, neither the photograph nor the written text provides any information about the identity of these individuals; they are rendered anonymous examples of a social phenomenon. Furthermore, the composition of the photograph, with the individuals spread across the image, suggests that

Fig. 2.2. The opening pages of Charles S. Johnson's "How Much is the Migration a Flight from Persecution?" Opportunity *(Sept. 1923): 272–73.*

they were anything but a united force; instead, each seems isolated and distanced from the other. It is difficult to imagine how they might have worked together to overcome their poverty, especially given the absence of laborers in the prime of their working ages. It seems up to the readers or the viewers of this image—the employers Johnson mentioned, for example—to bring about changes that might alleviate the poverty depicted here. The photograph, then, elicits aid from readers, allowing them to see black Southerners as potential objects of charity. Johnson may have been able to redefine migrants, but his text and the photograph reaffirm conceptions of African Americans in the South as victims rather than agents of change.

A third example of the kind of illustrated sociological or social work study that appeared so often in *Opportunity* even more clearly reveals the dynamics of empowerment enacted in these texts. Here, again, the implied differences between the readers and the subjects of the studies are problematic. The main argument in "Where Negroes Live In Philadelphia," written by A. L. Manly and published in the May 1923 issue, is that housing problems faced by African Americans were not unique. "Negroes are neither the only nor the worst sufferers from the adverse effects of bad housing," Manly insisted, and his point is reinforced by a photograph of an alleyway crowded with women of different races (10). Significantly, the caption reads, "Negroes Are Neither the Only Nor the Worst Sufferers" (see fig. 2.3); the repetition of Manly's conclusion suggests the degree to which the photograph complements his written argument, as well as the importance of that argument. Housing conditions had been one of the primary targets of reform movements in the 1890s and 1900s. Texts that garnered attention and motivated action often included visual elements, like Jacob Riis's photographs of the impoverished immigrants who inhabited areas like the Bowery or an exhibit of photographs of tenement houses organized by the Charity Organization Society in 1900.[17] But in cities in the North in the 1920s, the problem of overcrowding was increasingly associated with African Americans, particularly because of the Great Migration. Manly's argument disrupts that tendency, and the photograph reminds readers of the broader dimensions of the problem, particularly because it visually echoes familiar images, like Riis's, of immigrants. In *Opportunity,* then, these written and visual texts work together to keep readers from assuming that housing is only a problem for African Americans; in other words, it prevents them from labeling housing "a Negro problem."

In that way, Manly's illustrated text—as do others like it—serves the purpose of expository texts in providing information and challenging assumptions about social conditions. However, this pair of texts also sends a problematic message about the capabilities of its subjects and its readers. Manly used a good deal of data to establish the effects of poor housing practices, such as overcrowding. He also argued that high rents prevented residents from being able to save enough money to eventually buy their own homes. He ended with a call for change; specifically, the establishment of a

> well organized heavily financed organization whose purpose would be buying or taking on long time improvement lease, the old dilapidated houses and converting them into homes of comfort and respectability, not for colored people, not for white people, but for all the unfortunate peoples who now inhabit the "slum" districts. (15)

Manly's essay is exactly the kind of study that would have been helpful for clearing up misunderstandings about African Americans and for motivating readers to become involved in changing social situations, with its careful description of the conditions and its clear call for action. But implicitly, the essay also falls into the trap of suggesting that its subjects were helpless to change their own lives, since Manly represented the residents here as poor, while the people he looked to for bringing about change had to be wealthy if they were to contribute to his "well-financed" organization. Furthermore,

Where Negroes Live In Philadelphia

By A. L. MANLY
Armstrong Association of Philadelphia

If the housing standard of a community is of the mud hut variety the fact of living in a mud hut is normal to it and need occasion no excitement or shame. If, however, the standard is higher, the assumption is that the community knows better and in order to maintain a proper balance it becomes the duty of all the units of that community to work together in the effort to maintain that standard.

In most of the cities of the North unofficial but effectively rigid lines are drawn prescribing the bounds of habitation for different racial groups. So long as the several groups remain within the bounds set, there is little disposition to regard them as a problem. It is the attempted emergence from these bounds which sets in motion the sugges-tion of social, economic and health prob-lems.

In Philadel-phia the same general hous-ing deficien-cies exist that in other cities lead to con-gestion in cer-tain districts, overcrowding and its at-tendant evils in the poorer sections, due in turn to the s h o r tage of houses a n d the enormous rents charged for those that are available. There are sec-tions where the vast ma-jority of the population is r e p resented by a distinc-

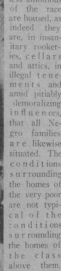

"Negroes Are Neither the Only Nor the Worst Sufferers"

tive racial group; but as strange as it may seem Negroes are neither the only nor the worst suf-ferers from the adverse effects of bad housing.

The Whittier Center made a survey of Negro occupants in two districts in Philadelphia and draws rather unusual conclusions. Of the very bad areas the report says: "Such areas differ in no wise from the bad housing districts occu-

pied by other races. The Negro who has little or no income or no steady or assured income, has to suffer from the same gross evils of insani-tation that afflict his Italian or Jewish neighbor. He is the victim of the same greedy landlordism, the same municipal neglect, and he contributes to a like extent, through his own slovenliness, to the filth surrounding him."

Contrasted with the above the report goes into details of the better type of house occupied by Negroes. It says: "The group is normal, not sub-normal. If among such persons conditions were found to be bad, it would be safe to assume that the strata lower down in industry and ambi-tion were more poorly housed. The reverse of this would be true. It would not follow that because t h e less ambitious of the race are housed, as indeed they are, in insan-itary rooker-ies, c e l l a r s and attics, in illegal t e n e-m e n t s and amid pitiably demoralizing i n fl u e n ces, that all Ne-gro families a r e likewise situated. The c o n d i t i o n s s u r rounding the homes of the very poor are not typi-c a l o f t h e : o n d i t i o n s s u r rounding the homes of the class above them.

Very few of the houses were occupied by their owners. Low as is the percentage of homes privately owned in Philadelphia by all classes, yet the number of such among the colored people is still lower. In the city at large 26.1% of the houses are occupied by their owners, leaving about 74% occupied by tenants. In this study of 1158 houses, only 57, or 5% were privated owned; 95% of the families being tenants. This per-

Fig. 2.3. The opening page of A. L. Manly's "Where Negroes Live In Philadelphia." Opportunity *(May 1923): 10.*

rather than demonstrating how readers and subjects might have worked together to ameliorate these situations, Manly's focus on these residents as "sufferers" casts them in a passive role from which it is not apparent that any collective action will be possible. What was needed, then, was for people who were different from these subjects to step in and help change the situation. While this push toward action certainly could have had the positive effect of inspiring readers to act, it hardly empowered the people who were the focus of his study.

The problem with this kind of argument is made clear in discussions about the advantages and drawbacks of soliciting charity. While the backing of donors and philanthropists obviously played an important role in making social work possible, it also potentially set up or maintained a system of dependence. This danger was spelled out, for example, by Eugene Kinckle Jones in an essay he published in *The Messenger* in 1917. In laying out guidelines for the development of social work among African Americans, Jones was critical of efforts to help African Americans through "material aid given with no special desire to render the recipient independent" ("Social Work among Negroes" 26). Such an approach boiled down to the distribution of alms, whereas "the best way to make a man good is to make him more or less independent of alms" (26).[18] The challenge for a magazine like *Opportunity*, then, was to motivate readers to act—but also to promote and encourage the independence of African Americans and to enhance readers' awareness of that independence even as they offered their assistance.

Expository essays thus have both advantages and limitations. They prove useful to *Opportunity*'s efforts to provide information about African Americans and to be taken seriously as a source of objective information. These texts helpfully identify problems that need attention, and they undermine particular identifications for African Americans, work against perceptions of African Americans as victims of violence, and assert certain understandings of African Americans' characteristics. In that sense, they demonstrate the ways that expository texts could be used to send particular messages about African Americans to the magazine's readers. But sociological and social work essays also fail to demonstrate that African Americans were active participants in American institutions. *Opportunity*'s contributors, though, found ways to make this obvious in other texts.

To some extent, the magazine's writers demonstrate African Americans' achievements simply through expository studies with a more positive focus. The essays that demonstrate problems faced by African Americans are complemented by others that highlight the ways that African Americans already were overcoming these obstacles. These essays share some of the topics typical in sociology and social work, such as labor relations and education, but they emphasize what was going right in these fields, rather than merely identifying problems. Furthermore, when they do identify problems, they establish that the problems result from conditions, and that as conditions changed, not only African Americans but also companies, schools, communities—in short, American society as a whole—would benefit.

The most common focus of such essays was on African American workers. Essays about workers demonstrate the magazine's efforts to challenge assumptions about African Americans and to define them as important contributors to American institutions. The question of African Americans' work habits and success as employees was a frequent topic in *Opportunity* in its first years. For example, the first issue included reports on two experiments with "Negro Labor and the Industries." The writers of both articles described the efforts of their companies to offer African American employees "a square deal," and both explained the benefits the companies reaped from these efforts: faithful, loyal, and honest work from the men hired. J. O. Houze's description of employment practices at his company, National Malleable Casting Company, seems particularly aimed at correcting false impressions of African American workers. For example, he acknowledged the rumor "that Negroes are unreliable" but emphasized that his company had found African American employees to be steady workers with low rates of absenteeism (21). That is only one of many assumptions about African American workers that Houze contradicted with the experiences of his company. He insisted throughout his essay that the company was "entirely satisfied with the results we are getting" from African American employees (21). Edward McClelland reported similarly satisfactory results with the use of "Negro Labor" at his company, Westinghouse Electric and Manufacturing Corporation, arguing that African American workers were an important source of labor for industries. He concluded, "we are convinced that [the Negro] has the making of a man just the same as an average white man has, if he is properly treated" (23). Two small photographs are included with the reports; they show African American employees hard at work, thus supporting the arguments presented by Houze and McClelland.

These reports on the work of African Americans in industries, and the others like them published in early issues of *Opportunity*, make a number of points clear. First, again, is their usefulness for providing information about African Americans. As an editorial headnote explains, accounts from employers about "the fitness of these men for their new positions" were infrequent (20). These two personnel managers had been asked "to recount frankly their experience" (20); the essays are their testimonies. The facts that the reports are identified as frank assessments and that they are written by the employers themselves add to both the reliability of the information presented and the credibility of the magazine as a whole. The fact that they are illustrated further enhances the persuasiveness of the arguments, for it means they include visual evidence as well as the written testimony of the employers. Second, these essays suggest that any previous problems with African American workers were caused by discriminatory practices, not by any difference in the workers themselves. For example, McClelland pointed out that Westinghouse began hiring African Americans "in any considerable numbers" only in 1916 (22–23), thus alluding to the discriminatory practices in employment that were only recently being challenged. Now that that situation was being fixed, the company was discovering the value of African Americans as employees.

Another essay on African American workers furthers this process of redefinition. This one, a short essay on "Shop Representation" by Charles M. Mills, was published in the April 1923 issue with a photograph of twelve of the African American workers at the Standard Oil Company refinery in Baton Rouge, Louisiana (see fig. 2.4). Mills explained that African American employees at the oil company's plants were "included in a representation plan on the same basis as the white employees," with elected representatives serving as liaisons between them and managers (25). The goals were to make sure that African American workers knew that their concerns were being heard and to make sure that their needs were being met. Mills used a quote from one of the employees at the Baton Rouge plant to emphasize that the benefits of this plan included increased devotion and greater output on the part of the workers: "I guarantee you that this black man is going to do everything he can to influence every Negro in the Standard Oil Company to give an honest days [sic] work" (25). This assertion of the value of equal inclusion, in economic terms of efficient work, is also an implicit argument against the belief that African Americans were lazy workers; it identifies them as dedicated workers who motivate each other. The photograph of the twelve employees, standing on the front steps of the building with "STANDARD OIL CO.—LA." above them, reinforces this point. Their position on the front steps of Standard Oil's building visually suggests the company's interest in its black workers, and the suits and ties that most of them wear show their professionalism, as do their serious facial expressions. The written text provides the explanation of the system; the photograph provides the image of the professional, dedicated black men as evidence of how well it was working. Together, written and visual texts demonstrate the logistics and the results of treating black workers with the same respect as white workers.

Shop Representation

By Charles M. Mills

The Standard Oil Company of New Jersey has established an industrial representation plan through which elected representatives of the employes and the management meet in joint conferences to discuss the problems of wages, hours, working conditions, and grievances.

In its refineries at Charleston (S. C.) and Baton Rouge (La.) where it has a large percentage of colored employes, they are included in a representation plan on the same basis as the white employes. While the plan in the Charleston refinery was started in November, 1921, the organization in the Baton Rouge refinery has been conducted successfully since 1920. At Charleston four colored representatives are chosen out of 125 colored employes at the plant, while the Baton Rouge there are twelve colored representatives for 1,500 negro employes. These representatives are chosen at an annual election by secret ballot, in which all employes of the plant are privileged to vote. Any employe can be chosen as representative, the term of office being for one year. Fifty per cent of the representatives are re-elected.

The main purpose of the industrial representation plan is to bring management and men together in joint conferences so that petty differences may be ironed out and a basis established for conference on fundamental questions, such as wages, hours, and working conditions.

Fundamentally, the industrial representation plan has effected the negro in granting to him adequate justice. If any employe feels that he has been taken advantage of, he is privileged to go to his representative in that department, who in turn takes the matter up with the employe's foreman. If the matter is not settled there, there is a line of appeal directly to management. In this way satisfaction is guaranteed to the colored employe.

The annual joint conference recently held at Baton Rouge, at which the writer was present, was a remarkable occasion. The Negro representatives present surely appreciated the effect that the industrial representation plan had made upon them. As one of the Negro employes said at the meeting, "The Standard Oil Company has done more for the Negro in this part of the country than any other Company. I guarantee you that this black man is going to do everything he can to influence every Negro in the Standard Oil Company to give an honest days work as I fully appreciate what you are doing for us. For the first time the Negro has got justice, for the Company has reached down and picked the black man up."

Shop Representatives, Baton Rouge Refinery

Fig. 2.4. Charles M. Mills's "Shop Representation." Opportunity *(April 1923): 25.*

These arguments about African American employees were especially important given working conditions for African Americans in the 1920s. Too often, African Americans were excluded from unions, as Du Bois had emphasized in editorials in *The Crisis* in the 1910s.[19] In many cases, they became strikebreakers. Unfortunately, this led to resentment and tension between white and black workers, and this antagonism was sometimes encouraged by union organizers as a way of increasing their membership. In fact, hostilities over employment were among the factors that contributed to the riots in East St. Louis in 1917 (Lewis, *Du Bois* I: 536–37). The essays in *Opportunity* steered readers' attention away from tensions between black and white workers and instead emphasized benefits reaped by companies that treated African Americans fairly. Their argument, aimed at employers, was that hiring African Americans would create not problems but the benefits of increased efficiency and productivity.

Essays about African American workers, in short, define the characteristics of this group of people in positive terms. *Opportunity* also defined African American identity through the characteristics of other groups, particularly those involved in African American institutions. For example, essays about black colleges emphasized the development of the character of African American graduates and their preparation for roles in American society. In March 1923, essays on Howard University, Virginia Union University, and Shaw University were the first in a series on "Our Negro Colleges" that ran through a number of issues. These essays repeatedly emphasize these institutions' contributions to the training and development of African Americans who would take leadership roles within the race. But the writers of these essays drew attention to the national as well as the racial significance of these institutions. D. O. W. Holmes's description of Howard University is characteristic. Holmes argued that Howard had grown since its founding in 1867 to become "the acknowledged leader in the field of Negro education, a university truly national in its character" (10). He insisted that Howard's two thousand students

> constitute a social fact whose significance in America is practically infinite.... And since this large body of students is being prepared primarily for places of leadership in a group making up one-tenth of the total population of our great democracy, the importance of its work and its influence in the solution of the great economic and social problems which face the nation cannot be overestimated.... The work of no other single college or university in America is of equal importance as a national influence. (10–11)

Holmes continued with this kind of praise through the remainder of his article, emphasizing Howard's significance to the nation as a whole, often by explaining the roles that its African American students would take in American businesses, politics, and professions. His discussion is particularly important, given that the focus of African American colleges had been the subject of public debate in the 1910s. In 1917, a study was released by the United States Bureau of Education and the Phelps-Stokes Fund on African American higher education; it was critical of colleges and universities that offered liberal educations to African Americans. Du Bois, of course, was furious, and he defended the need for the higher education of African Americans in a series of essays in *The Crisis* (Lewis, *Du Bois* I: 547–51). The controversy continued into the 1920s, especially over the leadership and ideals of black colleges.[20] The essays in *Opportunity* again sidestepped the controversy but emphasized the rights and capabilities of African Americans, particularly focusing on the contributions they would be able to make to American institutions thanks to their education at colleges like Howard.

In articles like these, *Opportunity* engaged in ongoing debates about the racism and discrimination faced by African Americans in areas like employment and education. But these essays transcend the limited focus on existing problems—typical both of sociological and social work essays but also of Du Bois's protest texts—by turning their primary attention to the abilities of African Americans to overcome obstacles and to the benefits to be gained by all parties involved if greater opportunities for African Americans were granted.

Opportunity also went beyond the typical focus of sociological and social work essays in its inclusion of news stories that recorded the achievements of African Americans. These redefine African American identity in positive terms by drawing attention to the achievements of individual African Americans. For example, the June 1923 issue included a short feature on George B. Anderson, a student at an integrated high school in New York City; it was accompanied by a portrait photograph of him (see fig. 2.5). The written text, "One Negro Boy's Record," describes his selection to tutor his fellow students in geometry because of his high standing as a student. Of the twenty students who were chosen to serve in this role, Anderson was the only African American. The text also mentions his goal of studying law at Columbia. Anderson, with his high goals and his early success, is a reminder to readers of the achievements and potential of African Americans. Anderson also serves as an inspiration for other African American students. The photograph works with the written text to emphasize both points: Anderson stands, carefully dressed, perhaps in a school uniform, with what looks like a diploma or a certificate of achievement in his hands. He does not smile but has a serious look on his face that befits his status as a scholar and the stately backdrop of the photograph, with the large window and heavy drapes. He

THE NATIONAL NEGRO MEMORIAL AT WASHINGTON

Underwood and Underwood

A MEMORIAL TO NEGRO HEROES

A Movement has been launched in Washington to erect a National Memorial Building "to commemorate the heroic deeds of Negro soldiers and sailors who fought in all wars of our country." The association for this purpose was formed in 1916 and its scope has widened after the war. The Governors of several states have by request appointed representative commissioners from their respective states to cooperate with the association. The building as planned will be an imposing collonaded structure not only to serve heroes of the Negro race, but as an educational temple where statues of colored leaders may be placed.

ONE NEGRO BOY'S RECORD

During the *Boys' Week*, celebrated recently in the DeWitt Clinton High School of New York City, George B. Anderson was chosen on account of his high standing to teach. He taught in the General Science class of second year boys, on the subject of the Eye. It was concluded by the regular teacher of this class and the student body that George conducted the lesson creditably indeed. Because of this he had occasion to teach another day while a teachers' meeting was taking place.

There are two sessions in the DeWitt Clinton High School, the morning and the afternoon. Those boys who are deficient in a subject have the opportunity of being helped by the boys of the afternoon session. Thus George was selected for his Plane Geometry Class to tutor in the named subject.

In tutoring, the boys are organized into a *Mathematics Squad*. This is composed of twenty boys of high standing. George was selected because of this and represented his race by being the only colored boy of the Squad. He is now 16 years of age and his ambition is to enter Columbia and study law. His father is a veteran letter carrier and is attached to the Williamsbridge P. O., New York City.

SHORTAGE OF NEGRO PHYSICIANS

The American Medical Association has recently raised a question about doing something to increase the output of capable Negro physicians for practice among Negroes. It is stated that only about fifty first class Negro physicians are graduated annually from first class medical schools to serve a Negro population of ten million which is still growing. The high morbidity and mortality rate among Negroes and the disposition frequently to regard the efforts of white physicians to improve sanitary conditions as racial criticism, this association thinks, make necessary more Negro physicians. Of eighty-one first class medical schools in the United States only two are devoted entirely to training of Negro Medical students.

GEORGE B. ANDERSON

Fig. 2.5. George B. Anderson, the subject of "One Negro Boy's Record." Opportunity *(June 1923): 27.*

embodies and demonstrates the dedicated attitude of a youth committed to pursuit of his goals, and the prop he holds is a particularly evocative reminder to those who see this image that he is on the way to accomplishing these goals.

Other examples of African Americans' achievements include a story on "the World's Fastest Mail Sorter," a woman whose picture and accomplishments were featured in the January 1923 issue; a photograph of Charles Anderson, on the occasion of his reappointment to his post as collector of internal revenue, in the May 1923 issue; and, the following month, a photograph of an African American track and football star at Washington and Jefferson University. Such news stories appeared in every issue; they focused on Boy Scouts, librarians, police officers, artists and musicians, actors, recipients of honorary degrees from noted universities—in short, individuals who were meeting with success in almost every possible field. In the written texts, information about these achievers was presented without elaboration, with only the relevant facts, adding to the impression that *Opportunity* was a reliable source of information about such achievements. As with the affirmative texts in *The Crisis*, these accounts are paired with photographs of the African Americans who had succeeded in their endeavors. Here, too, the composite texts are convincing evidence of African Americans' accomplishments. The difference here is that *Opportunity* depicted leaders in their professions, like Charles Anderson, but also blue-collar workers, sports figures, and youngsters. As a result, *Opportunity* offered a more inclusive portrait of African American identity than did *The Crisis* in the 1910s.

Opportunity also used news stories and photographs to encourage the overcoming of racism and to emphasize the benefits of fair treatment of African Americans. These news texts simultaneously asserted the positive characteristics of African Americans and the advantages for American society of extending opportunities to African Americans. For example, most YMCAs in the early 1920s were segregated, which meant that separate facilities had to be built for African Americans. Rather than focusing on the discriminatory practices clear in this situation, *Opportunity* emphasized that important character traits and even positive interracial relations were developing at the segregated facilities. A brief article by B. W. Overton on the Cincinnati YMCA in the February 1923 issue, for instance, identifies the role of the YMCA in the development of certain characteristics among African Americans. The four photographs included with the article show the YMCA building, its basketball team, a formal dinner conference held in its facilities, and a mid-day meeting at a Cincinnati industrial plant (see fig. 2.6). They show African Americans in the roles of outstanding athletes, the social elite, and productive workers, and the article makes explicit the importance of

tion, nor does it believe that it has found the solution to the race problem which is to be made secure over night. It does believe, however, in the language of George Madden Martin, that prejudices are stubborn, that it is not a task for limited sympathies and petty natures; that it is not a task that can be done by machinery or mere organization; that it is a spiritual task, a task to be carried out in the spirit and according to the ethics of the Man of Galilee. These principles emphasize first the truth that contact is necessary in the solution of any human problem. Differences are at first minimized then they disappear. In order that the Movement be motivated by Christian principles, the leaders perfected a duly organized commission with membership representing thirteen states and headquarters in Atlanta, Georgia. In addition to this Commission, each of the thirteen states has a Commission directing the work of the Commission in each

state. Some eight hundred of the twelve hundred counties in the Southern States have organized.

It is probably known that in 37 years, from 1885 to 1922, there have been 437 lynchings in Georgia and only one indictment. It is probably not known that in the year 1922, alone, there have been four indictments out of eight cases of lynchings; four persons sent to the penitentiary and 22 indictments returned. In most of the cases the evidence was collected by the Inter-racial Secretaries and Committees in Georgia.

What the Commission needs more than perhaps anything else is the confidence of the community, white and colored, in the Commission itself. It seeks the sympathy and co-operation of the members of the churches of Jesus Christ in America and social organizations to the end that this greatest problem confronting the American people today may be settled by the principles of justice, fair play, and according to the teachings of Jesus Christ.

The Cincinnati "Y"
By B. W. Overton,

The Ninth Street Branch of the Y.M.C.A. is one of the fourteen participating organizations in the investment of $350,000 by Julius Rosenwald in buildings for Negroes. The work in this city was organized in 1912, and the building opened in 1916. The annual operating budget has increased from $17,778 in 1916 to $50,703. The building represents an investment of

ganization conducts extensive programs through which others are reached. Some of the work of this character—building institution is told in the accompanying pictures.

Building of the Ninth Street Branch of the Cincinnati Y. M. C. A.

Ohio Basket Ball Champions and Mid-West Contenders.

$111,545, contains 46 dormitory rooms, a completely equipped gymnasium and swimming pool. Aside from its 289 boys in membership, the or-

One of the Dinner Conferences of the Cincinnati "Y."

Mid-day Meeting in a Cincinnati Industrial Plant.

Fig. 2.6. Programs at the Cincinnati YMCA, described by B. W. Overton. Opportunity *(Feb. 1923): 14.*

these images: the last line of the written text states, "Some of the work of this character-building institution is told in the accompanying pictures" (14). The institution's contribution to national culture is implicit: the emphasis on its "character-building" nature, and the array of images included with the written text, underlines its roles in making its users productive in social organizations and industries, as well as athletics. The article also pays tribute to connections between black and white Americans in its attention to the fact that the YMCA was funded in large part by Julius Rosenwald, the white president of Sears, Roebuck who contributed generously to cities that would put money and effort toward building YMCAs for African Americans. The emphasis on Rosenwald's role in establishing this branch underlines the fact that positive interracial relations were occurring, and that national culture was improving as a result.

That argument is even more clear in a story published in the "Bulletin Board" column in the September 1923 issue. It details the racism faced by an African American student, Charles C. Dogan, who had been chosen to read the Declaration of Independence at his high school as part of a Fourth of July celebration. The written text, headlined "Democracy in Boston," explains that Dogan's selection had been protested because he was black. But the mayor of Boston had responded that the protest was "devoid of Americanism, so destitute of all knowledge of the principle and practices of our government, and so offensively and stupidly impertinent" (285). The text ends by noting that Dogan did read the declaration to great acclaim. The photograph accompanying the text shows him standing with what are apparently the white male dignitaries of the city, reading the declaration, on a platform draped with American flags (see fig. 2.7). The fact that the photograph is a snapshot, which looks as "realistic" in its spontaneity as the documentary photographs discussed previously, turns it into evidence of changing practices. In addition, the cropping of the photograph to include as much as possible of the flag-draped platform—as well as the caption, "Charles C. Dogan, reading the Declaration of Independence"—links the participation of this student with the practice of American ideals. It is only a partial inclusion: the fact that all of the dignitaries are white men demonstrates the absence of African Americans and white women from leadership positions, and the controversy over Dogan's role reveals continuing racism. But the story and photograph offer a vision of what a nation moving toward more inclusiveness might look like. Significantly, the fact that the platform is draped with not one but three American flags underlines the significance of the American ideals strengthened by Dogan's participation in this ceremony.

The mix of illustrated expository essays and news stories and photographs in *Opportunity,* then, proves to be an effective combination. The es-

Bulletin Board

INDUSTRY

According to figures compiled by the Georgia Bankers' Association, 229,000 Negroes have left Georgia for the North within the past three and a half years, or since the beginning of 1920. The figures show, moreover, that 77,500 of this number left during the first six months of the current year. In Georgia there are now 46,676 vacant farm dwellings and 55,524 idle plows. Based upon a production of $500 to the plow, which is very low, it will be observed that Georgia's loss of wealth from her farms this year will amount to the sum of more than $27,000,000; in a decade to more than $250,000,000.

The National Federation of Colored Farmers has been organized, with headquarters in Richmond, Va. Mr. Charles E. Hall is at the head of the federation. The purposes of the organizers are to enroll every Negro farmer in the country into membership, to develop co-operative marketing, better farming, diversified crops and increased production, and to secure for colored farmers all of the benefits enjoyed by the farmers of other races.

It has been estimated that Negroes in Chicago have more than $20,000,000 deposited in the various local banks. The resources of two of the colored banks are: the Douglass National, $646,536.57; Binga State, $976,-940.59. The Binga State Bank has purchased property at 35th and State Streets, and is preparing to erect an exclusive bank building to cost practically $200,000.

DEMOCRACY IN BOSTON

The Boston Post of June 27 had the following report: "The Protestants, Thomas F. Armstrong, J. Frank McClelland, and Frank Dalton of Charlotte, N. C., declared to Mayor Curley in a letter: " 'The Boston Post, of June 5, carries the announcement that you have selected Charles C. Dogan, honor pupil at English High School, to read the Declaration of Independence from the balcony of the Old State House in connection with the July Fourth exercises.

" 'Being former Bostonians and still residents of Boston, in spirit if not in body, and, further, knowing the Negroes as we know them, we protest such an appointment on the grounds of a deliberate insult to the Boston school boy and the average Bostonian.

" 'The South would not allow such an appointment to be made and we believe, knowing both sides as we do, that what this section of the country will not tolerate, should not be accepted by the city of our birth.

" 'We make the above protest aware that the question of race has never been settled, but we feel, as all here do, in the supremacy of the white race. May we have the honor of hearing from you?'

"Mayor Curley answered, in part: 'I have seldom received a letter from any source so lacking in good manners, so devoid of Ameri-

Charles C. Dogan, reading the Declaration of Independence.

canism, so destitute of all knowledge of the principle and practises of our government, and so offensively and stupidly impertinent. . . . When men claiming birth and former residence in Boston are guilty of the gross discourtesy you have committed, and its bad manners are emphasized by a betrayal of the principles and an insult to the traditions of their birthplace, they become at once deserving of scorn and contempt. . .

" 'Charles C. Dogan was selected for the honor conferred on him for excellent reasons; he has shown a competence and capacity in the generous rivalry of school life to make him a worthy choice; he is an "honor pupil", that is to say, a pupil of more than ordinary attainments; his choice has the approbation of his fellow pupils; and his selection to read the immortal Declaration is an expression of our recognition of the services of his race in Massachusetts to human freedom and democratic government. One of his race died in the streets of Boston in defense of human rights —Crispus Attucks—and Boston has raised a monument to his memory on Boston Common; and thousands of his race fought and died to preserve the union in the War of the Rebellion, and to "make the world safe for democracy" in the World War. Any man of any race, color or creed, who is willing and worthy to serve the Flag and die for the Republic, is worthy to have his place in the Sun of American Democracy.

Fig. 2.7. Charles C. Dogan, reading the Declaration of Independence at Boston's Fourth of July celebration, the subject of "Democracy in Boston." Opportunity *(Sept. 1923): 285.*

says and documentary photographs establish the magazine's identity as a reliable source of information about African Americans. The creators of these
texts draw their readers' attention to particular aspects of African American
identity, and they encourage their readers to contribute to the amelioration
of existing problems. But by adding news stories and photographs, the creators of the magazine went beyond the conventions of the fields of sociology
and social work in ways that make its portrait of African Americans more
empowering for its subjects. The combination of texts, then, turns into a
multi-pronged response to the racism that faced African Americans in the
early 1920s and a multi-media redefinition of African American identity.

Opportunity's insistent resistance to protest—the fact that it noted racism only to emphasize African Americans' ability to overcome discrimination—earned the magazine criticism from some readers for being too
optimistic. Comparing *Opportunity* to *The Crisis*—or to the even more
pronounced protest published in periodicals like *Negro World* or the *Chicago
Defender*—makes it clear that *Opportunity* and the NUL were much closer
in philosophy to Booker T. Washington than to Du Bois.[21] But in the context
of the early 1920s, when many texts in the white media asserted that African
Americans were incapable of integration, *Opportunity* played an important
role in demonstrating that integration was possible, and its emphasis on the
benefits of integration for not just African Americans but also for American
industries and institutions was significant. *Opportunity*'s optimism, then,
inserted a note of hopefulness into the ongoing discussions about race relations in the United States and about the possibilities of positive developments. *Opportunity*, in short, provided an important counterpoint to the example of protest in *The Crisis;* in representing a very different response to
the continuing racism and discrimination against African Americans, it
draws our attention to the range of responses African Americans had to the
social realities of the early 1920s.

But even Charles S. Johnson had doubts about the success of efforts to
undermine racism. David Levering Lewis, in fact, argues that Johnson,
"more accurately than perhaps any other Afro-American intellectual," understood the depths of American racism after World War I (*When Harlem
Was in Vogue* 48). Johnson's sociological training also led him to appreciate
the difficulty of using texts to change public opinion. When he discussed the
shaping of public opinion in that address he delivered in May 1923, he mentioned that people have a tendency to dismiss information that challenges
their already-held beliefs ("Public Opinion and The Negro" 201). Drawing

on a recently published book by Walter Lippman called *Public Opinion,* Johnson discussed the power of "the picture within our heads" to shape our understanding of new information (202). What that meant for *Opportunity* was that the magazine had to be exceptionally compelling if it was to have the desired effect on readers' ideas. As Johnson would write years later about the role of the magazine, "What was necessary was a revolution and a revelation sufficient in intensity to disturb the age-old customary cynicisms" ("The Negro Renaissance" 85). As *Opportunity* developed, Johnson continued to search for strategies of representation that would have this kind of impact—and, by the mid-to-late 1920s, it was the arts, rather than expository essays, that became the magazine's primary means toward that end.

3

The Arts as a Social Tool:
Mixing Media in *The Crisis*
and *Opportunity*

Despite the differences between The Crisis *in the 1910s and* Opportunity in the early 1920s, by the mid-1920s the two magazines shared an important similarity: both reflected the importance of the arts in representing African Americans in the years leading up to and constituting the Harlem Renaissance. Though the arts lay beyond the scope of each magazine as it was originally defined, both Du Bois and Johnson began to include reviews of literature, performance, and visual arts not long after the founding of their magazines. By the mid-1920s, both placed a great deal of emphasis on the potential of the arts to influence ideas about African Americans, and the pages of their magazines are full of discussions of the ability of literature and other arts to help change attitudes toward and treatment of African Americans. The main question debated in the two magazines is not so much whether the arts could contribute to changing ideas about African Americans but how they might do so most effectively.

The hope that the arts—especially literature—would contribute to the end of racism is an aspect of the Harlem Renaissance that has gotten a good deal of attention from scholars of the movement. But participants in the Harlem Renaissance used the arts in ways that have yet to be fully assessed, and *The Crisis* and *Opportunity* record their explorations of the potential of the arts to communicate ideas about African Americans. Both magazines capitalized on relatively obvious uses of the arts: to demonstrate the skills and talents of African Americans and, like expository and news texts, to provide more images of African Americans. The arts also added an important dimension to the revelations of expository and news texts: they established the realm of culture as one in which the achievements of African Americans were clear. In addition, the magazines highlighted the distinctive capabilities of the arts, particularly to reveal more about the "inner lives" of African Americans than other kinds of expository or affirmative texts. Furthermore, at their best, creative texts in *The Crisis* and *Opportunity* push readers to a more critical understanding of how texts work, because they subtly draw attention to what is left out of other texts. On each of these points, Du Bois and Johnson both enhanced the ability of the arts to provide information about African Americans by combining visual and written texts and by drawing connections among the arts. When they or their contributors discussed images of African Americans, their attention often ranged from literature to performance to music to other kinds of texts. Furthermore, individual issues of both magazines often included essays about and reproductions of many kinds of art and literature, and creative texts were often paired into particularly suggestive composite texts.

The inclusion of the arts in *The Crisis* and *Opportunity* did not replace other kinds of texts in either magazine; instead, the resulting combinations of expository and creative texts suggest the degree to which participants in the Harlem Renaissance saw the arts as working with other kinds of texts to redefine African American identity and to undermine racism. Clearly the contributors to these magazines did not see literature or any of the arts as isolated media but rather as related elements in a rich cultural mix. If we are true to that vision when we study *The Crisis* and *Opportunity,* we will be better able to assess the ability of the magazines to use texts to influence public opinion about African Americans.

Attention to the arts in *The Crisis* and *Opportunity* began early in each magazine's development, but it became particularly pronounced through the mid-1920s.[1] Scholars of the Harlem Renaissance have explored certain aspects of the use of the arts in the two magazines, including the hope that the arts would help change ideas about African Americans.[2] They also have given extensive attention to the themes, techniques, and quality of the literature of the movement, and scholarship on participants' work in music, painting and sculpture, photography, and film is increasing. But this work tends to remain within disciplinary boundaries. Literary critics most often concentrate solely on the literature of the movement, art historians and critics on the visual arts, and so on.[3] This focus on individual arts does not register the fact that many participants in the Harlem Renaissance combined texts in many different media and discussed the ways the arts could work together to create especially vivid and compelling depictions of African Americans. Analyzing the discussion and presentation of the arts in *The Crisis* and

Opportunity allows us to recover participants' multi-media interests, and it reveals some of their most innovative ideas about the potential of creative texts to influence readers' ideas about African Americans.[4]

On a more practical note, including the arts in *The Crisis* and *Opportunity* must have helped both magazines boost their circulation. The arts added entertainment to the purposes served by the magazines, and they certainly drew in readers who were less interested in their more sociological or political texts. But the arts were never presented as "mere" entertainment: from the start, as they included and discussed the arts, contributors to both magazines emphasized the role of creative texts in influencing public opinion about African Americans. Du Bois began including the arts in *The Crisis* within months of the magazine's founding. Line drawings and photographs graced the covers in the first six months, and cartoons by John Henry Adams appeared in these early issues. The first piece of literature—a poem by Leslie Pinckney Hill called "The Teacher"—was published in January 1911. The magazine's first literary contest was announced the following year. In the call for entries, Du Bois began to outline his sense of purpose for creative work: he wrote that he hoped that works of fiction might present "pictures of the real colored America" ("Short Story Competition" 189). In an essay he published in another magazine in 1913, Du Bois hinted that these new "pictures" of African Americans would take many forms. He emphasized the importance of the spirituals and literature, and he closed by noting the work of African American painters, actors, and composers ("The Negro in Literature and Art" 862–67). His discussion of literature is the most extended section of the essay, but the fact that he preceded and followed that discussion with references to other kinds of creative work communicates a sense of connection among these various kinds of texts. Significantly, that essay appeared the same year Du Bois first formulated plans for a pageant to represent the achievements of black people throughout history. This elaborate theatrical event, eventually named "The Star of Ethiopia," included music, actors, and dramatic stage sets; it thus brought together work in many different media. It was first presented in conjunction with an exhibit in New York City in 1913, celebrating the fiftieth anniversary of the Emancipation Proclamation; it was next staged, in expanded form, in Washington, D.C., in 1915 and then embarked on a tour of many different cities. Du Bois described the pageant and its success in a series of editorials and essays in *The Crisis,* and although it was quite costly and labor intensive to stage, this multi-media extravaganza was valued by him and others as "a force for breaking down prejudice."[5]

The mix of arts in the pageant was repeated on the pages of the magazine, where the idea that the arts would help undermine racism was often emphasized. In April 1915, when Du Bois outlined "The Immediate Program of the American Negro," he included "a revival of art and literature" as an important component in efforts to achieve equality (312). This revival would be significant, Du Bois emphasized, because of what it would reveal about both the talents of African American artists and the fitness of African Americans as subjects for literary portrayals. Du Bois asserted that "we should set the black man before the world as both a creative artist and a strong subject for artistic treatment" (312). In the following years, Du Bois's inclusion of creative texts in *The Crisis* increased, and he often repeated his calls for further work of this kind. In April 1920, for example, he mentioned with pride the inclusion in *The Crisis* of poetry, prose, cartoons, and cover art. He also encouraged more African American writers to create: "A renaissance of American Negro literature is due," he asserted ("Negro Writers" 299).[6] In June 1922, he called for a summer gathering of African American artists and writers, which might nurture their talents and enhance the relations among them ("An Institute of Negro Literature and Art" 58). Four years later, he acknowledged that focusing the attention of *The Crisis* and the NAACP on the arts might have seemed inappropriate, given the identity of the NAACP as "a group of radicals trying to bring new things into the world, . . . struggling for the right of black men to be ordinary human beings" ("Criteria of Negro Art" 290). But he defended the arts as "part of the great fight we are carrying on" and as representing "a forward and an upward look—a pushing onward" (290). For Du Bois, then, the arts served the same ends as the protest and affirmative texts in *The Crisis*.[7]

The importance of the arts also was hinted at in *Opportunity*'s first issues. Explanatory editorials in the first two issues indicated that the arts would play an important role in efforts to change perceptions of the race. Eugene Kinckle Jones focused exclusively on the magazine's presentation of facts and information in "'Cooperation' and 'Opportunity,'" but the anonymous writer of "1923" noted, "The weary struggle of the Negro population for status thru self-improvement and recognition, aided by their friends, goes on" and called for a new effort against difficulties faced by African Americans as well as "an increased technique for dealing with them" (3). In the second issue of *Opportunity*, the writer of "Why We Are" explained that that increased technique would include facts and information but also the arts. "There are aspects of the cultural side of Negro life that have been long neglected" (3), this writer asserted, and the contributors to *Opportunity* would write about and illustrate those aspects of Negro life: drama, music, art, and literature by African Americans. The importance of the creative arts in the magazine also was signaled by the fact that the first issue included an essay on "Our Young Negro Artists." This review of two exhibits, one in New

York City and the other in Boston, included reproductions of six portraits by African American painters. There were only a few creative pieces in this and other early issues, but the August 1923 issue included a call for submissions on the table of contents, asking readers to send in creative writing, drawings, paintings, and photographs, as well as news stories and "authentic articles." Starting that month most issues included at least one or two pieces of fiction or poetry.

By the mid-1920s, creative texts were included in every issue of both magazines. Any given issue might include a review of a performance by a singer, two or three reviews of new books of fiction or poetry, and an announcement of an exhibit of visual art. News items might mention the work of actors, singers, writers, and painters, as well as politicians, professionals, and sports figures. The issue probably also would include at least two or three poems, a short story or two, and possibly a play.[8] The importance of the arts—and of different kinds of art—to both magazines is further underlined by the fact that both Du Bois and Johnson ran contests for creative artists in 1925, 1926, and 1927, and that they included categories for artists working in different media.[9] Both editors preceded each contest with numerous calls for submissions, and the magazines published many of the winning entries in the months following the announcements of the results. Du Bois included categories for written, visual, and musical texts: artists could submit stories, plays, poems, essays, or illustrations in the 1925 and 1926 *Crisis* contests, and Du Bois added a category for songs for the 1927 contest ("The Amy Spingarn Prizes in Literature and Art" 247; "KRIGWA 1926" 67–68; "Krigwa, 1927" 191–93). The 1925 *Opportunity* contest included categories for stories, poems, plays, essays, and "personal experience sketches"; a category for music was added for the 1926 and 1927 contests; and "constructive journalism" was included in the 1926 contest ("Opportunity Literary Contest" 228; "The Contest" 292; "The Holstein Prizes" 319). Literature was clearly the main focus of both contests, but the inclusion of categories for other kinds of creative texts is further evidence that both editors believed in the importance of work in many media.

In those years, both magazines were clearly established as important sources of creative work and forums for discussions of that work. Including the arts probably enhanced the ability of the magazines' other texts to do their work: by drawing in readers, the creative texts in these two magazines attracted a larger audience for their expository and editorial texts. More people, then, would have found Du Bois's editorials and *Opportunity*'s essays. This was particularly true when the magazines published literature serially, as *The Crisis* did with a number of short stories in the 1910s and early 1920s. By dividing the stories into sections and running them in subsequent issues, the magazines ensured their readers' continued attention.

But the arts also complement the expository and affirmative texts in *The Crisis* and *Opportunity* in important ways. First, the arts, like propaganda and news texts, helped participants in the Harlem Renaissance counteract the limited nature of images of African Americans available in American popular culture. Du Bois, for example, when he announced a symposium on "The Negro in Art" complained that too many depictions of African Americans showed only the "sordid, foolish, and criminal among Negroes" ("A Questionnaire" 165). He emphasized the role literature and other arts by African Americans could play in focusing on different types of African Americans; in so doing, they might expand their readers' perceptions of and ideas about African Americans. Numerous writers in *Opportunity*, too, emphasized the potential of the arts to enhance their audiences' knowledge about African Americans: one contributor argued, for example, that literature provided an opportunity "for Negroes themselves to replace their outworn representations in fiction faithfully and incidentally to make themselves better understood" ("An Opportunity for Negro Writers" 258). The two magazines, then, used creative texts just as they used news stories or propaganda texts, to introduce their readers to sides of African American life that they had not yet encountered and to thus alter public opinion of African Americans for the good by supplanting existing stereotypes. In short, their efforts to redefine African American identity and undermine racism took on many forms; the arts was one of many tools.

This potential of creative texts to offer new images of African Americans was frequently emphasized in reviews of novels by black writers. For example, Montgomery Gregory, in his *Opportunity* review of Jean Toomer's book *Cane,* praised the author's realistic representation of African Americans. He emphasized that Toomer's portraits of African Americans counteracted past representations of African Americans by white American writers, which he called works of "alien exploitation" that had led to the acceptance of "caricatures of the race . . . as bona fide portraits" (374). Toomer, in contrast, presented more accurate portraits, and Gregory argued that they demonstrated the unmistakable power of literary portraiture to correct mistaken impressions of the race. Similarly, when he reviewed Jessie Fauset's *There Is Confusion,* Gregory identified the "great value" of the novel as its interpretation of "the better elements of our life to those who know us only as domestic servants, 'uncles,' or criminals" (181). Texts like this, in other words, were important because they presented images of a class of African Americans that was not often portrayed elsewhere. Similar arguments were made in both magazines about many novels, plays, and poetry collections.

Another way that the arts complemented news and expository texts was that they provided additional proof of the skills and talents of African Americans. Demonstrating and asserting the quality of the work of African American artists and writers was of great concern to contributors to both *The Crisis* and *Opportunity,* particularly because they often assumed that assessments of African Americans in general were greatly affected by the quality of art they produced. In other words, evidence of creative abilities was another kind of information the arts provided about African Americans. While news stories recorded African Americans' contributions in education, politics, and other fields, short stories, poems, and illustrations recorded African Americans' achievements in the arts. It is significant, then, that both magazines emphasized the racial identity of the African American writers and artists whose work they included. For example, when *Opportunity* announced the winners of its contests, it included not only their names but also photographs of most of them. These photographs make visible the race of the writers, who, as did the individuals featured in news stories, served as role models for other African Americans. In both magazines, many reviews of works of literature or art included portraits of the writers or artists. For example, reviews of Fauset's and Toomer's novels in both magazines included photographs of the two writers (Du Bois and Locke; Gregory). Significantly, Gregory in his assessment of *Cane* almost immediately identified Toomer as "a young Negro," as if to ensure that the work of this light-skinned writer was counted as a credit to his race (374).

The ability of the arts to provide images of African Americans and to demonstrate their talents was even further enhanced when essays or creative texts were paired with drawings. For instance, in a feature on "Black Verse," written by Frank Horne for the November 1924 issue of *Opportunity,* Horne's comments on the work of African American poets are illustrated by drawings of James Weldon Johnson, Countee Cullen, and Leslie Pinckney Hill by Francis C. Holbrook (see fig. 3.1 for one page). Similarly, a series of essays on spirituals and folk songs by African Americans that appeared in the November 1925 issue of *Opportunity* was accompanied by three drawings by Aaron Douglas. Each of the drawings is titled with a line of a spiritual, making the connection between the illustration and the song explicit. In one pair, Arthur Huff Fauset includes a number of excerpts from spirituals to demonstrate the range of emotions expressed in them and their evocative capabilities ("The Negro's Cycle of Song" 333–35), while Douglas's illustration captures a moment of prayer in a suggestive black-and-white drawing (see fig. 3.2). Such combinations of written and visual texts become multi-media demonstrations of the quality of the work of many different kinds of artists.

Black Verse

By FRANK S. HORNE

". . . And do not ask the poor man not to sing, For song is all he has."—ROBERT NATHAN.

FROM the Trinity College Press, Durham, North Carolina, comes an "Anthology of Verse by American Negroes," edited by Newman Ivey White, Ph.D., Professor of English at Trinity College, and Walter Clinton Jackson, Vice President of the North Carolina College of Women, with an introduction by James Hardy Dillard, Ph.D., L.L.D., President of the Jeanes Foundation and the John F. Slater Fund.

We have here something more than just another anthology. It distinguishes itself, on the one side, by coming from the heart of the Southland, by its utter impartiality, and its scholarly completeness; on the other, by its lack of direction in development, absence of personality, and faultiness of viewpoint.

The professors have been most diligent. There is evidence of concentrated application and profound probing into obscure poetical sources. The book is redolent of the South, the schoolroom, and the professorial dictum. The work is scholarly, and the treatment is both critical and sympathetic to some degree. It at least demonstrates that these two southern scholars have looked upon this definite body of literary production, and deemed it worthy of their recognition. But for all that, the anthology is sluggish; it lacks distinction and verve. It possesses neither the vigor and raciness of Professor Talley's folk lore collection, nor the poetical finesse and judgment of James Weldon Johnson's "Book of American Negro Poetry." The book lacks, in a sense, personality. To a student of the subject, the work is undeniably a worthy contribution; but to the reader of verse, it is a volume he can as well get along without.

In an effort to achieve completeness, the authors have included several worthy features. There is a more or less critical and historical general "Introduction"; brief biographies of the authors accompanying the selections; and a mass of "Bibliographical and Critical Notes" at the end. We shall consider them each in turn. The general "Introduction" is truly more historical than critical. The professors, not being poets, lack the poetical judgment and the insight that is so evident in James Weldon Johnson's "Essay on the Negro's Creative Genius" which serves so aptly as an introduction to his own admirable collection. In essence the two viewpoints stand sharply contrasted when it comes to the question of the ultimate contribution of the Negro to American poetry. The professors, after correctly stating that the constant themes of religion and race in Negro poetry contribute nothing new, go on to say: "There is, however, a kind of Negro humor that deals in a distinctively racial manner with the Negro's love of music, talk, animals, meetings, dancing, loafing and fishing, and is best exemplified in the poems of Dunbar, Allen, and Davis. In this direction, the Negro is perhaps likely to make a purely racial contribution to American poetry. Otherwise, his contribution is apt to be individual and not racial in character." And there you have it! The compilers of this volume appear to believe that the "loud guffaw and the wide grin" are the paramount expressions of Negro aesthetics. At this point, I join the company of Johnson, Braithwaite, and DuBois, and vehemently dissent. The Negro poet has long since forsaken the jester's tatterdemalion. His contribution is more subtle and pregnant; more sensitive to the adventures of his own harassed soul. And in support might be offered such examples as "Self-Determination", by Leslie Pinckney Hill; "When I Die", by Fenton Johnson; "Fifty Years", by James Weldon Johnson; "And What Shall You Say", by Joseph Cotter, Jr.,—I offer you William Stanley Braithwaite, Jessie Redmond Fauset, and Claude McKay—and I offer you the youngest

James Weldon Johnson

Fig. 3.1. The opening page of "Black Verse," written by Frank S. Horne with illustrations by Francis C. Holbrook. Opportunity *(Nov. 1924): 330.*

The Negro's Cycle of Song - A Review

By ARTHUR HUFF FAUSET

I'm goin' to heaven on eagle's wing,
All don't see me, goin' to hear me sing.

THE pity of it is that all who read this splendid volume must content themselves with the mere seeing. Negro song is not something to be looked at; to appreciate it and understand it you must hear it.

Odum and Johnson, the compilers of the volume, both heard and saw; better than that, they devoured what came across their paths, and apparently made a good meal of it. Seldom have we had the pleasure of encountering such perfect comprehension of the Negro on the part of white investigators. For say what you will, the Negro is a difficult "problem." Like the Irishman's flea, it's hard to put your finger squarely upon him. Sometimes he seems to defy analysis.

His songs, like himself, are a problem. As I stated above, they must be heard to be fully appreciated and understood. In cold type they are words, ofttimes—and what crude vehicles are words for suggesting the pulsations, the quiverings, and the trippings of the soul! Sometimes in the case of these songs they approach the inanity of nonsense-syllables.

Small wonder. They have arisen from every conceivable condition of mind and body, and from circumstances innumerable. The wonder is not that they are as they are, but that they even exist. What right have Negroes to be singing anyhow! . . . But that's the whole secret.

The songs have their own general characteristics, of course, which make their origin very apparent, but as to classification, they simply defy any method of classifying.

They scan and they don't.

They are full of sense and they are so much nonsense.

They are sad and droll at the same time.

They contain evidences of profound philosophical reflection couched in expressions which have no parallels for naivete.

Depending on your point of view, they might be everything, nothing, more than anything, less than anything.

Now, can you beat that?

This is a choice sample:

I got de blues, but too damn mean to cry.

THE NEGRO AND HIS SONGS, By *Howard W. Odum, Ph.D., and Guy B. Johnson, A.M.* Published by the *University of North Carolina Press.* Price $3.00.

The epitome of dolefulness. Nevertheless I laughed when I read it.

Take this:

When I git to heaven gwine to ease, ease,
Me an' my God goin' do as we please,
Settin' down side o' holy Lamb.

Or this:

Of all de beastes in de woods,
I'd rather be a tick;
I'd climb up roun' my true love's neck,
An' there I'd stick,
Jus' to see her roll dem snow-white eyes.

The following is certainly a jewel:

Someone stole a chicken in our neighborhood,
They 'rested me on suspicion, it was understood.
They carried me 'fo' a jury—how guilty I did flee.
'Cause my name was signed at de head, de jury said was me.

"I couldn't hear nobody pray."   BY DOUGLAS

Fig. 3.2. "I Couldn't Hear Nobody Pray," an illustration by Aaron Douglas accompanying Arthur Huff Fauset's "The Negro's Cycle of Song." Opportunity *(Nov. 1925): 333.*

Significantly, many works of fiction and poetry were also illustrated in both *The Crisis* and *Opportunity.* In *The Crisis,* illustrated works of literature appeared as early as April 1911, when the magazine published a portrait of William Stanley Braithwaite with a written tribute to his poetry and his work as an anthologist. Illustrated poems and stories appeared in the magazine throughout the 1910s and into the 1920s. A number of Jessie Fauset's stories, for example, were illustrated either with photographs or with drawings by Laura Wheeler. Similar paired texts appeared in both *The Crisis* and *Opportunity* in the 1920s. A particularly striking example is the poem "The Black Runner," by Georgia Douglas Johnson, published with an illustration by Aaron Douglas in the September 1925 issue of *Opportunity* (see fig. 3.3). The poem emphasizes the power and vitality of the speaker. In short, vivid sentences and phrases, punctuated with exclamation points, Johnson describes the runner's pursuit of the "deeds to be done" and the "goals to be won," emphasizing the faith of the runner that he will be able to accomplish them: "I can! And I must!" Douglas's drawing visually asserts his ability: the runner is as muscular as typical representations of a Greek god; his skyward glance and his smile reveal his confidence; and the dust cloud that billows up behind him is an effect of the speed and the impact of his footsteps. While the poem communicates the runner's goals and attitude, then, Douglas invests his illustration with visual symbols that show his power. This paired text, then, offers new images of African Americans through its contents—the written and visual images of the strong black man—but also because it demonstrates the talents of both the writer and the illustrator. Other illustrated poems—like James Weldon Johnson's "To America" in *The Crisis* or Langston Hughes's "To Midnight Nan at Leroy's" in *Opportunity*—similarly provide both written and visual examples of African Americans' creative skills (see fig. 3.4).

These paired creative texts also hint at a belief of contributors to both magazines that the potential of the arts to influence public opinion about African Americans was greatest when different kinds of arts were brought together. This understanding is made particularly clear in contributors' discussion of the arts in wide-ranging essays. For example, in an unsigned editorial called "The New Generation" in the March 1924 issue of *Opportunity,* the writer referred to a number of books about African Americans, including *Cane,* that "point to a gentle awakening among a large mass of the reading public which until recently would take its pictures from virulent Negro baiters only, or remain indifferent" (68). With this comment, the writer implied a connection between literary and visual portraiture; he or she then tied in performance by turning to the influence of Broadway shows with African American characters and periodicals that direct positive attention to

Fig. 3.3. Georgia Douglas Johnson's "The Black Runner," illustrated by Aaron Douglas. Opportunity *(Sept. 1925): frontispiece.*

To Midnight Nan at Leroy's

By LANGSTON HUGHES

STRUT and wiggle,
Shameless gal,
Wouldn't no good fellow
Be your pal?

Hear dat music . . .
Jungle night.
Hear dat music . . .
And the moon was white.

Sing your Blues song,
Pretty baby;
You want lovin', . .
And you don't mean maybe.

Jungle lover . . .
Night black boy . . .
Two against the moon
And the moon was joy.

Strut and wiggle,
Shameless Nan,
Wouldn't no good fellow
Be your man?

DOUGLAS

Fig. 3.4. Langston Hughes's "To Midnight Nan at Leroy's," illustrated by Aaron Douglas. Opportunity *(Jan. 1926): 23.*

African Americans. All combine, the writer concluded, to inspire "the new group of young Negro writers," who were "leaving to the old school its labored lamentations and protests, read only by those who agree with them, and [were] writing about life" (68). The author then emphasized the social and political impact of this change of focus: "This is a healthy state for race relations. This freedom of discussion and new curiosity may well be regarded a first effectual blow in the destruction of those barriers of mutual ignorance and prejudice, hatred and fear, which long have throttled understanding" (68). In this articulation of effects of the arts on public opinion and the move between literature and Broadway, this writer implied that different arts worked together to promote changes in perception.

At the same time, though, the idea that the arts could undermine racism by providing positive images of African Americans was often seen as in tension with the importance of the quality of creative work by African Americans. This dilemma was particularly clear in *The Crisis*. Du Bois had strong ideas about the need for positive images of African Americans and clear definitions of what constituted positive images, and he could be so outspoken on this issue that he sparked a good deal of resistance from writers, artists, and critics who disagreed with him.[10] The resulting conflicts are articulated particularly clearly in his 1926 symposium on "The Negro in Art." Du Bois announced the symposium in February, offering a series of questions about how African Americans "should be pictured by writers and portrayed by artists" ("A Questionnaire" 165). He printed answers submitted by twenty-two publishers, editors, writers, and readers of *The Crisis* between March and November of 1926. Many of the respondents argued that writers and artists should be free to create whatever kind of images they wanted to, and that to demand certain kinds of images was to put too many limits on the creative processes. Du Bois disagreed, as he made clear in October when he published "Criteria of Negro Art." The essay is the source of Du Bois's oft-quoted proclamation of the "bounden duty" of African Americans to create, realize, and preserve Beauty, and of the need for art to work as propaganda (296).[11] It is a stark contrast to the calls for freedom voiced by so many of the other contributors to the symposium.

These debates about the duty or the freedom of the artist were ongoing in *The Crisis,* and they also were carried on in the pages of *Opportunity*. Just as they did in *The Crisis,* contributors to *Opportunity* articulated a range of opinions about the appropriate content of the arts. For example, Countee Cullen, who served as assistant editor for the magazine and wrote a monthly column, "The Dark Tower," from 1926 to 1928, used his column in March 1928 to argue that:

> whether they relish the situation or not, Negroes should be concerned with making good impressions. They cannot do this by throwing wide every door of the racial entourage, to the wholesale gaze of the world at large. Decency demands that some things be kept secret; diplomacy demands it; the world loses its respect for violators of this code. . . .
>
> Let art portray things as they are, no matter what the consequences, no matter who is hurt, is a blind bit of philosophy. (90)

Cullen's comments are in line with Du Bois's argument against "art for art's sake"; they parallel Du Bois's call for the arts to work as propaganda. In contrast, Alain Locke warned in *Opportunity* of the dangers of subjecting the arts to "the irrelevant social values of 'representative' and 'unrepresentative,' 'favorable' and 'unfavorable'" ("To Certain of Our Phillistines" 155). Locke insisted that such a tendency toward demanding that the arts provide only positive images of African Americans, which he labeled "Phillistinism," "cannot be tolerated" (155). These two comments represent opposite ends of the spectrum of opinion; different positions on that spectrum were articulated by other contributors to both magazines throughout the 1920s.[12]

These debates reveal the dangers of expecting the arts to function in the same way that affirmative texts or news stories did, and they reveal the assumptions of many of the participants of the Harlem Renaissance that creative work was distinct from expository or news texts. For the highest quality work to be produced, many argued, the freedom of the artist needed to be protected—even if that meant that he or she did not produce "positive" images of African Americans. While the arts fit into efforts to redefine African American identity and undermine racism carried out in other kinds of texts, then, their inclusion in *The Crisis* and *Opportunity* also raises questions about whether the demands of the creative process made it unproductive to expect them to serve the same purposes as propaganda and affirmation.

The inclusion of creative texts in *The Crisis* and *Opportunity* also reveals, however, that the arts had other properties that made them particularly beneficial to the struggle over representation, and both magazines capitalized on these aspects of the arts when they combined written and visual texts. Key among these was the fact that the arts encourage recognition for African Americans as fully rounded human beings in a way that expository and news texts do not. The arts reveal aspects of African Americans' experiences that escape depiction in expository and news texts, and the ability of the arts to shed light on African Americans' inner lives and to demonstrate African Americans' talents of self-expression proved vital to the magazines' efforts to redefine African American identity.

One of the crucial advantages of the arts, as contributors to both magazines often emphasized, was that they reveal intangible aspects of the lives of their subjects. When, for instance, Willis Richardson wrote in *The Crisis* about "The Hope of a Negro Drama," he emphasized the need for not "merely plays with Negro characters," and not necessarily "propaganda" plays, but for plays that show "the soul of a people" (338). When Jessie Fauset announced the winners of a short story contest in June 1923, she called for more "writers who will be able to express our needs, our thoughts, our fancies" ("The Prize Story Competition" 58). When Locke praised her novel *There Is Confusion* in February 1924, he insisted that the book was important, in part, because it was "a race story told from the inside" (Du Bois and Locke 162). As such, it could show how "the race situation in this country" affected African Americans psychologically (163). Simultaneously, though, it also showed that the conflicts and dilemmas faced by its characters "are those more universal ones of human nature" (163). These reviewers, in short, emphasized that literature and the arts could reveal what Locke would call in *The New Negro* the "inner" life of African Americans ("Foreword" ix).

Similar arguments were made in many issues of *Opportunity*. For example, the May 1925 issue announced the winners of that year's contest and included an editorial, "Out of the Shadow," emphasizing the importance of their work. The writer argued that, in this creative work, "amazingly interesting stories about real Negroes . . . have come to light, revealing pictures, compelling in their sheer charm and underlying humanity" (131). These texts went beyond the scope of expository texts: "We expect of literature, nowadays, to reveal with some measure of faithfulness something of the life of a people; something of those subtle forces which sustain their hopes and joys, stiffens [*sic*] them in sorrow" (131). These subtle forces might be more internal than external, more emotional than material. The "life" that might be captured in the creative texts, if so, goes beyond the physical realities of African Americans' lives that are recorded in so many expository and news texts.

Other discussions of creative texts emphasize more explicitly that the insight they offer into the emotions and desires of their subjects makes creative texts an important complement to the images presented in other texts. Where essays and news stories describe social forces, job performance, academic accomplishments, and so on, creative texts provide information about aspects of African Americans' lives that cannot be measured in expository texts. The need for a focus on the internal lives of African Americans as well as more external studies was emphasized repeatedly by contributors to *Opportunity*. Charles Johnson, for example, opened his review of the novel *Nigger* with this proclamation: "Scientific treatises on the relations of white and black in this country are more accurate, but a novel . . . gets under the skin" (30). His comment implies effectiveness for both factual and fictional texts, but for different reasons: the persuasive nature of accuracy—the revelation of information—on one hand, and the ability of a work of fiction to explore the inner lives of its subjects. If "getting under the skin" implies that a work of art—a novel, in this case—can depict the inner, emotional workings of a character, that person appears human to readers in a way that he or she would not if only an external view were offered.

"Getting under the skin" also can be read another way. If racial differences are physically represented by skin color, to get under the skin is to move beyond that perceived difference. What is discovered are shared human values. In that sense, the ability of the arts to reveal the inner lives of African Americans was posited as an advantage for building a sense of connection between black and white Americans. Contributors to *Opportunity* in particular often emphasized that the result might be improved race relations. For example, one writer suggested that literature's ability to reveal "the life and longings and emotional experiences of the Negro people" might help inspire the "interest and kindred feeling" of readers ("An Opportunity for Negro Writers" 258). Esther Fulks Scott, writing about a mixed-race audience for a play about African Americans, argued, "The feeling of interest in each other was noticeable to such an extent one wondered if such a movement would not tend effectively to break down race prejudice" (21). That interest did not depend on finding out that "they" were just like "us": few contributors to the magazine argued that there was no difference between black and white Americans. Instead, when they asserted differences, they emphasized that bonds across racial lines were possible in spite of those differences. For example, the writer of "On Writing About Negroes" argued that literature in particular reveals "the undeniably human touch which affirms brotherhood both in likenesses and in differences" (227). Drawing a parallel to the importance of "Oriental Art" in revealing "the heart of Asia," the writer of "A Contest Number" emphasized that "fellowship can be found in beauty of whatever origin" (173). Art, in short, revealed the humanity of its subjects. As Johnson concluded in his review of *Nigger,* the book was worthy of acclaim because in it, "The Negro is pictured as a human being capable of some aspirations and standards enough to feel his disappointment over failure to attain them" (30). As Locke argued about the work of a writer whose characters were African, the importance was finding "the common human denominator" ("The Colonial Literature of France" 334).

The connection between emotional revelation and improved race relations was even more explicitly asserted in the announcements of *Opportunity*'s literary contests. The contest announcements and bits of advice for potential entrants allowed Johnson and other contributors to the magazine to outline their criteria and their hopes for quality work of literature and art. For example, the writer of the opening essay of the September 1924 issue, "An Opportunity for Negro Writers," laid out the hopes of *Opportunity* for work by African American writers:

> There is an extreme usefulness for the cause of inter-racial good-will as well as racial culture and American literature in interpreting the life and longings and emotional experiences of the Negro people to their shrinking and spiritually alien neighbors; of flushing old festers of hate and disgruntlement by becoming triumphantly articulate; of forcing the interest and kindred feeling of the rest of the world by sheer force of the humanness and beauty of one's own story. (258)

This statement, in bringing together the cause of "inter-racial good-will," the exposure of "the life and longings and emotional experiences of the Negro people," and the idea of interest and kindred feelings emerging from "the sheer force of the humanness" of the story, links each of the concepts discussed previously. It makes clear how, as Edna Worthley Underwood, one of the 1925 contest judges, claimed, "Art should be—and undoubtedly will be —the powerful and compelling liaison officer between nations and races" (qtd. in "The Contest" 130).

Revealing points of shared humanity was an important way creative texts might have been more likely than expository or news texts to encourage a sense of connection between readers and subjects. Again, this was especially important if the readers in question were white. One of the assertions of the Chicago Commission on Race Relations was that "between the races, differences were so minimal as to make nonsense of sustained enmity" (Lewis, *When Harlem Was in Vogue* 47). But many white Americans—and perhaps black Americans, too—believed so strongly in the fundamental differences between black and white Americans that that point was lost.[13] The protest texts in *The Crisis* and the expository texts in *Opportunity*, as we have seen, often failed to communicate much about the identity of their African American subjects and only rarely offered any insight into their thoughts and feelings. The creative arts, in contrast, revealed the emotional lives of African Americans. Significantly, these texts showed that their dreams and desires were the same as anyone's: respect, opportunities, and so on.

The creative arts, then, played a crucial role in both magazines in offering kinds of insights that expository or news texts could not. *Opportunity* went a step further on this point than did *The Crisis* when the former integrated the arts into its efforts to battle racism by demonstrating and nurturing improved interracial relations. By using creative texts to offer white readers insights into the inner lives of African Americans, *Opportunity* capitalized on the ability of the arts to draw attention to points of connection and similarity between the readers and the subjects of these texts. These insights encouraged white readers, more than did expository or news texts, to understand African Americans as people just like themselves. The very need to do so, of course, is a reminder of the extent of the racism that pervaded the 1920s; the use of the arts, *Opportunity* shows, was an important way to address and challenge that reality at that time.

Another advantage of the arts in both magazines was that they could be used to educate readers about the processes of representation. Perhaps even more effectively than protest or affirmation, or expository or news texts, the arts suggest the limitations of any individual text. This point becomes particularly clear in both magazines when written and visual texts are paired in ways that suggest that a complete understanding of the topics at hand depends upon an integrated reading of related texts.

In some combinations of creative written and visual texts, the illustration simply offers a visual representation of the events in the story or poem. For example, in "The Treasure of the Poor," a short story by the French writer Jean Richepin that was translated into English by Jessie Fauset and published in the December 1917 issue of *The Crisis*, an impoverished elderly couple is befriended by a cat who leads them to an abandoned home in the woods. Three pen-and-ink drawings by Laura Wheeler depict the moment when the couple meets the cat and show the couple enjoying the home; in other words, they offer readers a visual depiction of key moments in the story. The relationship between the visual and written texts is one of quotation, in which "[t]he artist produces a picture which is a visual double for the word" (Kooistra 15). This kind of relation between written and visual texts can also be found in other pairings of creative texts, such as Fauset's "The Sleeper Wakes," published in *The Crisis* in August, September, and October 1920 with drawings by Wheeler. Here, the role of the illustration as offering a visual rendition of a moment in the text is emphasized by the fact that each of the drawings is coupled with a caption that is a quotation from Fauset's story. Similar relationships between written and visual creative texts can be found in numerous issues of *The Crisis* and *Opportunity*; the point of such pairings seems to be to catch readers' attention and draw them into the written texts with which they were printed.

The photographs that accompany Fauset's story "Emmy," in contrast, demonstrate the degree to which illustrations can move beyond mere quotation and draw attention to significant details in the written text. In this story, published in 1912 and 1913 in *The Crisis*, Emmy is a relatively dark-skinned young woman whose relationship with the much lighter Archie is put into danger by the fact that he can pass as white—unless he marries Emmy, in which case his own identity as African American will become clear. In the first installment of the story, a photograph shows Emmy smiling into a mirror; the caption indicates that she is thinking happily of Archie's love for her (see fig. 3.5). However, the photograph accompanying the second half of the story shows Emmy sitting dejected; the caption indicates that she is musing on the tragedy of their broken relationship (see fig. 3.6). In the photographs, the reader sees Emmy's skin color, and the contrast between her joy and her sadness in the two images underlines the heartbreak brought by the effects of racism. The illustrations, then, add emphasis to the theme of

"Why should I mind, Archie," she asked that faithful squire as they walked home in the afternoon through the pleasant "main" street. Archie had brought her home from school ever since she could remember. He was two years older than she; tall, strong and beautiful, and her final arbiter.

If any of the boys in your class say anything to you, you let me know. I licked Bill Jennings the other day for calling me a 'guiney.' Wish I were a good, sure-enough brown like you, and then everybody'd know just what I am."

Archie's clear olive skin and aquiline fea-

"ARCHIE LOVES YOU, GIRL," SHE SAID TO THE FACE IN THE GLASS.

Archie stopped to watch a spider.

"See how he does it, Emmy! See him bring that thread over! Gee, if I could swing a bridge across the pond as easy as that! What d'you say? Why should you mind? Oh, I don't guess there's anything for us to mind about. It's white people, they're always minding—I don't know why.

tures made his Negro ancestry difficult of belief.

"But," persisted Emmy, "what difference does it make?"

"Oh, I'll tell you some other time," he returned vaguely. "Can't you ask questions though? Look, it's going to rain. That means uncle won't need me in the field this

Fig. 3.5. The first illustration for "Emmy," by Jessie Fauset. The Crisis *(Dec. 1912): 80.*

SHE SAID: "NOW THIS, I SUPPOSE, IS WHAT THEY CALL A TRAGEDY."

Fig. 3.6. The second illustration for "Emmy," by Jessie Fauset. The Crisis (Jan. 1913): 135.

the story; they offer the reader another way to understand the impact of racism and appreciate its effect.

Other illustrated stories and poems demonstrate even more complex relationships between the written and visual texts, and these become particularly useful for the education of readers. For example, an early illustrated story in *The Crisis* vividly reminds readers how little they perceive if they depend only upon one kind of text. Charles Chesnutt's "The Doll" was printed in the April 1912 issue. The story focuses on Tom Taylor, a successful black barber, and his mental struggle about how he should treat one of his white patrons. Taylor and his shop are well known and well respected by his regular customers, but one white man decides to test his restraint. While Taylor is shaving him, the customer, a Southern colonel, tells his white companion the story of how he murdered a black man years before. As it turns out, the murdered man was Taylor's father, and the barber wages a mighty battle in interested, too, in watching the barber, who, it was evident, was repressing some powerful emotion. It seemed very probable to the judge that the barber might resent this cool recital of murder and outrage. He did not know what might be true of the Negroes in the South, but he had been judge of a police court in one period of his upward career, and he had found colored people prone to sudden rages, when under the influence of strong emotion, handy with edged tools, and apt to cut thick and deep, nor always careful about the color of the cuticle. The barber's feelings were plainly stirred, and the judge, a student of human nature, was curious to see if he would be moved to utterance. It would have been no novelty—patrons of the shop often discussed race questions with the barber. It was evident that the colonel was trying an experiment to demonstrate his contention in the lobby above. But the judge could not know the barber's intimate relation to the story, nor did it occur to him that the barber might conceive any deadly purpose because of a purely impersonal grievance. The barber's hand did not even tremble.

In the barber's mind, however, the whirlwind of emotions had passed lightly over the general and settled upon the particular injury. So strong, for the moment, was the homicidal impulse that it would have prevailed already had not the noisy opening of the door to admit a patron diverted the barber's attention and set in motion a current of ideas which fought for the colonel's life. The barber's glance toward the door, from force of habit, took in the whole shop. It was a handsome shop, and had been to the barber a matter of more than merely personal pride. Prominent among a struggling people, as yet scarcely beyond the threshold of citizenship, he had long been looked upon, and had become accustomed to regard himself, as a representative man, by whose failure or success his race would be tested. Should he slay this man now beneath his hand, this beautiful shop would be lost to his people. Years before the whole trade had been theirs. One by one the colored master barbers, trained in the slovenly old ways, had been forced to the wall by white competition, until his shop was one of the few good ones remaining in

the hands of men of his race. Many an envious eye had been cast upon it. The lease had only a year to run. Strong pressure, he knew, had been exerted by a white rival to secure the reversion. The barber had the hotel proprietor's promise of a renewal; but he knew full well that should he lose the shop no colored man would succeed him; a center of industry, a medium of friendly contact with white men, would be lost to his people—many a good turn had the barber been able to do for them while he had the ear—literally had the ear—of some influential citizen, or held some aspirant for public office by the

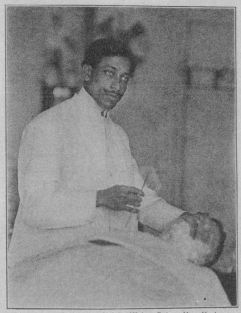

Arranged and photographed by Walter Baker, New York

"If the razor went to its goal he would not be able to fulfil his promise to Daisy!" (p. 252.)

throat. Of the ten barbers in the shop all but one were married, with families dependent upon them for support. One was sending a son to college; another was buying a home. The unmarried one was in his spare hours studying a profession, with the hope of returning to practice it among his people in a Southern State. Their fates were all, in a measure, dependent upon the proprietor of the shop. Should he yield to the impulse which was swaying him their livelihood would be placed in jeopardy. For what white man, while the memory of this tragic event should last,

Fig. 3.7. The photograph accompanying Charles Chesnutt's "The Doll." *The Crisis* (Apr. 1912): 251.

his mind. He has long dreamed of killing his father's murderer, and with one simple movement, he could slit the colonel's throat. But he knows that he himself would be killed if he did so, and that his actions also would have severe repercussions for his employees, his family, and even the relations between black and white residents of the city. With that in mind, he allows the colonel to leave unharmed.

The story makes a number of points clear. The first is the colonel's complete lack of awareness of the danger into which he put himself. He knows that the barber was the victim's son; in fact, he purposely goes to his shop and tells the story to his friend to demonstrate, as he argues, that African Americans "will neither resent an insult, nor defend a right, nor avenge a wrong" (248). He is so convinced of this that he closes his eyes while he is shaved; he is thus blind to the struggle of the barber (249). Readers know that the events are much more complicated than the colonel's narrative indicates; once he has told his version of the events, Chesnutt narrated what Taylor knows happened. The differences between the two tellings of Taylor's father's murder are a stunning reminder that there are many versions of any one story. Furthermore, the story is illustrated with a photograph that makes the partial knowledge of any one text even more evident. It shows Taylor, razor in hand, pausing for a moment over the reclined body of the colonel (see fig. 3.7). This is the moment, surely, when he weighs his options and decides whether to commit murder. But the photograph reveals no such turmoil: it seems as though the barber is just glancing off into the distance, momentarily distracted from his job. It is only when readers view the photograph with the story that they understand what he is thinking at that moment. The pairing of photograph and story, then, underlines the extent to which a photograph offers only an external view of the barber; readers need the written text to fill in what the visual image cannot tell.

Such pairings of literature with visual texts continued in *The Crisis* through the 1910s and into the 1920s. *Opportunity* did not include such revealing combinations in its first issues, but as its coverage of the arts increased in 1924 and 1925, composite texts became more frequent, and they culminated in a feature that combines the work of poet Langston Hughes and illustrator Aaron Douglas. This set of paired poems and drawings was printed in the October 1926 issue; by this time, both Hughes's and Douglas's work had appeared repeatedly in *The Crisis* and *Opportunity*, so readers would have recognized the poet and artist as two of the up-and-coming participants in the New Negro movement. But the feature also demonstrates particularly clearly the degree to which complicated understandings of African Americans' lives depended upon readings of multiple texts. One poem and illustration combination appears on the cover of the issue; the others appear inside the magazine on a two-page spread. Each of the illustrations is titled with a line or a phrase from the corresponding poem, which makes the connections between them explicit. The feature also works music into the equation: Hughes's poetry is a tribute, in form and content, to the blues. The poems, particularly in their evocation of the blues, record the difficulties of life in America for blacks, but with Douglas's drawings, they also demonstrate the possibilities of overcoming those difficulties.

In *The Dream Keeper,* a collection of poems that Hughes published in 1933, Hughes included a one-paragraph "Note on Blues" that illuminates the form of the poems that appeared in this feature. Hughes described the blues as having "a strict poetic pattern: one long line, repeated, and a third line to rhyme with the first two" (30). Such lines are often called "the repeat line" and "the response line," and Hughes in many of his poems broke them in half, so each stanza became six lines, with the third and fourth repeating the first and second and the fifth and sixth becoming the response (Chinitz 178). In terms of content, Hughes wrote that the spirituals "are often songs about escaping from trouble, going to heaven and living happily ever after," while the blues "are songs about being in the midst of trouble, friendless, hungry, disappointed in love, right here on earth" (*Dream Keeper* 30). But the blues, he insisted, have a transformative potential: the mood is "almost always despondency, but when they are sung people laugh" (30). In the collaboration with Douglas, Hughes used both the spirituals and the blues as models for the form and the content of his poems, but it is Douglas's drawings that make clear the transformation occurring for Hughes's subjects.

The first paired poem and illustration appear on the cover of the issue. Douglas's drawing sits above Hughes's "Feet o' Jesus" (see fig. 3.8). Hughes's speaker situates himself "At de feet o' Jesus," surrounded by "Sorrow like a sea," and he begs Jesus to "reach out yo' hand" to him. But in Douglas's illustration, the figure stands tall, not humbled as Hughes's speaker might be, but broad shouldered and strong. Furthermore, while the poem captures the speaker in his moment of supplication, the beams of light falling from above in Douglas's illustration suggest that his prayers have reached the heavens. In fact, the slanted, darker beam on the right almost forms a platform on which he can ascend. Douglas's illustration makes visible, then, the possibility of "escaping from trouble, going to heaven and living happily ever after" that Hughes identified as characteristic of the spirituals.

That possibility of escape, and the religious focus of "Feet o' Jesus," sets it apart from the more secular poems on the inside spread, but the transformative possibilities continue to be an important part of the pairs. Inside the issue, the five paired poems and illustrations focus on worldly troubles and transcendence of them. The poems describe the problems of their speakers;

Fig. 3.8. The cover of *Opportunity,* the month that "Two Artists" ran. The poem is by Langston Hughes, and the illustration is by Aaron Douglas. Opportunity *(Oct. 1926): cover.*

Douglas's drawings move beyond the content of the poems to demonstrate the individuals' transcendence of those difficulties. For example, things are so bad for the speaker of "Lonesome Place" that he is "Weary, weary, / Weary as can be." The poem offers no hope that he will overcome these troubles; in fact, the poem hints at the possibility that he will drown himself, "Cause there ain't no worries / Where de waters go." But Douglas offered in his image, "Weary as I Can Be," a far more optimistic picture of the speaker: he is dignified, wearing a stylish hat, reclining regally on the side of the river (see fig. 3.9). Douglas showed him at peace with his surroundings. Douglas similarly transformed Hughes's speakers in "Bound No'th Blues" and "Hard Luck." He portrayed the speaker in the former as a tall, strong, black man who, though he carries a heavy load, strides purposefully toward his future (see fig. 3.10). There is far more optimism in his image, then, than in Hughes's poem about the loneliness of the road and the distance ahead of him. The "Hard Luck" figure, who Hughes left feeling hopeless—"I don't know what / Po' weary me can do"—in Douglas's illustration at least looks at his bad luck card without flinching (see fig. 3.10). Hughes thus took the characteristic focus of the blues on the hardships his African American subjects must face, but Douglas made the transformative aspects of the music visible by showing the subjects' ability to overcome those hardships.

The poem "Misery" and Douglas's "Play de Blues" have a similar relationship. They are worth closer analysis, since they both explicitly focus on the blues and because the illustration again brings up the importance of collaboration between individuals. Hughes structured this poem around four-line rather than six-line stanzas; the repeating lines are shortened into individual lines, as if to offer an example of a variation within the typical form of the blues. But the focus, again, is on the worldly troubles of the speaker, who calls for the blues to ease her misery in an opening stanza:

> Play de blues for me.
> Play de blues for me.
> No other music
> 'Ll ease ma misery.

In this case, her troubles stem from a "no-good man" who has "Done [her] wrong," and only the blues, she declares, can help her through her misery. Douglas's drawing, "Play de Blues," likewise makes clear the importance of the music. A woman, presumably the speaker in Hughes's poem, stands behind a piano player, who leans back and looks up at the music that flows from the top of his piano, drawn by Douglas as wavy black and white bands. The woman too looks toward the music; she raises her left hand as if to touch it. She is broad shouldered and strong looking (see fig. 3.10). If Hughes focused on her misery, Douglas gave the reader an image of her perhaps after she has heard the music, after it has eased her sorrow. She has been transformed and uplifted by the blues.

Douglas's illustration, by showing both the woman and the piano player, also draws attention to the connection between the two figures. In doing so,

TWO ARTISTS

Poems by LANGSTON HUGHES

Drawings by AARON DOUGLAS

I NEEDS A DIME FOR BEER

Down an' Out

If you loves me
Help me when I'm down an' out.
If you loves me
Help me when I'm down an' out.
Cause I'm a po' gal that
Nobody gives a damn about.

'Stalment man's done took ma clothes
An' rent time's most nigh here.
'Stalment man's done took ma clothes,
Rent time's most nigh here.
I'd like to buy a straightenin' comb
An' I needs a dime for beer.

Talk about yo' friendly friends
Bein' kind to you.
Talk about yo' friendly friends
Bein' kind to you:
Just let yo'self git down an' out
An' then see what they'll do.

Lonesome Place

I got to leave this town.
It's a lonesome place.
Got to leave this town cause
It's a lonesome place.
A po', po' boy can't
Find a friendly face.

Goin' down to de river
Flowin' deep an' slow.
Goin' down to de river
Deep an' slow,—
Cause there ain't no worries
Where de waters go.

I'm weary, weary,
Weary as I can be.
Weary, weary,
Weary as can be.
This life's so weary,
'S 'bout to overcome me.

WEARY AS I CAN BE

Fig. 3.9. The first page of "Two Artists." Opportunity *(Oct. 1926): 314.*

ON DE NO'THERN ROAD

Bound No'th Blues

Goin' down de road, Lord,
Goin' down de road.
Down de road, Lord,
Way, way down de road.
Got to find somebody
To help me carry this load.
Road's in front o' me,
Nothin' to do but walk.
Road's in front o' me,
Walk . . . and walk . . . and walk.
I'd like to meet a good friend
To come along an' talk.
Road, road, road, O!
Road, road . . . road . . . road, road!
Road, road, road, O!
On de No'thern road.
These Mississippi towns ain't
Fit for a hoppin' toad.

Misery

PLAY DE BLUES

Play de blues for me.
Play de blues for me.
No other music
'Ll ease ma misery.

Sing a soothin' song.
Said a soothin' song.
Cause de man I love's done
Done me wrong.

Can't you understand,
O, understand
A good woman's cryin'
For a no-good man?

Black gal like me,
Black gal like me
'S got to hear a blues
For her misery.

Hard Luck

Cause you don't love me
Is awful, awful hard.
Gypsy done showed me
Ma bad luck card.

There ain't no good left
In this world for me.
Gypsy done tole me,—
Unlucky as can be.

I don't know what
Po' weary me can do.
Gypsy says I'd kill ma self
If I was you.

MA BAD LUCK CARD

Fig. 3.10. The second page of "Two Artists." Opportunity *(Oct. 1926): 315.*

it also draws attention to a key feature of the blues: that it forges connections between people. Hughes saw the blues as a collaborative art form; the connection might be among a number of musicians, or a piano player and a singer, or the performers and the listeners, but in any case the bond formed between them is behind the change in mood that Hughes described in *The Dream Keeper* and that is visible in Douglas's illustration. Furthermore, because the illustration makes the woman's transformation more obvious, the combination of the poem and the illustration also results in a stronger argument about the importance of the blues. Hughes believed that black music "was crucial to any understanding of black American culture" (Rampersad, "Langston Hughes" 30); poems like "Misery," in form and content, communicate that importance to Hughes's readers.

Overall, this feature by Hughes and Douglas shows the ways that poetry and the visual arts, particularly when paired, can suggest the complicated experiences of African Americans, illuminating both their troubles and their transcendence. This is most clearly shown in the combination of written and visual texts; either, on their own, would tell only part of the story. The same could be said of the photograph and story by Chesnutt; in short, these paired texts demonstrate that the best understanding of the situations depicted comes through a combination of texts. This is a significant lesson for readers of *The Crisis* and *Opportunity* about the processes of representation: given the prevalence of racist images of African Americans in the 1920s, it was particularly important that these two magazines did as much as possible to convince readers that they needed to be critical consumers of images.

By pairing the arts, then, both Du Bois and Johnson showed their readers that a true understanding of a subject required information gleaned from multiple sources. This is true, as the previous examples demonstrate, in the creative pairs. But that message applies as well to each magazine as a whole. This chapter and the previous two have each focused on certain kinds of paired texts in the magazines: protest and affirmation, essays and news stories, literature and the visual arts. But, in truth, any one issue might include all of these. Each issue became a multi-media, multi-genre text, and to truly appreciate their inclusive strategies of representation, we need to explore the ways these various kinds of texts came together into complex wholes in the magazines.

We can come to an understanding of this aspect of the magazines by exploring how different kinds of texts work together in individual issues to send complicated and persuasive messages about their topics. Practically any of either magazine's issues from the early to mid-1920s could be selected as such an example, but the complementary relations among different kinds of texts are most obvious in special issues that were each devoted to one particular topic. *The Crisis*, as we have seen, ran such special issues regularly, focusing on graduates, children, certain cities, soldiers, and so on. In the 1920s, *Opportunity* published a number of special issues on the arts. The May 1925 issue, for example, was the "Contest Number," while the May 1926 issue was an "Art Number" that included many of the winning entries from that year's contest.

Such special issues follow a pattern established in the May 1924 issue, which was devoted to African art and featured a compelling mix of editorials, expository essays, poems, and illustrations. In its focus, the issue participated in a conversation about the significance of African art that had been going on for more than a decade in the pages of *The Crisis*. Du Bois's magazine had printed an illustrated essay by Mary Dunlap Maclean in March 1911, in which she argued that recently discovered art and artifacts demonstrated the significance of African civilizations in world history. In the following years, *The Crisis* often carried notices about ongoing reassessments of African culture and their significance for evaluations of African American culture, and the topic also was repeated in many issues of *Opportunity*. In the early years of the twentieth century, art collectors in Europe had begun to collect and exhibit African art, and writers in both magazines used this growing appreciation of African art to call for a reassessment of ideas about race and culture that would have implications for African Americans. The *Opportunity* issue in May 1924 is a remarkably extensive and persuasive example of this argument.[14]

The issue's attention to African art begins in its editorial section, with a piece devoted, in title at least, to "Dr. Barnes." It emphasizes the white millionaire's significance to readers who might have heard of him but did not fully appreciate the importance of his extensive collection of African art. It also emphasizes his role and the role of the Barnes Foundation in promoting "serious study and exclusive research into the field" of African art (133). But more of the editorial's focus is on the art; the writer emphasizes that it was already being appreciated in Europe and that with its reevaluation in America would come "a new valuation of the contribution of Negroes, past and yet possible, to American life and culture" (133). Immediately following this editorial are three long essays by Locke, Barnes, and Paul Guillaume, the owner of a gallery of African art in Paris and, according to Locke, the "ardent pioneer and champion" of studies of African art ("A Note on African Art" 134). The three writers expanded upon the points made in the editorial, particularly emphasizing the influence of African art on European artists by listing a number of European painters, sculptors, and musicians whose work had been shaped by African aesthetics. This influence was so significant, Locke wrote, that the African art object had "become the corner-stone of a new and more universal aesthetic that has all but revolutionized the theory of art and considerably modified its practice" (134). This point is particularly persuasive because of its presentation in both editorials and essays; the four written texts have a cumulative effect.

The essays also emphasize the significance of this appreciation to African Americans. As Locke asserted, a reevaluation of African culture might lead to a greater sense of pride in African Americans' history: "Nothing," he insisted, "is more galvanizing than the sense of a cultural past" (138). Locke's argument echoed those made by other contributors to *Opportunity*. For example, the August 1923 issue included a long, unsigned review of works included in an exhibit of African art at the Brooklyn Museum. The writer of this review, "The Creative Art of Negroes," pointed out that this display of African art countered the prevailing assumption that ancient Africa had no culture—an assumption that profoundly affected assessments of black culture in the United States:

> Negroes are everywhere judged by the level of culture of their African forbears and expected to reflect it. Actually they are a part of the American scene in culture, tradition, education and history, tho not a large part. But it is all they have or know anything about. Judgment, however, has been passed upon the civilization of African tribes. They have none. (240)

Art, the writer continued, disproves this: "art is an evidence of culture and civilization, even tho the civilization follows a different and unfamiliar direction dictated by a different environment and by technical limitations" (240). The sophistication of African art "cannot be made to fit" the consciousness of Americans and their "categories of Negro traits," and thus will force Americans to alter their assumptions about African Americans (240). When readers encountered the same argument in the May 1924 issue, then, its recurrence might have made it more persuasive. So, too, would the illustrations that appeared with it. The essays by Locke, Barnes, and Guillaume all include photographs of the works from Barnes's collection (see fig. 3.11 for one page). In including these photographs, the issue takes on more of the power of the two collections to foster appreciation for African art. The magazine brings the work to readers who cannot visit Paris or see Barnes's collection. The photographs provide examples of sculpture and masks; they demonstrate significant aspects of the art, particularly the range of styles used by the creators of these works.

The layout of this issue also makes another point clear. In his essay, Locke asserted the influence of this art on other creative work in a range of

Soutine, for example, is to a certain extent, the work of the African emotion in a new setting. In the same way the sculpture of Archipenko, Lipschitz and of Epstein is impregnated with Africanism. The music of Berard, Satie, Poulene, Auric, Honegger—in short, all that which is interesting since Debussy, is African. One can say as much also of the poetry since Raimbaud up to Blaise Cendrars and Reverdy, including Apollinaire. Gobineau has aptly written that "The source from which the arts have sprung is concealed in the blood of the blacks": it is necessary to know this source. But the influence of Negro art on the imagination of the artist is far from having given its full content. We are in the presence of an art eminently suggestive and revealing; an art which touches miraculously the extreme limits of perfection, an art which one can qualify *Sybarritique,* so exquisite is its refinement, but it is a divine art which never weakens, never disappoints. What a delight for the knowing eye of today; that personal quality is not found in the arts of the high epochs of Greece, of China, or even of Egypt where the perfect work seems the end of a dream which will never reawaken.

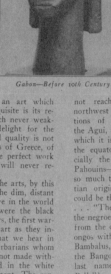

Gabon—Before 10th Century

African art, the most modern of the arts, by this spirit is also the most ancient. In the dim, distant epochs, the men who were first active in the world after the silence of the centuries were the black men. These men were the first creators, the first warriors, the first poets; they invented art as they invented fire; it is later, probably, that we hear in the East of other men, the white barbarians whom they conquered. The conquest was not made without a large infusion of black blood in the white element. The consequence was that the whites, thus regenerated, conquered the blacks, who fled into their forest, from which they were never dislodged. They left, however, the white ethnic traces of their presence in the north and in the east of Africa. These are the Semites and Chamites, mysteriously submitting to the fatality of a somnabulistic tra-

Bushongo—15th Century

dition, lethargic continuators of the spirit of a formidable civilization. Having injected the artistic virus into the barbarian world, they took refuge in their secret religious and social practices and continued to materialize in wood their religious emotions. Grandiose and disconcerting, that took place several millenaires before our era. From the heart of Africa, hypothetical site of the fabled Atlantide, those people, those empires, emigrated in consequence of frightful calamities or cataclysms. Instinctively they turned toward the sea—their pact with the forest was broken. Then they fixed the homesteads which we consider in our present ethnical classifications. The central stock divided into three branches, one went toward the northwest, the other to the southwest, the third remained on the equator but did not reach to the coast of Guinea. In the northwest they are, therefore, the populations of the Nigers, the Bobos, the Baoules, the Agui, the Gouros, the Dan, and so many others which it is not possible to enumerate here. Below the equator and in the southwest they are especially the M'Fangs, the most beautiful of the Pahouins—at whose elegance Europeans marvel so much that they attribute it wrongly to Egyptian origin without dreaming that the contrary could be the truth. A disconcerted traveler writes: . . . "The M'Fangs are the least negro of all the negroes." On the equator, but quite a distance from the coast, are the pastoral races of the Bushongos with their sub-tribes of names so poetic, the Bambalus, the Gwembis, the Bakele, the Yungu, the Bangongo, (in the dialect of the country the last name mentioned signifies "People of the Bells").

The collection of Negro art in the Barnes Foundation is rich in works coming from the races of these different sources. *In this collection besides it will be noted that the epochs have been for the first time definitely fixed.* In order to determine the epochs where these sculptures have been executed diverse elements of

Soudan—Niger—10th Century

Fig. 3.11. A page from *Opportunity*'s special issue on African art. Opportunity *(May 1924): 141.* Top: Reliquary Guardian Head, Gabon Fang Peoples, BF #A124. Lower left: Mask, Guro Peoples, BF #A106. Lower right: Mask, Bamana Peoples, BF #A224.

media. In addition to emphasizing the importance of African art to visual
aesthetics and to assessments of African Americans, he argued that the reconsideration of African aesthetics in the plastic arts had led to an opening
up of racial aesthetics in different arts. He wrote, "A new movement in one of
the arts in most cases communicates itself to the others, and after the influence in plastic art, the flare for things African began shortly to express itself
in poetry and music" ("A Note on African Art" 137). This point is demonstrated by three poems that follow the three articles on African art: "Africa,"
by Claude McKay; "Africa," by Lewis G. Alexander; and "Our Land," by
Langston Hughes. Each of the three poems, as the titles indicate, is a celebration of Africa: each demonstrates Locke's point that the celebration of
"things African" caused by the appreciation of African aesthetics also influenced poetry by African Americans. Importantly, these three poems are then
followed by a number of essays that report on the Civic Club dinner that
Charles Johnson hosted in March 1924 as a way of drawing attention to African American writers. The articles in *Opportunity* summarize the events at
the dinner, listing the names of the writers who had read their work and
transcribing the comments of the speakers who had paid tribute to that
work and to the work of their predecessors. By placing these tributes to the
work of African American writers just after the three poems, and placing
those just after the articles about African art, *Opportunity* allows the texts to
build on one another; the result is a demonstration of the skills of African
and African American artists, shown through both expository and creative
texts and through both written and visual texts.

Closing this chapter with this special issue draws attention to what
would follow: the discussion here of the importance of African art would be
echoed in arguments about African Americans' American identity, and
Africa and African culture would become important elements in the promotion of a unified African American identity and culture. But this issue,
with its discussion of the Civic Club dinner that had just happened, also al-
ludes to the kinds of collaborative illustrated volumes that would be published in 1925 and 1926. *The Crisis* and *Opportunity* both continued, of
course, but their ongoing representations of African Americans and their
monthly definitions of African American identity soon were complemented
by a series of single-volume works, each of which would stretch toward a definitive collective portrait of African Americans. It was the Civic Club dinner
that inspired the editor of the *Survey Graphic,* Paul Kellogg, to devote an
issue to Harlem; it was that issue that became the basis of Locke's anthology,

The New Negro; and it was at least in part in response to *The New Negro* that the young black writers and artists launched their literary and arts magazine *Fire!!*. These volumes are different in nature from these two periodicals, but they would build upon both the themes and the strategies of representation found in the magazines.

Significantly, each of these volumes would continue the practice demonstrated by the magazines of combining different kinds of texts. They would mix propaganda and news texts, and visual and written texts. They also would grant the arts the position of importance they took in *The Crisis* and *Opportunity*. Protest and affirmative texts, as we have seen, proved essential tools for Du Bois's critique of American racism in *The Crisis* in the 1910s. Expository and news texts were useful, when Johnson used them in *Opportunity* in the early 1920s, for revealing the continuing obstacles faced by African Americans but also their growing achievements. But the arts complemented these other kinds of texts, and the arts, with their potential to "get under the skin," also proved helpful to efforts to forge connections between black and white Americans. The arts, then, proved crucial to the representation of African Americans in *The Crisis* and *Opportunity*. The two magazines offer important lessons in the ways that the arts can provide information and shape public opinion about their subjects. Perhaps the most important lesson, though, is that the transformation of ideas is most likely to happen when it encompasses the work of artists and writers who created many different kinds of texts.

4

Survey Graphic's Harlem Issue: Defining the New Negro as American

When the special issue of Survey Graphic *magazine* on Harlem was published in March 1925, it became one of a number of publications in which magazines with predominantly white readerships focused their attention on the New Negro movement. Edited by Alain Locke and including texts primarily from African American contributors, the Harlem issue of the *Survey Graphic* was an important opportunity for African Americans to offer their own representations of themselves and their own definitions of African American identity. As Du Bois and Johnson did in *The Crisis* and *Opportunity,* Locke used the texts in the *Survey Graphic* issue to present new images of African Americans, ones that could correct what Locke called the "grotesque . . . distortions of journalism" covering African Americans ("Harlem" 629). On some level, the texts in the issue merely provide information about African Americans. But a number of arguments about African Americans emerge from these texts: they redefine the relationship between black and white Americans, assert African Americans' importance in American society, and demonstrate African Americans' contributions to American culture. In short, the texts in the *Survey Graphic* issue claim a place in America for African Americans, and they show the relevance of class, gender, and race consciousness to African Americans' attempts to redefine themselves as American.

But the texts in the *Survey Graphic* issue reveal that asserting an American identity for African Americans was a contested effort. Like *The Crisis* and *Opportunity,* the *Survey Graphic* issue contains many different kinds of texts—expository essays, fiction, poetry, photographs, and visual portraits. Many of these texts follow conventions of representation that were common in this magazine and others like it that represented "exotic" groups of people primarily to white American readers. There is an ethnographic quality to this issue, and the connotations of some of its individual texts have the potential to limit their creators' ability to claim an American identity for African Americans. Contributors to the magazine, then, had to struggle to transform these conventions to suit their own ends. In effect, the *Survey Graphic* issue shows the difficulty of using an established publication to offer new images of African Americans, and it also allows us to explore whether and how participants in the Harlem Renaissance successfully appropriated existing strategies of representation and used them to redefine themselves.

As we shall see, the contributors to the *Survey Graphic* issue were able to overcome the ambiguous implications of individual texts, particularly by creating narratives that challenge notions of identity as static or that break down assumed differences between groups of people. New definitions of American and African American identity emerge from these texts; as we analyze them, we will come to a better understanding of the potential of the strategies of representation in the magazine as well as of the complexities and challenges of claiming an American identity and reshaping it in the process.[1]

At first glance, the most obvious goal of the issue is to introduce the African American residents of Harlem to readers who, presumably, were unfamiliar with the area and its inhabitants. The issue opens with a series of expository essays that present information about Harlem's residents, the historical development of the community, the challenges faced by black workers, and the migrants and immigrants who had moved to the city in recent decades. Portraits by the Bavarian artist Winold Reiss offer visual images of "Harlem Types" and "Negro Women." Later in the issue, creative texts and essays about art and literature demonstrate the cultural accomplishments of African Americans and identify African art as an important foundation for African American culture. Finally, the issue closes with a series of essays about "race contacts." These describe the integration of African Americans in American society but also hint at the racism still faced by African Americans. In short, the contents of the issue provide a written and visual introduction to the area and its residents, to the cultural achievements of African Americans, and to a number of aspects of their life experiences.

These texts effectively put African Americans on display for the readers of the magazine, in ways that both help and hinder its contributors' efforts to challenge conventional representations of African Americans. In the 1920s, African Americans were not often included in definitions of American identity. After all, the term used to refer to African Americans was "Negroes." Many of the contributors to the *Survey Graphic* issue, however, implicitly or explicitly defined African Americans as American, either by using the names "Negro Americans" or "American Negroes" or by laying out arguments that established African Americans' contributions to American institutions, society, or culture. One of the insights offered by the issue, then, is that it demonstrates the strategies African Americans used to claim an American identity. Furthermore, it reveals that defining themselves as American was closely tied to establishing equality with white Americans. Asserting equality was both a condition of and a result of claiming an American identity—in other words, when African Americans established bonds between themselves and white Americans, they were able to define themselves as American, but defining themselves as American also allowed them to establish themselves in relationships of equality with white Americans.

However, a special issue of the *Survey Graphic* was in some ways an inherently problematic place to assert African Americans' equality with white Americans and their American identity, as the history of the magazine indicates. *Survey Graphic* grew out of a series of magazines that began with *Charities* in 1897; one of the main goals of this publication was to provide information to its relatively wealthy readers that would help them decide to which organizations they should donate their money (Chambers 7–10). As the magazine grew, its focus expanded to include information that would help its readers understand the needs of groups of people and the social conditions that contributed to those needs. The editors hoped that this information and understanding, in turn, might inspire the benevolence of its readers and might ensure that social workers and philanthropists were working as efficiently and effectively as possible (Chambers 28–31).

By the time Paul Kellogg started work as an assistant editor in 1902, the magazine had evolved into *Charities and the Commons,* and its focus had broadened to include service and reform, charities and the settlement movement, practice and social action, and, increasingly, social research (Chambers 28). This last goal hints at the extent to which the magazine was meant to provide information to its readers to teach them about others. This social research, in theory, would then enable readers to establish and contribute to programs that effectively addressed problems in various communities. In 1909, Kellogg renamed the magazine *Survey* to reflect its mission of "social exploration" of the New World (Chambers 42–44). He saw his readers as a group of professionals that could form an "elite corps" that might work together to contribute to national social progress (Chambers 45). Implicitly, then, the readers of the magazine were understood as different from its subjects, particularly in terms of their ability to understand developments and administer aid.[2]

The magazine also often included visual displays of its subjects that reinforce this sense of difference between its readers and subjects. Kellogg split *Survey* into *Survey Graphic* and *Survey Midmonthly* in 1923 in an effort to reach a broader audience with *Survey Graphic* and to make the format of the magazine more compelling. *Survey Graphic*, which came out at the beginning of each month, was intended for a more general audience than the *Midmonthly*, which came out weekly during the month and was geared toward a readership of social workers and professionals in related fields (Chambers 84–85). *Survey Graphic*, as its name implies, placed particular emphasis on visual texts. Issues often included photographs, cartoons, graphs and charts, and etchings, as well as essays, poems, and personality sketches. The visual texts were meant "to engage the attention of a wide audience by use of graphic and literary arts in partnership with the social sciences, to catch the eye and the heart as well as the intellect" (Chambers 105). The editors' goal for *Survey Graphic* was in line with their aims for the magazine's forerunners: they still meant to present information that would contribute to their readers' knowledge and spur the forces of social change, and they believed that using illustrations would increase the magazine's potential impact. But the visual texts also often included portraits and photographs of members of the communities the magazine studied; not only cultural artifacts, then, but also people were put on display.[3]

This implicit othering enacted by visual texts is particularly evident when the *Survey Graphic*'s visual texts fit into the tradition of representing groups of people in "type studies." These photographic portraits of anonymous subjects became popular in Europe and the United States in the mid-1800s, when they were used to catalog groups of people, serving as visual demonstrations of their identifying features. In the nineteenth century, for example, type studies were used in Europe to depict the features of criminals and the insane (Sekula 343–89). In the United States, although type studies sometimes focused on white Americans, they most often took as their subjects ethnic minorities or foreigners. Even when type studies were done on residents of the United States, they often treated their subjects as specimens, as if they were a separate group of people, set apart and different from their viewers. For example, type studies of prison inmates produced by Mathew Brady in 1846 were meant to "show how to read a criminal head" (Trachtenberg 57). For a series of photographs of African slaves working in South Carolina in 1850, photographer J. T. Zealy stripped his subjects naked, representing these human beings as "examples or specimens of a 'type'—a type, moreover, of complete otherness" (Trachtenberg 54; see also 53–60). By the 1920s, photography had become an important component in anthropologic studies; Bronislaw Malinowski, for example, used photographs to visually introduce readers to the people he studied in Southeast Papua New Guinea (Goin 67–72).

Type studies send complicated messages about the identity of the people they depict. The conventions of type studies in many ways implicitly support the othering of their subjects. First, they reduce the complexity of their subjects' identity to a single factor—their status as slaves or prisoners, in the above examples. This simplification of their subjects' identity is reinforced by the fact that type studies generally include very little if any information about their subjects' lives, and that they only rarely include their names. Second, type studies fail to communicate the diversity within the groups of people presented. Type studies imply that the millions of individuals who make up a group—African slaves, for example—can be easily represented by a few examples. Simultaneously, though, type studies can also assert the humanity of their subjects. The subjects of Zealy's daguerreotypes, for instance, are able to preserve some aspect of their dignity through the directness with which they stare through the camera lens at their viewers (Trachtenberg 56, 59–60). Despite the dehumanizing conventions of the way they are represented, then, the subjects of these studies are able to establish relationships between themselves and their viewers. Overall, then, type studies were charged texts in the 1920s; they had the potential to both distance and connect their viewers and their subjects.

The *Survey Graphic* often included type studies of the groups of people it portrayed. In the Harlem issue, Reiss's portraits fit into the genre, as the title of his first series, "Harlem Types," makes particularly clear. These type studies also fit into another trend in the magazine. In the 1920s, the *Survey Graphic* began to pay tribute to renaissance movements and to the people who provided the political and cultural momentum to these movements. The magazine published a number of special issues in the early 1920s that focused on cultural nationalist movements in Ireland, Mexico, and Russia. Kellogg and the *Survey* editors lauded the increase in self-definition in these movements, and they therefore turned their pages over to members of the communities they portrayed. For the November 1921 issue on the renaissance in Ireland, for example, *Survey* reporter Savel Zimand traveled the country and interviewed the people he found there; the issue is filled with essays written in response to his questions, as well as poetry, samples of Irish art, and painted portraits of "Irish Types." Likewise, the March 1923 issue on the movement in Russia includes work by Russian politicians, essayists, historians, creative writers, and visual artists: woodcuts, lithographs, poster art, photographs, and paintings and drawings of "Russian Faces." Although the editors of the *Survey Graphic* had final control over these issues, they allowed the subjects of the issues to take an active role in creating their own repre-

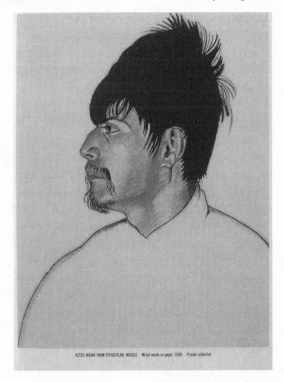

AZTEC INDIAN FROM TEPOZOTLAN, MEXICO   Mixed media on paper, 1920   Private collection

Fig. 4.1. A portrait by Winold Reiss that shows the style he used in the *Survey Graphic's* special issue on Mexico. *Reproduced from Stewart 1.*

sentations of themselves. The issues thus show the members of these communities to be articulate, capable of self-assertion, and active in the processes of social change.

The Harlem issue fit into the conventions established in these special issues of the *Survey Graphic* magazine. In fact, the Harlem issue is quite similar to the special issue on Mexico, which was published in May 1924. The issue focuses on recent developments in Mexico, and it includes type studies by Reiss and essays about "The New Yucatan," "The New Conquest," "Why We Are Different," and "The Revolution in Intellectual Life," in which writers emphasized the changes occurring in Mexican society and culture. This focus on new developments in Mexican communities would be echoed in the Harlem issue in essays like Locke's "Enter the New Negro." In his pastel portraits of Mexicans, Reiss sketched in the clothing of his subjects, devoting greater attention to faces and hair (see fig. 4.1 for an example)—just as he would in his portraits of African Americans in the Harlem issue. The similarities between the two issues suggest parallels between the situation in Mexico and the New Negro movement. The editors, in fact, made this connection explicit: in the table of contents of the Harlem issue, they pointed out that "Winold Reiss's studies of Mexican types will be vividly remembered by readers of the Mexican Number" (627). In their introduction to the issue, they also likened the movement among African Americans to movements around the world, like those in Ireland, Russia, and Mexico. The fact that the Harlem issue appeared in the context of these special issues about movements in other countries and that the editors reminded readers of the parallels emphasizes the importance of the New Negro movement on an international scale. Implicitly, it defines American culture as undergoing the same types of progress and development that were being seen in other parts of the world, thanks to its African American residents. But the similarities in the representation of the New Negro and of other cultural movements also contribute to the marginalization of African Americans in the United States; the implication that the New Negro movement is much like these movements in other countries positions African Americans as exotic outsiders in America, more like foreigners than American citizens.

However, Kellogg's ideas about what he wanted the Harlem issue to show about African Americans fit with its contributors' emphasis on the identity of African Americans as American. The Harlem issue was not the first special issue of the *Survey Graphic* or its predecessors to focus on African Americans. In 1905, Kellogg ran an issue on "The Negro in Cities of the North," which included essays by W. E. B. Du Bois and Booker T. Washington (Chambers 21). Kellogg apparently had been thinking about updating this special issue on African Americans for some time before he put plans in motion for the Harlem issue. At the Civic Club dinner hosted by Charles S. Johnson in March 1924, Kellogg heard tributes to the work of African American writers by luminaries like Du Bois and Carl Van Doren as well as readings by Walter White, Georgia Douglas Johnson, Jessie Fauset, Countee Cullen, and Gwendolyn Bennett. This concentration of talent convinced Kellogg to propose an entire issue of the *Survey Graphic* on Harlem.[4] He knew that he wanted to focus on African Americans' achievements. On the day after the Civic Club dinner, Kellogg wrote a letter to a friend describing his idea of updating the 1905 issue with a special issue of the *Survey Graphic* that would portray African Americans in a single community and would shift its focus from "Negro needs, and Negro grievances, to the Negro's contributions" (qtd. in Chambers 113). Rather than looking at African Americans as a problem to be dealt with or as a burden on American society, Kellogg wanted to represent them as active contributors to it.

Kellogg also immediately turned the issue over to African Americans, thus allowing African Americans to define themselves. When the issue on Harlem was published a year later, the *Survey Graphic* editors signaled this turning over of its pages to African American commentators on the table of contents, where it listed Locke as responsible for "the concept of this issue, for painstaking collaboration in its preparation," and for a number of articles in it (627), and where it identified the many other African American contributors to the issue. The fact that the texts in the issue were created by African Americans made the *Survey Graphic* issue unique:

> For the first time a major publication with national circulation turned over its pages not to a discussion of "the Negro problem" (usually as portrayed by white authors), but to an exploration of the dynamics of cultural life in the Negro community as Negro leaders themselves perceived it. (Chambers 115)

Furthermore, the fact that African Americans represented themselves in the issue is crucial to their ability to redefine their relationship with white readers. It was almost as if the readers were engaged in a conversation with the contributors to the issue, with the contributors passing along their insights and knowledge. The relationship thus established between readers and writers suggests a measure of equality that makes it easier for African Americans to define themselves as American. Furthermore, in this position as guides, the contributors to the magazine are able to show themselves—and, by extension, African Americans as a whole—to be articulate, capable of defining themselves, and capable of contributing to social change.

But this relationship is primarily established between readers of the magazine and leading African Americans. Locke's identity as a member of the African American elite, for example, is clear. Locke and Kellogg had known each other for a number of years by the time of Johnson's dinner; Locke had contributed a number of essays to other issues of the *Survey Graphic*. In fact, the two had already discussed a special issue.[5] By the time Kellogg appointed Locke editor of the *Survey Graphic* issue, Locke had become relatively well known in Harlem and quite well educated. He had graduated from Harvard in 1907, studied at Oxford as the first African American Rhodes Scholar, and then studied at the University of Berlin and the College de France. He returned to the United States and joined the faculty at Howard University in 1912, living in Washington, D.C., but spending much of his time in Harlem. By the early 1920s he had begun writing articles for *Opportunity, The Crisis,* and *Survey,* as well as other magazines.[6] Charles Johnson came to see him as "a natural 'press agent' for the Harlem Renaissance" (Lewis, *When Harlem Was in Vogue* 150). Locke's familiarity with the editors of the *Survey* magazines and his connections to others involved in the New Negro movement made him a logical choice for editor of the special issue on Harlem. But it is Locke's position as one of the elite of the race that was most emphasized by the editors of the *Survey Graphic.* In the table of contents, they described Locke as "himself a brilliant exemplar of that poise and insight which are happy omens for the Negro's future" (627). They mentioned his background at Harvard, Oxford, and Berlin, and his position as a professor of philosophy (627). It is as a member of the elite, then, that Locke wrote to the magazine's readers. Other contributors to the issue—men like Charles S. Johnson, James Weldon Johnson, and Du Bois—might have been recognized by readers as African American leaders. Just in case, though, they are identified in the table of contents as writers, editors, and officers in important organizations like the NAACP and the NUL. The contributors whose names might have been less familiar to readers of the magazine—Albert C. Barnes, for example, or Eunice Hunter or Elise McDougald—are similarly identified by their accomplishments and their leadership roles. The African Americans who led this tour of Harlem, these identifications made clear, were the elite of the race.

In contrast, there is far less attention to the African American folk. One significant difference between the coverage of movements in Mexico, Ireland, Russia, and Harlem is that each of the first three includes significant attention to the folk arts of the communities being studied. The illustrated essays that describe and show the work of the Mexican, Irish, and Russian folk artists position them as creators of culture. In contrast, the Harlem issue includes no such coverage. There is one brief essay by Locke on African art, and a few photographs of sculpture and masks are included. But there is no visual evidence of African American folk creations in America. The African American folk, instead, are depicted in Reiss's portraits and in photographs of Harlem, and they are discussed in a few of the essays. But the absence of any extensive discussion of their work hides their self-expressiveness; it leaves readers with no understanding of their ability to assert and express themselves in the arts. If active contributions to cultural developments establish connections between readers and subjects of the *Survey Graphic,* the Harlem issue implies that those connections can happen across racial lines but not across class lines. In other words, class rather than race becomes the factor that divides readers and subjects.

The issue, then, sends complicated messages about possible connections between black and white Americans. The complexity of those relationships, in fact, is immediately reflected in two advertisements for the NUL and *The Crisis,* which are the very first texts readers encounter. The two-page ad for the NUL explicitly encourages the development of positive relationships between black and white Americans: it emphasizes the role of both black and white participants in the organization's activities and its efforts to promote social change. The first page of the ad is a description of the league's programs, and the second is a letter from Eugene Kinckle Jones, executive secretary of the NUL, addressed "Dear Survey Reader." Both pages emphasize the focus of the NUL on improving living and working conditions for African

Americans in America, and both emphasize the role of black and white Americans in these goals. Jones, for example, explained, "All League Boards, national and local, are composed of leading white and colored citizens, thus guaranteeing the best inter-racial thought on our common community problems growing out of race contacts" (623). This seems to be an appeal to the *Survey Graphic*'s white readers to take part in this organization, and Jones in fact ended his letter by inviting readers to become members of the NUL or make contributions to it. The NUL, then, appealed to readers as an organization in which black and white members would work together toward their goals, which in turn implies interaction and even equality among its members.

In contrast, the ad for *The Crisis* is aimed at white readers and presents African Americans as a mysterious other to them. This full-page ad addresses readers who want to be able to study and understand African Americans. It opens,

> Would you like to know how it feels to be an American Negro?
> Would you like to know what Negroes are thinking and doing?
> Would you like to see their daily life pictured?
> Would you like to see "facts" as Negroes see them? (624)

These questions imply a difference between "you" and "American Negroes"; the questions situate African Americans as objects of study and *The Crisis* as a source of information about "them." The fact that this ad appears in the *Survey Graphic* suggests that the NAACP saw the magazine as having mostly white readers; more importantly, it assumes distance rather than connections between its white readers and black subjects.[7]

The advertisement for *The Crisis* speaks to the degree to which one of the implicit purposes of a publication like it, or like the *Survey Graphic* issue, was for African Americans to put themselves on display for white readers, in hopes of changing the ideas those readers had about African Americans. That same dynamic, and even more explicit assumptions that readers of the *Survey Graphic* issue were white, were articulated in response to an exhibit of portraits by Reiss at the Harlem Branch of the New York Public Library, which opened the day the issue was published. Visitors to the exhibit expressed concern about the images of African Americans being put forth both here and in the *Survey Graphic* issue, and many were upset that the individuals portrayed were not "representative" of the race. McDougald, herself a subject of one of the portraits, explained in a letter to Locke that one individual even wondered whether "the whole art side of the issue were a 'piece of subtle propaganda to prejudice the white reader.'"[8] Clearly that individual's concern was with how a white reader might interpret Reiss's portraits. That concern—how the texts in the issue might be read by the issue's presumed audience of white subscribers—underlines the importance of the issue's success at representing African Americans. If the readers of the issue thought of themselves as Kellogg did, as a group of elite white Americans, leaders in social work and social progress, the improvement in living conditions and the extension of democratic rights to others, they probably would have been interested in African Americans in the United States as a group to whom their good will might be extended—and they may have seen themselves as quite different from African Americans. For contributors to the issue, then, the challenge was to create a volume that convinced white readers to see African Americans not as wards of the state but as contributors to it, to see African Americans not as people who they could help uplift but as equals to themselves—to see African Americans, in short, as Americans just like themselves. It remains to be seen, then, whether they were able to control the inherent complications and contradictions of the types of texts they used, and whether they were able to use these strategies of representation to their advantage.

The text that most explicitly reflects and comments on the challenge of defining African Americans as American is Du Bois's short story, "The Black Man Brings His Gifts." The events in this story explicitly assert African Americans' American identity; they also speak to white Americans' resistance to that redefinition. Two of the characters in the story assert the contributions of African Americans to American society and culture, but other characters are vehemently opposed to acknowledging these contributions. The tension between these characters, and their differing opinions about African Americans' contributions to America, dramatize the efforts to represent African Americans in the issue and the challenge of redefining African American and American identity.

The story is set in a small town in Indiana, where residents are planning a pageant about "America's Making." It is just after World War I, and the pageant has been proposed as a way of reuniting the townspeople. Du Bois's narrator, a white resident who clearly holds a low opinion of "the colored folks" in town, explains that the town "had seven or eight races or nations, not counting the colored people," and needed "something to sort of bring us together after the war," something to promote "Americanization; a sort of wholesome getting together" (655). The story itself records the meeting of the planning committee that has been established to organize that pageant. Their chair, a professor at the local university, has been appointed because of concerns that immigrants in town—the Germans, Poles, Scandinavians, and Italians—would claim such a large role in America's making that "there'll be nothing left for the real Americans" (655). But as the committee considers different aspects of American culture, the chair repeatedly brings up another issue that proves to be the undoing of the committee and of the pageant itself: the contributions of African Americans to America. The committee offers labor, music, architecture, painting, inventions, dancing, literature, education, democracy, exploration, and finally religion as important aspects of American culture. In each field, the chair demonstrates the importance of the work of African Americans. He even invites in an African American woman to speak for herself about the accomplishments of African Americans. The assertions of this "college woman," particularly her question of whether America could be America without African Americans, is the straw that breaks the committee's back: they give up on the pageant and angrily leave the room. The pageant about America's making, it is clear, will not occur in this town; neither will the "wholesome getting together" for which the narrator had hoped.[9]

Du Bois's story raises a number of points about American society, the development of American culture, and the possibility of social change. First, there is a perceived need for Americanization in this town; the disunity in the town is taken to be a problem. The town's desire to overcome that disunity with a pageant that will bring people together raises the possibility of altering attitudes; addressing the question of America's making forces them to consider who had made contributions to the nation and opens up a space for the recognition of African Americans' roles. Second, dramatizing the committee's consideration of America's making allowed Du Bois to make a number of explicit and extended arguments about the contributions of African Americans to various aspects of American society and culture. The professor's attempts to convince the committee members of these points gave Du Bois an excuse to include details and evidence that prove his case, including the names of important African American composers, writers, painters, and educators, as well as lists of the kinds of labor, inventions, and stories they had contributed. But the story also highlights the resistance of white Americans to the idea that African Americans had made important contributions to American culture. The committee members' first reaction to the professor's assertions is somewhat benign, but it progressively hardens. When the professor initially asks whether African Americans ought to be included in the pageant, the narrator mentions, "That took us a bit by surprise as we hadn't thought of them at all" (655). The "awfully aristocratic Southern lady" on the committee, Mrs. Cadwalader Lee, is open enough to propose putting together a "small auxiliary colored committee" and decides she'll ask her cook to take part. On the question of labor, she proposes "a very interesting darky scene": the pageant could include a cotton-hoeing episode, during which the African American participants could sing "Negro ditties." As a bonus, they would be able to serve food and clean up afterward (655–56). This response to the question of African Americans' participation and Mrs. Lee's ideas about how to include them hints at white Americans' lack of awareness of African Americans' contributions to American culture and their willingness to acknowledge it only to a very limited extent. They can conceive of the role of African Americans only in demeaning terms and in connection to work as servants.

The professor's repeated presentation of the evidence of other kinds of work by African Americans pushes the committee members further than they are willing to go. When the professor gets to literature and points out that Joel Chandler Harris's Uncle Remus tales are "thoroughly African," thus proving African Americans' contributions to American literature, Mrs. Lee sniffs that she will not be able to participate in the pageant (657). Clearly she wants no part in an event that reflects the breadth and importance of African Americans' contributions to American culture. While she may have been willing to include African Americans in the pageant, it is clear that their presence would have been acceptable to her only if they stayed in certain roles. Nor is she willing to include African Americans in the planning of the pageant: when the professor invites the African American woman to participate in the meeting, Mrs. Lee sails out of the room. She is unable to accept African Americans as significant contributors to American culture or as participants in the discussion of America's making; correspondingly, she refuses to participate in situations where African Americans are on equal footing with herself. Mrs. Lee's reaction, in short, exemplifies the resistance of white Americans to the idea that African Americans were important contributors to American culture.[10]

The story's ending, with the failure of the pageant to materialize and the corresponding failure of Americanization, makes clear the consequences of these racist practices and beliefs. But since it also demonstrates the silencing of those who would move America beyond those ideas, and the resistance of Americans to the arguments presented by "others," the story ends pessimistically. The story's inclusion in the *Survey Graphic* issue, though, suggests a way beyond that impasse. By drawing attention to the racism of Americans, the contributions of African Americans, and the consequences of continued discrimination, Du Bois provided a message that goes beyond the ending of the story. Du Bois, as the writer of the story, was not silenced; he illuminated the contributions of African Americans. The readers of his story might recognize the dangers the committee members did not and respond very differently than they did.

But even Du Bois's act of storytelling is problematic, particularly because of its implications about gender and about who is able to speak. Du Bois's title, "The Black Man Brings His Gifts," is perplexing because there is not a single black male character in the story. The only black character is the college woman, but she is silenced not only by the committee members but also by Du Bois, who summarized rather than recorded her words. And while the fact that the committee walks out on her reflects primarily the racism and sexism of the committee, it also implies that her speech is ineffective. Du Bois, in contrast, was able to speak effectively as the writer of the story. Perhaps he is the "Black Man" of the title, and the gifts in question are those of his information and insight. The implication of the woman's college degree and the professor's role as chair of the committee is that only the elite will be heard; the implication of Du Bois's title and the fact that only he had the ability to make himself understood by his audience implies that only the black male elite will be heard.

Du Bois's story, then, records the magnitude of the challenge facing those who wanted to demonstrate African Americans' contributions to American culture. It also, though, raises the possibility that, through evidence of those contributions, African Americans' status as American might be granted. But the story also reveals the other discriminatory practices connected to racism, both by the white Americans and by Du Bois in his efforts to struggle against racism. The story, then, establishes the need for and the possibility of demonstrating African Americans' contributions to American culture but also the danger of failing to challenge other forms of discrimination in the process.

The conflict staged in the story also is embodied in the rest of the texts of the Harlem issue of the *Survey Graphic,* and the key question for our analysis of the issue is to what extent it successfully promotes acceptance of African Americans as American and respect for African Americans' contributions to American culture. We also can ask to what extent it undermines other forms of discrimination. In terms of claiming African Americans' American identity, breaking down the assumed distance between readers and subjects was an important first step. Though this was a complicated process, the success of contributors at bridging this apparent divide then allowed them to more persuasively demonstrate African Americans' contributions to American society and culture and to expose the racism, sexism, and xenophobia in American society. For the most part, contributors to the issue offered convincing critiques of these discriminatory ideas and their practice in America, and also they used the consequences of these acts to push for social change, particularly through warnings about the direction American society might take if its racist practices continued and positive visions about the potential of the nation to move beyond those practices. But their demonstration of the assimilation of African Americans, though crucial to their challenge to American racism, has problematic implications.

African Americans' identity as American is explicitly claimed in a number of texts in the *Survey Graphic* issue. The first is the advertisement for *The Crisis,* where the magazine promises insight into "how it feels to be an American Negro" (624). This designation continues in the table of contents, where the editors explained that "a dramatic flowering of a new race-spirit is taking place close at home—among American Negroes" (627). References to African Americans as "American Negroes" or "Negro Americans" are repeated throughout the issue. But this claim of African Americans' American identity, in these two texts and elsewhere, is coupled with a sense of difference between black and white Americans that undermines the assertion of African Americans' Americanness. The ad for *The Crisis,* as discussed earlier, simultaneously assumes that African Americans are a mysterious other to readers; that sense is reaffirmed by the description of African Americans in the table of contents. In many ways, the issue as a whole feeds into this sense, to the extent that making African Americans the subject of a special issue presumes that they are a group of people about whom little is known. The fact that the magazine often focused on foreign movements reinforces that sense of difference. So, too, do a number of texts in the issue.

These texts undermine the identification of African Americans as American to the extent that they allow readers to continue seeing African Americans as different than themselves. At first glance, a number of texts fall into that trap. For example, James Weldon Johnson's essay, "The Making of Harlem," is almost a visitor's guide to the area. Johnson's written description of Harlem and a series of visual images lead readers on a virtual tour. One of Johnson's first statements is that "Harlem is indeed the great Mecca for the sight-seer, the pleasure-seeker, the curious, the adventurous, the enterprising, the ambitious and the talented of the whole Negro world" (635); he thus implicitly identified Harlem's African American residents as objects to be studied and investigated by *Survey Graphic*'s readers. He provided a good deal of information about the history of the area to satisfy those readers' curiosity about its development (635–38), but the sense of African Americans being put on display is most obvious in the visual texts that accompany

THE MAKING OF HARLEM

new and shiny, rusty old ones, bursting at the seams, boxes and bundles and impedimenta of all sorts, including banjos, guitars, birds in cages and what not. Similar scenes were being enacted in cities and towns all over that region. The first wave of the great exodus of Negroes from the South was on. Great numbers of these migrants headed for New York or eventually got there, and naturally the majority went up into Harlem. But the Negro population of Harlem was not swollen by migrants from the South alone; the opportunity for Negro labor exerted its pull upon the Negroes of the West Indies, and those islanders in the course of time poured into Harlem to the number of twenty-five thousand or more.

These new-comers did not have to look for work; work looked for them, and at wages of which they had never even dreamed. And here is where the unlooked for, the unprecedented, the miraculous happened. According to all preconceived notions, these Negroes suddenly earning large sums of money for the first time in their lives should have had their heads turned; they should have squandered it in the most silly and absurd manners imaginable. Later, after the United States had entered the war and even Negroes in the South were making money fast, many stories in accord with the tradition came out of that section. There was the one about the colored man who went into a general store and on hearing a phonograph for the first time promptly ordered six of them, one for each child in the house. I shall not stop to discuss whether Negroes in the South did that sort of thing or not, but I do know that those who got to New York didn't. The Negroes of Harlem, for the greater part, worked and saved their money. Nobody knew how much they had saved until congestion made expansion necessary for tenants and ownership profitable for landlords, and they began to buy property. Persons who would never be suspected of having money bought property. The Rev. W. W. Brown, pastor of the Metropolitan Baptist Church, repeatedly made "Buy property" the text of his sermons. A large part of his congregation carried out the injunction. The church itself set an example by purchasing a magnificent brown stone church building on Seventh Avenue from a white congregation. Buying property be-

Photograph by Paul Thompson

Sadly as Harlem lacks space to play outdoors, there is no lack of the play spirit either inside Harlem's crowded homes or on the broad avenues that cut through it. Parades are almost of daily occurrence —whether the occasion be the arrival of a vaudeville troupe, the patriotic enthusiasm of a new organization, or a funeral

This sketch map shows approximately where Negroes live in Harlem, according to a housing survey made in 1924 by the New York Urban League. The fringe of houses in which both Negro and white tenants live is not indicated. The first houses occupied by Negroes were on 134th Street east of Lenox Avenue

came a fever. At the height of this activity, that is, 1920-21, it was not an uncommon thing for a colored washerwoman or cook to go into a real estate office and lay down from one thousand to five thousand dollars on a house. "Pig Foot Mary" is a character in Harlem. Everybody who knows the corner of Lenox Avenue and One Hundred and Thirty-fifth Street knows "Mary" and her stand and has been tempted by the smell of her pigsfeet, fried chicken and hot corn, even if he has not been a customer. "Mary," whose real name is Mrs. Mary Dean, bought the five-story apartment house at the corner of Seventh Avenue and One Hundred and Thirty-seventh Street at a price of $42,000. Later she sold it to the Y. W. C. A. for dormitory purposes. The Y. W. C. A. sold it recently to Adolph Howell, a leading colored undertaker, the price given being $72,000. Often companies of a half dozen men combined to buy a house—these combinations were and still are generally made up of West Indians—and would produce five or ten thousand dollars to put through the deal.

When the buying activity began to make itself

Fig. 4.2. The map and a photograph from James Weldon Johnson's "The Making of Harlem." *Locke, ed., "Harlem," 637.*

Johnson's description. The essay is published with six photographs and a map. Two photographs show crowds of African Americans near a subway station and at a parade. Another two photographs show residential areas, and the final pair shows the business district. The map, which lays out where

African Americans live in Harlem, would orient visitors and help them find the areas they might want to see (see fig. 4.2). These visual texts give readers unfamiliar with Harlem an idea of who and what they might see if they should visit; even more than that, these illustrations allow the reader of the magazine to become a voyeur who can look into Harlem from the safety of his or her own home.

Johnson's essay, with its visual texts, is just one example of the degree to which residents of Harlem are put on display for readers of the *Survey Graphic*. The implication of this is that the subjects of the issue are far removed and far different from its readers; they are presumed to be fascinating subjects for further study. They are also implicitly defined as unable to express themselves; they are held up, mute, for study by the readers of the magazine. This is even more clear in Reiss's first series of portraits, "Harlem Types." These seven portraits put the African American folk on display, beginning with "Congo: a familiar of the New York studios" and progressing through "A college lad" (see figs. 4.3–4.6). The series visually shows the readers of the issue the "types" of African Americans that they might meet in Harlem. The subjects of these portraits do not seem fully human, especially because readers receive no information about them, even their names; the titles of the portraits present only minimal information about the subjects, such as the status of each as a lawyer or as a student. Furthermore, the written commentary printed with the portraits, presumably written by Locke, only adds to this process of objectification.[11] Locke focused on what the portraits show about the importance of African Americans as the subjects of art. In his work, Locke explained, Reiss "has achieved what amounts to a revealing discovery of the significance, human and artistic, of one of the greatest dialects of human physiognomy, of some of the little understood but powerful idioms of nature's speech" (651). His only comment about the subject matter is that it demonstrates the "intriguing problems and promising resources available for the stimulation and enrichment of American art" (651). In effect, Locke reduced Reiss's human subjects to resources, to materials for study; his commentary steers clear of any kind of empowerment for the subjects. Locke did hint that these portraits are of human beings by praising Reiss's work as a move away from caricature that allows viewers to see "the serious, the tragic, the wistful" characteristics of their subjects (652). But he quickly returned to his emphasis on the aesthetics of the work. It can, Locke claimed, be an inspiration for "the Negro artist, still for the most part confronting timidly his own material" (652). Again, he reaffirmed the sense of these subjects as material rather than human beings.

Locke's description of Reiss's work also allows readers to assume a distance from the subjects of these portraits based on class and nationality. In

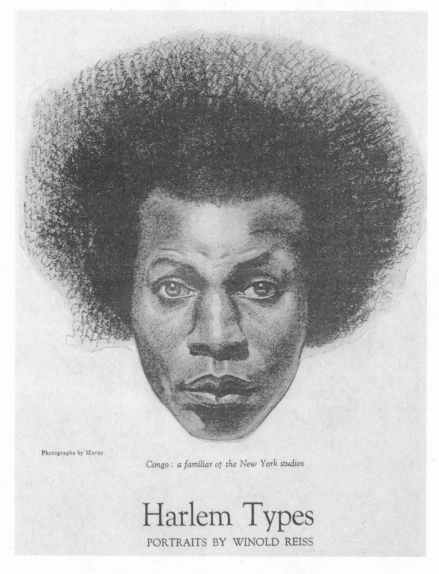

Photographs by Muray

Congo : a familiar of the New York studios

Harlem Types
PORTRAITS BY WINOLD REISS

Fig. 4.3. The first of Reiss's "Harlem Types": "Congo: a familiar of the New York studios." *Locke, ed., "Harlem," 651.*

the third paragraph of commentary on Reiss, Locke wrote of Reiss as "a master delineator of folk character," noting his studies of "the folk-types" of Sweden, Holland, the Black Forest, Tyrol, and America: the Black Foot Indians, the Pueblo people, Mexicans, and African Americans (653). Locke implicitly identified the subjects of the Harlem portraits as members of the

Mother and child

CONVENTIONS stand doubly in the way of artistic portrayal of Negro folk; certain narrowly arbitrary conventions of physical beauty, and as well, that inevitable inscrutability of things seen but not understood. Caricature has put upon the countenance of the Negro the mask of the comic and the grotesque, whereas in deeper truth and comprehension, nature or experience have put there the stamp of the very opposite, the serious, the tragic, the wistful. At times, too, there is a quality of soul that can only be called brooding and mystical. Here they are to be seen as we know them to be in fact. While it is a revealing interpretation for all, for the Negro artist, still for the most part confronting timidly his own material, there is certainly a particular stimulus and inspiration in this redeeming vision. Through it in all likelihood must come his best development in the field of the pictorial arts, for his capacity to express beauty depends vitally upon the capacity to see it in his own life and to generate it out of his own experience.

Young America: native-born

Fig. 4.4. Two more of Reiss's "Harlem Types": "Mother and child" and "Young America: native-born." *Locke, ed., "Harlem," 652.*

WINOLD REISS, son of Fritz Reiss, the landscape painter, pupil of Franz von Stuck of Munich, has become a master delineator of folk character by wide experience and definite specialization. With ever-ripening skill, he has studied and drawn the folk-types of Sweden, Holland, of the Black Forest and his own native Tyrol, and in America, the Black Foot Indians, the Pueblo people, the Mexicans, and now, the American Negro. His art owes its peculiar success as much to the philosophy of his approach as to his technical skill. He is a folk-lorist of the brush and palette, seeking always the folk character back of the individual, the psychology behind the physiognomy. In design also he looks not merely for decorative elements, but for the pattern of the culture from which it sprang. Without loss of naturalistic accuracy and individuality, he somehow subtly expresses the type, and without being any the less human, captures the racial and local. What Gauguin and his followers have done for the Far East, and the work of Ufer and Blumenschein and the Taos school for the Pueblo and Indian, seems about to be done for the Negro and Africa: in short, painting, the most local of arts, in terms of its own limitations even, is achieving universality.

A Boy Scout

A woman lawyer

Girl in the white blouse

653

Fig. 4.5. More of Reiss's "Harlem Types": "A Boy Scout," "A woman lawyer," and "Girl in the white blouse." *Locke, ed., "Harlem," 653.*

A college lad

Fig. 4.6. Harold Jackman, identified only as "A college lad," the last of Reiss's "Harlem Types." *Locke, ed., "Harlem," 654.*

African American folk, and he also connected these subjects to groups of people in other parts of the world. Doing so allows the readers of the *Survey Graphic* issue to see the African Americans depicted here as exotic others rather than as Americans. Like the conventions of the type studies, then, the written commentary about the portraits allows readers to interpret African Americans as an exotic group of people who needed to be studied and then aided. In that way, these texts undermine the assertion of the American identity of African Americans; they imply that African Americans are un-American, incapable of expressing or defining themselves and having little if any ability to contribute to American culture or social change.

There are hints, though, even in the portraits themselves, that Reiss's subjects are more than they might first appear. In a number of important ways, his portraits break out of the conventions of type studies. This is true even of the portraits in "Harlem Types," which actually send a more complicated message about African Americans than they seem to at first glance. Importantly, the subjects of these portraits do engage their viewers in a reciprocal gaze. For example, the individual referred to as "Congo," who may be male or female, stares directly out, through Reiss, at the reader (see fig. 4.3). That gaze sets up a relation of equality between the subject and Reiss, and in turn between the subject and the reader. While Reiss painted, looking at this young person, he or she studied Reiss. On the pages of the magazine, this person looks out at the reader as much as the reader looks at him or her. The girl in "Young America" and the subject of "A woman lawyer" also look directly out from the portraits (see fig. 4.4 and 4.5); their eyes hold a challenge to the readers that insists on the self-assertive abilities of these subjects.

The narrative of the portraits also demonstrates an important complication in terms of class distinctions. While the portraits depict the African American folk, they also offer a complicated message about who might be included in that class. On one hand, the series includes anonymous figures like the "Girl in the white blouse" who represent the masses, with no exceptional characteristics that set them apart (see fig. 4.5). On the other hand, that final full-page portrait of "A college lad," an unidentified Harold Jackman, well dressed in three-piece suit and tie (see fig. 4.6), and the smaller portrait of "A woman lawyer" (see fig. 4.5) represent the professional class of African Americans in Harlem. In this series, they broaden the concept of the folk from simply including the working-class masses to also including well-educated and professional African Americans. That being the case, the distance between the folk and the elite is not as great as it might have seemed to be. Furthermore, if the black folk are not so far away from the black elite, and the black elite are not so far away from the white elite, then the black folk and the white elite are not so far apart either. This suggests that categories of identity are more linked than separate.

The portraits also are arranged into narratives that demonstrate the assimilation of African Americans into American culture and society. This becomes another way of attacking rigid categories of identity and thus a challenge to racism. The progression of "Harlem Types" from "Congo" through "A college lad" records the Americanization of African Americans. The portrait of "Congo" includes only the disembodied head of this young individual, framed by his or her hair (see fig. 4.3). This image exoticizes its subject by floating his or her head in space, likening it to one of the African masks that were drawing the attention of the art world in the 1920s. The hair, worn in a relatively long Afro, would perhaps have been seen as another exoticizing feature in the 1920s. Each of the subjects on the following pages is more apparently American than "Congo"; this is particularly the case given that captions identify one girl as "Young America" and one boy as a member of the quintessentially American Boy Scouts. The "college lad" wears a three-piece suit that was the fashion for men in the 1920s (see fig. 4.6). White readers thus start with an image of a person who they can easily characterize as

Fig. 4.7. "A Woman from the Virgin Islands," the first of Reiss's "Four Portraits of Negro Women." *Locke, ed., "Harlem," 685.*

very different from themselves, but they end up looking at someone who probably does not look that different from themselves or their male friends. Reiss's second series of portraits demonstrates a similar move from foreign to American. "Four Portraits of Negro Women" opens with "A Woman from the Virgin Islands" (see fig. 4.7). Implicitly, she is a foreigner, although the United States recently had purchased the Virgin Islands. The next two portraits focus on women who work in Harlem, "The Librarian" and "Two Public School Teachers" (see figs. 4.8 and 4.9). McDougald is the subject of the final portrait (see fig. 4.10). The first three portraits are type studies: anonymous, these women represent others like them, as the "Harlem Types" had. The first woman is identified only by where she is from; the librarian and the teachers are identified by their jobs. But McDougald is named. She is the only subject to be named, in this series or in the first. Her portrait is the culmination of the shift from foreign to American; it also is the climax of the shift from anonymous type studies—depicting others far different from Americans—to portraits of individuals who serve as representative Americans.

A number of written texts that emphasize the assimilation of African Americans make this reading of the portraits more likely. The entire point of

Fig. 4.8. "The Librarian,"the
second of Reiss's "Four
Portraits of Negro Women."
Locke, ed., "Harlem," 686.

Melville Herskovits's essay "The Dilemma of Social Pattern," for example, is
that African Americans had become fully Americanized. Herskovits characterized Harlem as "a community just like any other American community.
The same pattern, only a different shade!" (676). He asked in the essay what
that means about Harlem's residents: "May it not then be true that the Negro has become acculturated to the prevailing white culture and has developed the patterns of culture typical of American life?" (676). His essay is full
of evidence that answers that question in the affirmative. Even Locke,
though he characterized Harlem as "the greatest Negro community the
world has known" in "Harlem" (629), emphasized the assimilation of African Americans into American ways of thinking: "The Negro mind reaches
out as yet to nothing but American wants, American ideas," he argued in
"Enter the New Negro" (633). If African Americans were becoming more
and more American, as these texts assert, then racism made less and less
sense. The texts in the issue that show African Americans' assimilation, in effect, bridge the assumed distance between "Negro" and "American." As that
distance narrows, the unreasonableness of racism becomes more clear.

McDougald's portrait also demonstrates a different point: the growing
articulateness of African Americans. McDougald was both seen and able to

Fig. 4.9. Reiss's portrait of two public schoolteachers, the third of his "Four Portraits of Negro Women." *Locke, ed., "Harlem," 687.*

speak out in the *Survey Graphic* issue: her essay, "The Double Task: The Struggle of Negro Women for Sex and Race Emancipation," appears immediately following her portrait. McDougald's portrait positions her as a type, implicitly; she appears as an educated African American woman who can impress *Survey Graphic*'s readers with her obvious poise and her sophistication. But she also serves as an individual, because she is named; significantly, she is an individual who clearly and forcefully expressed her opinions about the burden of sexism and racism that African American women face. This portrait and essay, then, together provide information about African Americans and demonstrate their ability to express themselves.

In addition to demonstrating McDougald's ability to assert herself, her essay implicitly attacks type studies. African American women, McDougald wrote, "vary in infinite degree" (689). That being the case, a few representative figures do nothing to communicate the differences among African American women. Moreover, she wrote, the problems that African American women face "cannot be thought of in mass" (689). She went on to consider the situations of elite African American women of leisure, of professional and business women, of women working in the trades and industries,

ELISE JOHNSON McDOUGALD

Fig. 4.10. Reiss's portrait of
Elise Johnson McDougald,
the last of his "Four Portraits
of Negro Women." *Locke,
ed., "Harlem," 688.*

and domestic and casual workers. She considered problems of low pay, racial discrimination in the workplace, and sexual inequalities, but she ended by noting the formation of African American women's organizations that work against these situations. Her essay, then, is a criticism and exposé of sexism, but it finishes with an emphasis on the ways that African American women were working to change their conditions. Their struggle, McDougald insisted, was a crucial aspect of the achievement of "the race's destiny" (691). In other words, she positioned African American women as a crucial force in the broader struggle of African Americans for equality and respect. In the same way, as the only person who is both seen and heard in this issue, her presence here suggests the important roles African American women would play in the New Negro movement.

McDougald—a college-educated, professional woman who persuasively argued against racism and sexism—is a foil to Du Bois's college woman. McDougald's essay suggests that the contributors to the issue may have been able to succeed where Du Bois's character failed. Furthermore, McDougald's argument against the typification enacted in the portraits makes it less likely that readers would have fallen into the trap of assuming fundamental differences between themselves and the subjects of those portraits. If they did not, they should have been more open to the arguments presented by other contributors to the issue.

These other contributors used a number of strategies to claim African Americans' American identity. A number of them asserted African Americans' contributions to American culture as a way of claiming this identity. Early in the issue, for example, Locke described the need for recognition of the contributions of African Americans in ways that echo Du Bois's story. In "Enter the New Negro," Locke explained that the greatest hope for increased respect for African Americans

> rests in the revaluation by white and black alike of the Negro in terms of his artistic endowments and cultural contributions, past and prospective. It must be increasingly recognized that the Negro has already made very substantial contributions, not only in his folk-art, music especially, which has always found appreciation, but in larger, though humbler and less acknowledged ways. . . . [H]e has contributed not only materially in labor and in social patience, but spiritually as well. (634)

In effect, Locke laid out a series of criteria for the kinds of contributions to national culture that are worthy of respect, and the texts in the remainder of the issue, in many ways, serve as evidence of these contributions.

A number of essays explicitly emphasize that those contributions have national significance. Locke himself, for example, argued in "Youth Speaks" that art by African Americans enriches American art (660); J. A. Rogers made the argument more explicitly about jazz, positing jazz as one of the "foremost exponent[s] of modern Americanism" (665). Jazz, Rogers emphasized, had transcended the status of being either "Negro" or "American"; instead, "it is of Negro origin plus the influence of the American environment. It is Negro-American" (666). If black music had attained this identity, certainly the creators of this music should have been able to claim it as well. In a slightly different vein, Albert Barnes, in "Negro Art and America," emphasized the contributions of African Americans to American culture based on assumptions about African Americans' essential differences from white Americans: art by African Americans, Barnes argued, reflects their "tremendous emotional endowment" (668). Barnes identified differences between black and white Americans: "The Negro has kept nearer to the ideal of man's harmony with nature and that, his blessing, has made him a vagrant in our arid, practical American life" (668). Those differences, he asserted, meant that art by African Americans adds missing elements to American culture. Poetry and music by African Americans, he argued, "is art of which America can well be proud" (668). Barnes concluded, "This mystic whom we have treated as a vagrant has proved his possession of a power to create out of his own soul and our own America, moving beauty of an individual character whose existence we never knew" (669). The potential, then, is that African Americans would participate in "the development of a richer American civilization to which he will contribute his full share" (669). Barnes's primitivist assumptions about African Americans are questionable generalizations about the race as a whole, but his argument that their work adds crucial elements to American culture positions the characteristics he assumed to be black also as distinctively American.

Other essays further develop Locke's claims that African Americans were contributing to American culture in material ways. For example, a good deal of emphasis in the *Survey Graphic* issue is put on the financial achievements of African Americans, as shown in a number of illustrated essays that measure monetary success through property ownership. In addition to providing readers with a tour of Harlem, James Weldon Johnson used "The Making of Harlem" to emphasize that African Americans, upon arriving in Harlem, "worked and saved their money"—and then bought property (637). Johnson detailed the accumulation of real estate by African Americans, concluding that, by the time he wrote the essay, "the total value of property in Harlem owned and controlled by colored people would at a conservative estimate amount to more than sixty million dollars. These figures are amazing," he emphasized, "especially when we take into account the short time in which they have been piled up" (638). These points are demonstrated visually by a number of photographs published with the essay, which depict buildings owned by African Americans. One photograph, for example, shows a residential area that is identified in its caption as "a block which has few rivals in the city for distinction of line and mass and its air of quiet dignity" (638). A similar argument is made in the final essay of the issue, George Haynes's "The Church and the Negro Spirit." Haynes's emphasis is on the taking over of church property by African Americans, which Haynes illustrated with photographs of seven churches in Harlem owned by African Americans. These two essays, after Locke's opening essays, frame the contents of the magazine; their position in the opening and the closing of the issue underlines the importance of financial wealth in the assertion of African Americans' position in American society. It is Johnson's essay that most explicitly connects the accumulation of property to Americanization, for Johnson emphasized toward the close of his essay the American identity of Harlem and Harlemites: "Harlem talks American, reads American, thinks

American. . . . The rapidity with which Negroes become good New Yorkers is one of the marvels to observers" (639).

A number of other texts detail different kinds of social contributions. Arthur Schomburg, for example, drew attention to the active contributions of African Americans to social change throughout American history in "The Negro Digs Up His Past." Schomburg emphasized the role of the Negro as "an active collaborator, and often a pioneer, in the struggle for his own freedom and advancement" (670). He also pointed out African Americans' contributions to social service and reform (671). Both points are demonstrated by visual texts printed with the essay: reproductions of the title pages of texts by African Americans that contributed to abolition and racial advancement. Schomburg left the question of African Americans' American identity implicit, but it is clear through his essay that African Americans had exerted important force toward change in American society.

In "The Tropics in New York," W. A. Domingo was more explicit about the role of black people in the shaping of American culture. Domingo focused in particular on the role of West Indians in the development of American society. "It is probably not realized, indeed, to what extent West Indian Negroes have contributed to the wealth, power and prestige of the United States," Domingo asserted (649), and he used his essay to demonstrate those contributions. In this case, his essay is illustrated not with visual texts but with poems by Claude McKay. Creative literature, then, is used as the example that shows West Indians' contributions to American culture. Given McKay's contributions to magazines of American literature like *Seven Arts;* the recognition of the quality of his work by writers like Max Eastman, who wrote the introduction to McKay's 1922 book of poetry, *Harlem Shadows;* McKay's status as a celebrity in Greenwich Village; and his role as an editor for *The Liberator,* McKay's contribution to American literature is beyond question.[12] His work is a useful tool with which to claim the importance of West Indians to American culture.

In short, in these essays African Americans were able to define themselves as crucial contributors to American culture and to its continued development. Far from being passive recipients of white Americans' interest or aid, African Americans showed themselves to be creating their own art and shaping their own conditions. The writers themselves demonstrated this dynamic: rather than allowing themselves to be depicted by white writers or artists, they asserted themselves, creating their own texts in which they could present their own arguments about African American identity and the role of African Americans in national culture. As they showed, the contributions of African Americans both improved American culture and reflected well upon it, by demonstrating the democratic potential of the nation. They revealed America to be a country in which racial discrimination did not prevent African Americans from contributing to a common national culture.

Fiction, advertisements, essays, music, poetry, visual art, finances, and even type studies thus are put to use in the *Survey Graphic* issue to establish a relationship between the issue's readers and subjects and to claim an American identity for African Americans. But there are a few omissions from the magazine and points of emphasis that also hint at the limiting aspects of this effort to define African Americans as American.

There are, for example, a number of references to American racism in the issue. In "Enter the New Negro," Locke characterized the racism in American society as "the great discrepancy between the American social creed and the American social practice" (633). Johnson, in his discussion of the takeover of real estate in Harlem by African Americans, mentioned the resistance of white residents to the spread of African Americans in the city. He pointed out the steps taken by whites to halt the accumulation of property by African Americans, such as "inducing financial institutions not to lend money or renew mortgages on properties occupied by colored people" (636). The continuing ownership of property by African Americans that Johnson detailed is evidence of the failure of these efforts. Such discriminatory practices also extended into the workplace and entertainment, as other writers demonstrated. Charles Johnson, for example, in his discussion of the employment of African Americans, pointed out that, on one hand, "Negro workers, it will be found, are freely employed in certain jobs requiring strength and bodily agility, but little skill"; on the other hand, "[r]acial orthodoxy seems to demand that the respective status of the white and Negro races be maintained as nearly intact as the interests of industry will permit" ("Black Workers" 643). Johnson convincingly demonstrated these points by providing statistics showing the numbers of African American workers in service and other low-skill jobs. Walter White's exposé of racism is focused on the social sphere: he opened "Color Lines" with an anecdote about Paul Robeson, after an enthusiastically received performance, being unable to find a restaurant in New York City that would serve him (680). The contrast between Robeson's success as an actor and the racism he faced on the street is evidence of the conflict between the values supposedly at the core of American society and the racism that was shot through it. As White pointed out, democracy may be a "proud boast" in America, but it was a "rarely practiced accomplishment of these United States" (681).

The creative literature in the issue supports this assertion. McKay's poems, included not only as support for Domingo's argument but also in the section of poetry, provide a strong indictment of American racism. Domingo closed his essay with the defiant final couplet from "If We Must Die": against the "murderous, cowardly pack," McKay called his readers to fight back, even if pressed to the wall and to death (650). In "White House" —titled here and in *The New Negro* "White Houses," against McKay's protests (Lewis, *When Harlem Was in Vogue* 151)—McKay articulated a similar resistance to persecution: "Oh I must keep my heart inviolate / Against the potent poison of your hate" (662). McKay did not explicitly identify the murderous pack or the reason behind the poison hate, but it is easy to read these poems, particularly in the context of the racism detailed in other texts in the issue, as responses to American racism.

But these texts do not fully reflect the magnitude of American racism in the 1920s. The only mention of the ongoing lynching of African Americans, for example, is an aside in which White alluded to his investigation of a number of murders and riots ("Color Lines" 681). The continued inability to pass the Dyer anti-lynching bill in the 1920s was another source of frustration that was not mentioned in this issue. Neither was Du Bois's interest in the Pan-African movement. Marcus Garvey and his black nationalist movement are mentioned twice in the Harlem issue, but the passing references by W. A. Domingo (650) and Kelly Miller (683) do not do justice to Garvey's immense popularity in the late 1910s and early 1920s. Perhaps Garvey's importance was undermined in the *Survey Graphic* issue because he was in jail at the time of its publication. But Du Bois's involvement in the Pan-African congresses continued through the late 1910s and the 1920s, so the complete absence of this movement from the *Survey Graphic* issue seems odd. Perhaps contributors to the issue understood the effort to define African Americans as one that prevented the assertion of a global African diaspora.

Another possible reason contributors barely hint at the importance of Garvey and his movement may have been that they wanted to avoid the connotations of Garvey's argument that racism in America was so entrenched that it would never be overcome. Instead, contributors to the issue presented compelling arguments about the need to end these practices, and they imagined a future in which American democracy would be more fully practiced. A number of the contributors made this point by emphasizing the benefits of an improved society for all Americans. For example, James Weldon Johnson emphasized that the fair treatment of African Americans encouraged them to contribute to the city: "New York guarantees its Negro citizens the fundamental rights of American citizenship and protects them in the exercise of those rights. In return the Negro loves New York and is proud of it, and contributes in his way to its greatness" ("The Making of Harlem" 639).

Locke argued that treating African Americans with respect and fairness would enhance American democracy. In "Enter the New Negro," he emphasized African Americans' importance to national culture, and, in fact, to the improvement of national culture. Locke argued that African Americans' inclusion in American society would allow for the full realization of America's promise: when the "the fullest sharing of American culture and institutions" was granted to African Americans, he asserted, democracy would be served and "American ideals" would be "progressively fulfilled and realized" (633). Later in the issue, Locke used the arts to further emphasize the benefits of treating African Americans with respect. In "Youth Speaks," Locke described the growth in attention being paid to African American poets and artists. When Americans listened to the messages these young African American creators offered, what they would find was a "new aesthetic and a new philosophy of life" (659). The talents of African Americans would enrich American art—but even more than that, these writers and artists would "offer through art an emancipating vision to America" (660). In Locke's assessment, African Americans would offer hope to America and would free America from the limits and the restraints of its own biases.

The vision offered by African American writers and artists, it is clear in the *Survey Graphic* issue, would be fully realized only in the future. The continuing racism in America, shown both in Du Bois's story and in a number of other texts in the issue, demonstrates that the ideal America—a nation that made good on its promise of democracy and one that fulfilled its full potential—still had to be worked for. But the *Survey Graphic* issue demonstrates the possibilities and the importance of working toward that ideal. Implicitly, it also makes clear that criticism is an important contribution to American culture: by offering their critiques of American society and pushing for its improvement, African Americans were demonstrating a model of citizenship that includes active participation in the shaping and the improving of American society.

The vision of American democracy offered in the *Survey Graphic* does have its limitations, for the issue replicates some of the very hierarchies it critiques. The issue makes clear that classism, sexism, and xenophobia had yet to be fully resolved. Even though the issue challenges the dichotomy between the folk and the elite, it also reinscribes the idea that it was the voices and opinions of the elite that mattered most. The absence of much evidence of black folk culture is telling. Furthermore, even when Locke drew attention to the importance of the folk, as he did in "Harlem" when he claimed that "it is the rank and file who are leading," he paired that mention of the role of the folk with a qualification: "No sane observer, however sympathetic to the new trend, would contend that the great masses are articulate as yet, but they stir, they move, they are more than physically restless" (630). And although Locke included McDougald's essay on the sexism faced by African American women, he failed to address the gender bias replicated by the issue. Only four of the issue's twenty-six contributors are women, and the masculinist pronouns used throughout to refer to the New Negro keep the experiences of African American women from being truly integrated into the issue's discussions. Finally, the emphasis on the assimilation of African Americans does little to challenge the assumption that immigrants and minorities had to blend into the dominant culture if they wanted to be treated with respect. If the *Survey Graphic* issue calls into being a future that moves beyond racism, that future, as it is embodied here, has its limitations, particularly in terms of the continuing marginalization of the African American folk, of African American women, and of those who do not conform to a model of Americanization.

The issue, furthermore, sets up a tension between Americanization and race consciousness. In "Enter the New Negro," Locke warned that, if African Americans continued to be treated poorly in America, the result would be a growth in a "deep feeling of race"; that separatism, he added, would be a force that would "encyst the Negro as a benign foreign body in the body politic" (632, 633). His point that "[t]he Negro mind reaches out as yet to nothing but American wants, American ideas" implies the threat of the opposite occurring if African Americans were not treated with respect (633). White, in his reflection on the racism faced even by celebrities like Robeson, even more explicitly drew the connection between oppression and race consciousness. He argued, "The constant hammering of three hundred years of oppression has resulted in a race consciousness among the Negroes of the United States which is amazing to those who know how powerful it is" ("Color Lines" 681–82). Both writers presented race consciousness as the result of racism and used it as a threat, a danger that might motivate greater efforts to overcome racial oppression. Doing so helped them push for social change—but it also kept them from being able to define the growth of race consciousness as a positive development.

Locke, as we shall see, did promote the pride, unity, and race consciousness of African Americans in *The New Negro*. This shift in focus suggests that perhaps his role as a guest editor of a special issue of a magazine with a largely white readership influenced what he showed about the New Negro. Or perhaps it was simply the centrality of assimilation to this definition of African Americans as American that led to the positioning of race consciousness as something to be avoided in this issue. In either case, the conventions of the *Survey Graphic* definitely led to other challenges for Locke, especially the need to undermine the presumed distance between the readers and the subjects of the magazine. Locke's ability to do so, both through the contents of the texts he included and through the conventions of representation enacted in those texts, is crucial to his success at offering through the issue a definition of African Americans as American. The chance to present this definition to the *Survey Graphic*'s regular readers was a major advantage to editing this special issue. Locke's challenge and his success suggest that using an already-established publication to promote one's own agenda can be a difficult—but potentially rewarding—undertaking.

It would remain for the creators of volumes that came after the *Survey Graphic* issue to imagine an America that would overcome the forms of discrimination that continued in this issue and to conceive of race pride as not a challenge to American identity but an important aspect of American society and American diversity. But the *Survey Graphic* issue does successfully bring into question many of the assumptions its readers might have had about African Americans. Though certainly its texts can be read in different ways, they convincingly establish African Americans' importance in American culture and society and bridge presumed gaps between "Negro" and "American." Defining themselves as American based on achievements, contributions, and assimilation allowed African Americans to appeal to American ideals and to use those to fight against racism. By emphasizing that Americanization was a process, by identifying the criteria for its achievements, and by demonstrating their fulfillment of those criteria, the contributors to the issue deconstructed the binary of American and un-American that shaped definitions of American and African American identity in the 1920s, often to the exclusion of African Americans. Their redefinition of African American identity allowed them to redefine American identity to their own advantage.

The Harlem issue of the *Survey Graphic* embodies what Locke in "Harlem" wrote about the city: the issue, like the city, offered "a new vision of opportunity, of social and economic freedom, of a spirit to seize, even in the face of an extortionate and heavy toll, a chance for the improvement of conditions" (629). The *Survey Graphic* issue, while it makes clear the steps that still had to be taken, helps us understand the importance of Americanness and American identity to that process.

5

Collective Identity in the Anthology: Representing the Race in *The New Negro*

Alain Locke's tour of Harlem in the Survey Graphic *issue* proved extremely popular. Two months before the issue hit the newsstands, in fact, Boni Brothers Publishers voiced an interest in republishing the material in expanded book form. In a letter dated January 15, 1925, *Survey Graphic* editor Paul Kellogg wrote to Locke: "Albert Boni of Boni Brothers (called) asking if it would be possible to arrange for the republication of the materials in our Harlem number in book form, perhaps next fall" (qtd. in Long 16). The success of the issue confirmed their desire to publish the book (Long 18). As Locke began to work on it, he used the contents of the magazine issue as its core, but he also expanded those contents in ways that dramatically altered his portrait of African Americans. His title is the first indication of those changes: "Harlem: Mecca of the New Negro" became *The New Negro: An Interpretation,* signaling a move away from the local focus of the magazine issue to a broader focus on the New Negro movement as a whole in the book. Like the *Survey Graphic* issue, *The New Negro* is an attempt to claim a particular identity for a group of people. But where the *Survey Graphic* issue records African Americans' efforts to define themselves as American, the focus of *The New Negro* shifts to the identity of African Americans as a race. While the argument that African Americans and African American culture were essential parts of American society and culture still is an important aspect of *The New Negro,* the book's primary emphasis is on African Americans' connections to one another rather than their connections to white Americans.

We can read *The New Negro,* then, as an attempt to define a collective identity for African Americans. In some ways, the book is similar to other collaborative illustrated volumes published during the Harlem Renaissance. For example, Locke focused on recording the changes occurring among

African Americans, an emphasis that links *The New Negro* to *The Crisis, Opportunity,* and even the *Survey Graphic* issue on Harlem: all share the goal of replacing stereotypes of African Americans with new, accurate images. Like those publications, *The New Negro* includes a range of texts. But *The New Negro* is a particularly clear example of efforts to demonstrate and encourage a growing sense of unity among African Americans. Locke believed that black people in the United States had only recently begun to develop a sense of shared identity, and he saw the fusion of diverse groups of African Americans into an integrated whole as a crucial part of the New Negro movement. His book records his attempts to promote a coming together of various groups of African Americans, a uniting of "dissimilar elements," as he called them in the book's title essay ("The New Negro" 6).

Locke's anthology constitutes an illuminating example of identity politics at work, and we can use *The New Negro* to explore the implications of such efforts to define collective identities. The book demonstrates both the advantages and the drawbacks of such projects: there are aspects of the book that are essentialist but also aspects that reflect the diversity and complexity of African American identity. To the extent that the book offers a relatively simple representation of the New Negro, it allows for a coherent first impression of African American identity that has practical benefits, particularly since it helps challenge and replace outdated and derogatory images of African Americans. In effect, the book offers a representation of the New Negro that Locke and other participants in the Harlem Renaissance could draw on and refer to again and again. But Locke's assertion of the shared experiences and ideas of African Americans raises the threat of implied homogeneity: to the extent that Locke's efforts to define the New Negro suggest that all African Americans were alike, or that African Americans had to have certain characteristics to fit into the race, it implicitly required the exclusion and omission of individuals and aspects of African Americans' lives that did not fit Locke's mold. Furthermore, to the extent that *The New Negro* allows readers to assume that all African Americans were alike, it does little to challenge the processes of stereotyping or the generalizing principle underlying racism. The question, then, is whether *The New Negro* is able to capitalize on the benefits of establishing a collective identity for African Americans without falling into the traps of essentialism and exclusion.

The answer lies, to a great extent, in the format of *The New Negro*. As a book that is focused on one group of people and uses a few central ideas as unifying themes, it promotes an awareness of the shared identity of African Americans. But because the book is a multi-media, multi-genre, collaborative anthology—one that includes more than 450 pages of essays, creative literature, drawings, portraits, and a bibliography—it simultaneously demonstrates the complexities of African American identity. The range of texts in the book draws attention to the diversity of African Americans' lives and experiences, especially because its texts, by many writers and artists, offer strikingly different—and sometimes conflicting—ideas about African Americans. As a result, the book as a whole challenges the idea of the race as a homogenous group. That point is driven home by the fact that Locke drew attention to this portrait of the New Negro as only one possible portrait, as one of many possible representations. The subtitle of the book—*An Interpretation*—as well as the placement of conflicting assessments of African American identity, the inclusion of competing arguments about aspects of African Americans' lives, and the closing bibliography all combine to draw readers' attention to the conflicts embodied in this definition of African American identity and the complexities that, despite its magnitude, it cannot reflect. By pushing readers to understand the book as one possible definition, these features encourage readers to be more critical of other partial definitions. The book demonstrates, then, the possibilities of anthologies as sites for the construction of collective identity and their potential to reflect both the unity of and the difference within the identities they construct.

There are some disappointing omissions and hierarchies present in the book, though. *The New Negro* reflects an unfortunate sexism and elitism as well as a failure to acknowledge a number of important aspects of African Americans' lives during the Harlem Renaissance, including the role of the blues and religion and the fact that homosexuality was an important aspect of African American identity. This point suggests the limits of how much difference or complexity an anthology with the goal of constructing a unified identity can contain; it also suggests the difficulty of challenging one form of oppression without falling into others. Still, in offering a coherent but expansive definition of African American identity, *The New Negro* promotes an understanding of collective identity that challenges the premises of racism, and it shows the usefulness of anthologies for the presentation of that concept.

An overview of the contents of *The New Negro* suggests both its simplifying and complicating messages about African American identity. As is the case for many anthologies that focus on a single group of people, it is the unifying impulses in *The New Negro* that are its most immediately perceived elements. The implication in the title that *the* New Negro is going to be easily summed up begins this sense of simplification. The suggestion that there is a single type of New Negro is reinforced by visual texts that immediately establish unifying themes and offer a relatively easily comprehended first impression of the New Negro. The book opens and closes with cover designs and endpapers by Winold Reiss, and the Africanist elements on these pages are echoed throughout the book by black-and-white drawings by Reiss and Aaron Douglas. These appear on the opening and closing pages of many of the essays and works of literature. They draw attention to the link between African Americans and Africans and turn that link into a motif of the book. The book also includes a series of portraits of the intellectual and creative leaders of the New Negro movement, such as Locke, W. E. B. Du Bois, and Charles S. Johnson; these portraits present a set of representative individuals who show the New Negro to be educated, sophisticated, dignified, and articulate. The portraits are placed throughout the volume, alongside the essays or creative texts by their subjects. Reproduced on glossy, heavy paper, they stand out from the rest of the book: a reader can easily flip through its pages and find the portraits. They make the progress and accomplishments of the New Negro an immediate emphasis of the book.

Beyond its initial sense of coherence, though, the volume contains a great deal of complexity in its representation of the New Negro. Again, this is partly a result of its format as an anthology. As Locke developed a fuller portrait of African Americans out of the texts he had included in the *Survey Graphic* issue, he added significantly to the contents of his book. While the magazine issue weighed in at about 100 pages, including quite a few pages of advertisements, *The New Negro* is more than 450 pages long. Much of the new material appears in its first section, "The Negro Renaissance," which focuses almost entirely on creative work. It takes up more than half of the book—nearly 270 pages. While the only written literature in the *Survey Graphic* was a short section of poetry, Du Bois's short story, and Rudolph Fisher's vignettes, *The New Negro* opens with more than 100 pages of fiction, poetry, and drama. This section of the book also includes essays about the importance of work by African American writers and artists as well as essays about African American music and folk culture. In addition, an essay on African art emphasizes the connection between African Americans and black Africans. It is only in the second section, "The New Negro in a New World," that Locke included sociological studies, reprinting, in expanded form, essays from the *Survey Graphic* issue and adding others. These essays take up a little more than 140 pages; they are a significant part of Locke's portrait, but they carry less weight than the creative texts. In addition to the drawings and portraits by Reiss and Douglas, the book includes black-and-white drawings by Miguel Covarrubias and four "type sketches" by Reiss, three of them the portraits of black women that appeared in the *Survey*

Graphic issue. The importance of these type studies is underlined by the fact that an image of "The Brown Madonna," a black woman holding a baby, appears as the frontispiece of the book. Like the other three type studies, this portrait complicates the use of the elite to demonstrate the characteristics of the New Negro. The book closes with an extensive bibliography compiled by Locke, Arthur A. Schomburg, and Arthur Huff Fauset (420). It includes lists of books, plays, music, folklore, and sociological studies by and about Africans, African Americans, and "the race problem" in America. This bibliography makes clear that there is much more to be learned about the New Negro than can be communicated by the texts in the book.[1]

Locke's use of an anthology to define African American identity fits into a long tradition of such efforts. Anthologies had been recognized as sites in which collective identities could be constructed well before the 1920s, both around the world and among African Americans.[2] Within the African American cultural tradition, the precedents of *The New Negro* include *Les Cenelles,* an anthology of poetry written by New Orleans Creoles. Published in 1845, it may be the earliest anthology of African American literature (Gates, *Loose Canons* 24–25). Booker T. Washington's 1900 *A New Negro for a New Century* is not a literary anthology, but it engages with the same process of defining collective identity, using portraits and biographies to assert a new identity for African Americans at the turn of the century. Even closer to the time of Locke's publication of *The New Negro,* James Weldon Johnson used his *Book of American Negro Poetry,* first published in 1922, to define an identity for African Americans based on their creative work. As Johnson emphasized in the preface to his book, the collection of literature by a particular group of people helped establish the identity and significance of that group:

> The final measure of the greatness of all peoples is the amount and standard of the literature and art they have produced. The world does not know that a people is great until that people produces great literature and art. No people that has produced great literature and art has ever been looked upon by the world as distinctly inferior. (9)

In collecting poetry by African Americans and publishing his anthology, in short, Johnson was implicitly asserting a definition of African Americans as literate, culturally sophisticated, and highly talented.

Anthologies tend to share certain features that make them both advantageous and problematic sites for the construction of collective identities, and they also reflect both the importance and the pitfalls of this process. For example, asserting a collective identity as unified and unifying, as an easily comprehended category, can be empowering. Defining a shared identity for a group can be "a condition for agency, for social change" (Gates, *Loose*

Canons 37), and anthologies can be very helpful texts to use toward that goal. They can be places "to construct and express a positive (communal) identity for contributors" (Franklin 10). A literary canon—often embodied, of course, in an anthology—can serve as a "commonplace book of our shared culture, in which we have written down the texts and titles that we want to remember, that had some special meaning for us" (Gates, *Loose Canons* 21). Through this function, a book like *The New Negro* might operate as a recording and an assertion of the ideas about African Americans that were important to African Americans in the 1920s. Furthermore, as one-time publications rather than periodicals, anthologies give a sense of permanence to the ideas and identities they represent. In fact, many of the scholars who have written about *The New Negro*, both during and after the Harlem Renaissance, have referred to it as offering a definitive portrait of the New Negro.[3] That assessment is not incorrect—and it in fact captures the way that Locke was using his anthology to offer a unified, relatively simple definition of African American identity. The benefit of this aspect of the book is that it offers readers an easily grasped concept of African American identity, one that clearly and powerfully contradicts the racist images of African Americans in popular culture.

But such defining projects also have drawbacks, particularly because asserting a collective identity that is unified and unifying can be exclusionary and limiting and can set up new hierarchies of oppression and exclusion. These aspects of the process were illuminated especially clearly in the 1980s and 1990s, when black feminists and other feminists of color began to explore and critique the limitations of white feminism, particularly in terms of its limited and homogenous constructions of the category woman.[4] Such analyses reveal that attempts to define collective identity often "[end] up excluding, marginalizing, or strategically stabilizing some aspect of identity that [they purport] to represent" (Franklin 26).

These potential consequences also have been noted by scholars who study the role of anthologies in determining the canons of American and African American literature. Anthologies that focus on work by a single group of people share the benefits and limitations of a certain degree of essentialism. By defining contributors by one aspect of their identity—such as their race or their gender—such anthologies imply that that single aspect of identity is the most (if not the only) significant factor about their contributors. Furthermore, to the degree that the anthologies attempt to offer a single definition of the identity in question, they imply that there are particular qualities essential to this identity. Scholars who focus on such works often approach this issue by raising questions about the people who are included in and excluded from membership in that group.[5]

But anthologies also can be helpful tools for drawing attention to the complexities of collective identity. In the case of *The New Negro*, the size of this book, the number of texts included, the fact that the texts are both creative and expository, written and visual, and the fact that the texts have such different focuses all draw readers' attention to the complexity of the portrait of the New Negro offered through the book. This complexity is, again, in some ways inherent in the fact that the book is an anthology. Anthologies' collaborative nature, for example, gives them the potential to include a range of voices and definitions of the identity in question. In effect, the fact that an anthology is a collection of texts by different contributors—and even a collection of texts in various genres—draws attention to the range of ideas and identities of contributors (Franklin 12). Furthermore, anthologies can emphasize the constructed nature of collaborative identities. Editors who draw attention to their selection processes and the texts they did not include reveal the provisionality both of their volume and the concept of identity it reflects.[6] Thus anthologies have the potential to set before their readers a variety of ideas and texts; the contradictions and complications embodied by these texts and ideas encourages them to understand the complexity of the identity or the canon being constructed.

A close study of Locke's book allows us to determine the extent to which it fulfills this potential—or the extent to which it offers a more problematic definition of African American identity. To develop a careful assessment of his volume, we will need to analyze both its essentializing impulses and its reflection of the diversity of African Americans' experiences and identities, for the simultaneous unity and complexity of the definition of African American identity in *The New Negro* are crucial to the book's ability to offer a coherent definition of African American identity but also to push its readers' thinking about race beyond simplicities. We need, then, to study the book as it was originally published, as a complex mix of written and visual texts.

Unfortunately, only a handful of studies of *The New Negro* exist, and most of these pay little if any attention to the combination of texts that appeared in the volume. These fail to register, then, the full dimensions of Locke's portrait.[7] Studies of *The New Negro*, furthermore, are hindered by the fact that reprints of the book often alter its contents and fail to include all of the texts that appeared in the original, thus subtly or drastically changing the portrait of African Americans that Locke created. One significant change, in fact, is in the title of the book: Locke's original *The New Negro: An Interpretation*, with its implicit assertion that many other interpretations are possible, has become *The New Negro: Voices of the Harlem Renaissance* in the 1969 and 1992 editions. Another significant change between the original and later editions concerns the dropping of the book's color portraits. The editions of the book published in 1969 and 1992 by Atheneum, for example, reproduce all of the written contents but omit Reiss's portraits.[8] The Arno edition of 1968 includes all of Reiss's work, but it reproduces the portraits in black and white, thus decreasing their impact.[9] Given the striking nature of the portraits in the original, their absence or black-and-white reproduction means these editions offer a significantly different definition of the New Negro. Returning to Locke's first edition of the book is essential, then. Most importantly, doing so allows us to recover the complexities of Locke's portrait of the New Negro and to consider with more accuracy the implications of his definition of African American identity and the strategies he used to construct that definition.

Locke made clear that his goal for *The New Negro* was to define African Americans, particularly to show the changes that were occurring among them. He gave emphasis to the growing unity of African Americans—and, in fact, of black people around the world. That sense of connection is asserted in a number of the texts in the book, but Locke himself defined it especially clearly in his essay "The New Negro." "Hitherto," he wrote, "it must be admitted that American Negroes have been a race more in name than in fact, or to be exact, more in sentiment than in experience" (7). But the growth of a "common consciousness" and "a life in common" was apparent in Harlem, where, Locke proclaimed, African Americans were seizing their first chances for "group expression and self-determination" (7). The book as a whole documents the complexity underlying that common consciousness, but its visual texts emphasize the shared aspects of African American identity.

Two unifying elements are evident even in the outside covers. The front and back cover each include a small graphic element. On the front, all that appears is the title of the book. On the back is an Africanist design, probably by Reiss. Without opening the book, then, readers can assume that it will focus on *the* New Negro, and that the link to Africa will be important. Inside the covers, visual texts continue to shape their impression of the New Negro. The endpapers, importantly, reinforce the link between the New Negro and Africa, through Reiss's Africanist aesthetics (see fig. 5.1). Printed in purple ink on a lavender background, these designs center around two seated human figures surrounded by exotic birds, cats, and plants. Reiss rendered these figures in stylized, flattened, geometric designs that evoke the aesthetics used in African masks. The reader who flips through the volume easily finds other similar drawings by both Reiss and Douglas. Reiss's black-and-

Fig. 5.1. One panel of Reiss's endpapers for *The New Negro. Locke, ed.,*
The New Negro.

white designs are used as headings to essays and as design elements at their
endings, and certain designs are repeated throughout the book (see fig. 5.2
for two examples). In effect, they unify the volume. Douglas's drawings feature similar design elements, most notably the sharply contrasting black-
and-white forms that are modeled on Africanist features (see fig. 5.3 for "An-

Fig. 5.2. Sample design work by Reiss from *The New Negro*. Locke, ed., The New Negro.

cestral," for example). Douglas's and Reiss's illustrations fill *The New Negro* with visual evocations of Africa; they are a constant assertion of the African background of black people in the United States. These visual texts "serve as 'ancestral' and culturally specific leitmotivs," becoming "a kind of graphic, African presence qualifying and surrounding all prose, poetry, and drama in the volume" (Baker 73). The link between African Americans and Africa is also reinforced in other texts, most notably in Locke's "The Legacy of the Ancestral Arts," a discussion of African art and its influence on ideas about African Americans. The endpapers, then, signal a theme that is carried through the volume when they link the New Negro to an African past.

The title page draws readers' attention to other unifying aspects of the book. It includes not the full title and subtitle but only the title: *The New Negro*. Without the qualification of the subtitle, that this is *An Interpretation,*

Fig. 5.3. Aaron Douglas's "Ancestral." In the 1927 reprint, this illustration was retitled "Rebirth" and moved to the fiction section. *Locke, ed.,* The New Negro, *268.*

the title immediately positions this book as a definitive portrait of this iden-tity. The definite article "the" is significant; it implies that this book does not offer a definition of "a" New Negro, but that the identity to be defined is a singular one. Throughout the book, Locke and other writers refer to the New Negro as a person; again, the sense is that the concept of the New Negro is so unified and uncomplicated that it can be represented by a single figure.

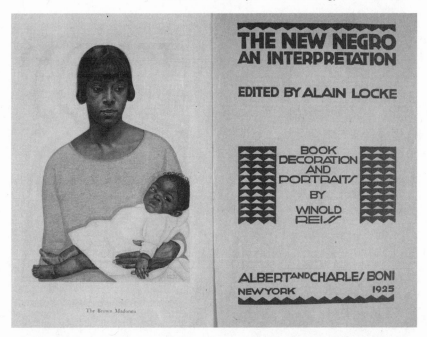

Fig. 5.4. Reiss's frontispiece portrait and the title page of *The New Negro*.
Locke, ed., The New Negro.

The title page also draws attention to Reiss's illustrations. Underneath the title is the identification of Locke as editor, and then, taking up about one quarter of the page, is an announcement of book decorations and portraits by Reiss (see fig. 5.4). Curious readers who flip through the rest of the book in search of the portraits will find them easily because they are on special paper and are printed in full color. The fact that Reiss's "The Brown Madonna" is the frontispiece encourages this activity. Both the woman and her baby look to their left; in fact, given that the woman's eyes are downcast, she looks almost directly at the announcement of Reiss's work. It is almost as if she wants readers to notice that announcement and to seek out the images. Readers who do so will discover Reiss's ten portraits of Locke, Du Bois, and their peers. They will find, as well, a "study" of Paul Robeson and a portrait entitled "Ancestral," a "type sketch" of a smiling black woman wrapped in a blanket and seated in front of a colorful cloth (see fig. 5.5). Readers also will find the three portraits of anonymous black women from the *Survey Graphic* issue; these are printed in black and white, but they, too, are printed on special paper.

These portraits focus readers' attention primarily on the elite of the race. While the two portrait series in the *Survey Graphic* issue both had focused

Fig. 5.5. Reiss's "Ancestral: a Type Study," which appeared in full color in *The New Negro. Locke, ed.,* The New Negro, *page facing 242.*

mostly on Harlem "types" and representatives of the working class, with only a few members of the elite, here the numbers are reversed. Locke and his peers are presented as sophisticated and dignified, in three-piece suits or dresses. The portrait of Locke himself is typical (see fig. 5.6). Locke sits, looking with dignity and calm assurance slightly to his right. His hands are together in front of him, as if he is idly turning a small object while he waits for his portrait to be finished. The pose allowed Reiss to draw attention to Locke's face and head as well as his hands; these are the only part of his body that Reiss fully rendered. The effect is an emphasis on Locke's intellect and the creativity represented in his hands: the portrait concentrates on the features Locke uses to carry out his intellectual work. At the same time, Reiss hints at the aspects of Locke's person that turn him into an embodiment of the New Negro. Locke, whose impressive achievements are listed in the list of "Who's Who of the Contributors" (415), in Reiss's portrait wears the clothing suited to his role as a member of the intellectual elite. He is dressed in a three-piece suit, complete with a tie and a handkerchief, carefully tucked into his breast pocket. Reiss rendered the other members of the elite in similarly sophisticated dress. These portraits provide the reader with a glance at the educated intellectuals that Locke described as "the more intelligent and

Fig. 5.6. Reiss's portrait of Alain Locke. *Locke, ed.,* The New Negro, *page facing 6.*

representative elements" of the race ("The New Negro" 9). Their images directly contradict the stereotyped, racist images of African Americans that would have been familiar in the 1920s. Even two of the four "type sketches" that appear in *The New Negro* portray individuals who appear to be relatively well off and sophisticated. The two schoolteachers wear Phi Beta Kappa keys that mark them as well educated (Stewart 54; see fig. 4.9); the librarian also reappears, dressed in a fur coat, gloves, and dressy hat (see fig. 4.8). Only the woman identified as "From the Tropic Isles" is dressed in clothes that might identify her as working class (see fig. 4.7).[10] The portraits, then, draw readers' attention to impressive representatives of the race.

The role of these individuals as demonstrating the potential of African Americans is underlined by the fact that many of the portraits are paired with written texts by their subjects. These paired texts shift the implications of the subject position. In the *Survey Graphic* issue, being put on display had a disempowering effect, particularly since readers learned little about the identity of the subjects of its portraits. But here, Reiss's subjects are seen to be articulate and fully capable of asserting themselves. For example, the portrait of Locke is placed within his opening essay, "The New Negro." As a result, Locke is both seen and heard, as was Elise Johnson McDougald in the *Survey Graphic* issue. In *The New Negro,* the portraits of Jean Toomer, Countee Cullen, Charles S. Johnson, James Weldon Johnson, Robert Russa Moton, McDougald, and Du Bois are likewise reproduced alongside the subjects' written contributions. Though the elite are put on display here, then, these subjects are not disempowered; in this case, their visual presence complements the presence of their arguments. These portraits, then, offer a depiction of the New Negro that draws attention to the elite of the race in a way that emphasizes their intellectual sophistication and their articulateness.

In short, *The New Negro* offers in the link to Africa and in the series of portraits a pair of unifying factors that lead to a relatively simple and easy-to-comprehend definition of African American identity. Furthermore, these aspects of African American identity implicitly contradict two racist assumptions about African Americans. The attention to African culture and the use of the elite to demonstrate African Americans' progress and potential conflicts with "the prevailing notion among most whites of blacks as not only physically and culturally inferior but without much hope of improvement" (Rampersad, "Introduction" xv). If readers were to put down the book at this point, having merely glanced through the visual texts of the volume, they still would walk away with a compelling, coherent impression of the New Negro. Such readers would comprehend the links among African Americans and between African Americans and Africa; they also would conceive of the New Negro as eloquent, articulate, sophisticated, and educated. This first impression is a helpful reference point, a concrete image that readers—or those attempting to revise definitions of African American identity—might draw on repeatedly. If a mental image of the New Negro needs to be called up, it easily could be.

For the readers who delve further into the book, however, a more complicated definition of African American identity emerges. This definition goes well beyond what is suggested by these visual texts, and the book in fact comes to challenge the impressions offered by these texts. The book, furthermore, undermines the notion that a simple and yet accurate understanding of African American identity can be achieved through a limited number of texts. These points are first suggested in Locke's "Foreword," a relatively short but complex opening essay that draws readers into the body of his book and gives them a hint of what they will find there. Embedded in the three brief pages of the essay are arguments about the role of texts in shaping ideas about collective identity as well as a preview of the definitions of African American identity to be found throughout the book.

The foreword comprises Locke's first step toward raising readers' awareness of the function of texts in shaping perceptions of African Americans. Locke identified the function of his book as being "to document the New Negro culturally and socially,—to register the transformations of the inner and outer life of the Negro in America that have so significantly taken place in the last few years" (ix).[11] That statement of purpose hints at the roles of different kinds of texts in this process: the word "document" links the volume to the kind of sociological studies of black culture that had been written by black and white intellectuals and hints at the role sociological essays play in Locke's construction of the New Negro. But, a few sentences later, Locke warned of the dangers of these kinds of studies, which, he explained, too often focus on statistics and offer an "external view" of the Negro that illuminates "the Negro problem rather than the Negro" (ix). To reveal the "internal world of the Negro mind and spirit" (ix), different kinds of texts were necessary. As Locke explained, "Whoever wishes to see the Negro in his essential traits, in the full perspective of his achievement and possibilities, must seek the enlightenment of that self-portraiture which the present developments of Negro culture are offering" (ix). In *The New Negro* the texts that represent these developments—the transcriptions, literature, and artwork by African Americans that Locke included, as well as essays about their creative work in other artistic fields—give readers insight into the inner lives of African Americans. A combination of different kinds of texts, then, offers the fullest portrayal of African American identity.

Locke also used his foreword to hint at the aspects of African American identity that characterize the New Negro. His primary focus was on the changes occurring among African Americans. These were, again, "transformations of the inner and outer life of the Negro in America" (ix). They were also, he asserted, undeniable: "There is ample evidence of a New Negro in the latest phases of social change and progress, but still more in the internal world of the Negro mind and spirit" (ix). These changes were so massive that Locke could write of the emergence of "a new figure on the national canvas and a new force in the foreground of affairs" (ix). A portrait that showed such changes would reveal the "achievement and possibilities" of the New Negro (ix). These changes, as readers would find later in the book, were practical and material, but Locke also emphasized here that they were changes in attitude as well. He insisted that the growth of self-expression and self-determination among African Americans amounted to "the resurgence of a people," the assertion of "a new soul," and the development of "a renewed race-spirit" (xi).

Those final comments hint at principles of the concept of race as a category of identity that are reflected in the rest of this book. Locke's emphasis here was on the fusion of "disunited and apathetic elements" of this group of people into a collective whole that was being unified and focused (xi). But this coming together of African Americans as a race did not imply their disconnection from other groups of people. In fact, Locke insisted that African American culture was closely connected to American culture. He positioned the "quickened centers of the lives of black folk" as signs of the revitalization of American culture, and vice versa: "America seeking a new spiritual expansion and artistic maturity, trying to found an American literature, a national art, and national music implies a Negro-American culture seeking the same satisfactions and objectives" (x). Locke presented this as evidence that "[s]eparate as it may be in color and substance, the culture of the Negro is of a pattern integral with the times and with its cultural setting" (x). He also drew parallels between the developments in African American culture and similar changes occurring around the world. "As in India, in China, in Egypt, Ireland, Russia, Bohemia, Palestine and Mexico, we are witnessing the resurgence of a people" (xi). The image of African Americans that Locke presented in *The New Negro,* then, is one of a fully modernized people with national significance, whose progress, as it is expressed through literature, art, and music, is in step with that of cultures around the world. Racial identity, then, is seen here not as a divisive force but simply one that links its members; it coexists with national and even global identities. Significantly, Locke closed the foreword by categorizing "the offerings of this book" as "the first fruits of the Negro Renaissance" (xi). Locke's reference here to the movement as the Negro Renaissance, rather than the New Negro Movement, links it to other "Renaissance" movements often discussed during the period, including those in Ireland and even in America in the previous decade.[12]

But the foreword also hints at the limiting aspects of Locke's definition of African American identity. The wording of Locke's references to the New Negro points to the kind of simplification and generalization that can accompany the concept of race. Locke's references to the "essential traits" of African Americans, for instance, draw attention to the limiting and exclusionary potential of his project (ix). Furthermore, by representing the New Negro as an individual whose progress sums up that of all black people in the United States, Locke opened up the possibility of monolithic ideas about African Americans. For example, in that statement of purpose, Locke's references to the transformation of the inner and outer life of the Negro in America—as well as his later discussion of "the Negro mind and spirit" (ix)—characterize African Americans as so similar that they can be represented or discussed as one individual. Locke's simplistic representation is different in intent, of course, from racist stereotypes and generalizations, but it shares with them the process of homogenizing a diverse group of people into one entity, and it fits into rather than challenges the categorization that makes racism possible. Locke's continual references to the New Negro as "him," furthermore, hint at the masculinist focus of his definition of African American identity. The foreword reveals, then, the ways that Locke's attempt at challenging racism by redefining African American identity ended up reinforcing other forms of hierarchies and oppressions.

Locke's foreword does outline the foundations on which the rest of the book builds. First, by throwing doubt on what other texts show about African American identity, Locke encouraged readers to consider whether texts offered true insights into African Americans' experiences and ideas, rather than assuming that they did. He also asserted that in many cases other texts failed to offer any real insight—and therefore he established the need for the new definition embodied in *The New Negro*. Second, Locke began to challenge established ideas about African Americans, particularly by emphasizing their capacity for change and their connection to other groups of people pressing for national and international modernization and progress. Locke positioned African Americans as part and parcel of global progress and progressive movements.

But Locke, in his foreword, could only assert these arguments. In theory, he could have expanded the essay a great deal, including details and evidence to support his arguments. But rather than capitalizing here on the persuasive possibilities of his expository text, he left the essay brief enough to serve as a quick introduction to the main ideas of the book. It is up to the following texts to support Locke's assertions and to convince readers of their accuracy.

Interestingly, though, readers who engage with the texts in the main part of the book—and who read them critically, as Locke encouraged them to do—find significant disagreement about even the primary factors that Locke used to assert the unity of African American identity. While there are texts that support the argument that African Americans were unified by their connection to Africa and represented by their intellectual elites, the book also includes many texts that throw those points into question.

Locke included in *The New Negro*, for example, texts that send competing messages about African Americans' connections to an African past. On one hand, a number of texts link African American culture to African culture. For example, Arthur Huff Fauset commented in his essay "American

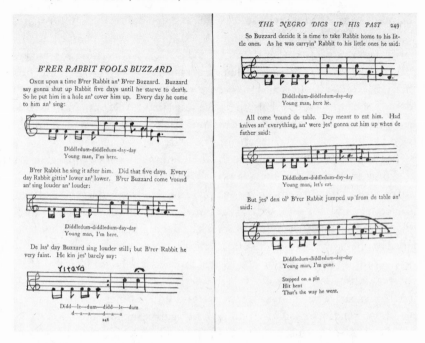

Fig. 5.7. "B'rer Rabbit Fools Buzzard" is one of two folktales transcribed in *The New Negro. Locke, ed., The New Negro, 248–49.*

Negro Folk Literature" that African American folktales were derived from African forms (239–40). Underlining this point are transcriptions of two African American folktales, "T'appin" and "B'rer Rabbit Fools Buzzard"; these follow his essay. A footnote indicates that both were collected in 1925 by Fauset, an anthropologist who focused on the collection and study of folklore. The first is identified as "Told by Cugo Lewis, Plateau, Alabama. Brought to America from West Coast Africa, 1859" (245). It is a subtle piece of evidence against the argument that Africans forgot all of their expressive traditions on the traumatic middle passage and arrived in America as blank slates—particularly since the story includes prayers for food, written in what presumably is an African language. The second story is not dated; most likely it is a more recent tale than the first. Notably, it is transcribed with bars of music that demonstrate how B'rer Buzzard sang to B'rer Rabbit and how B'rer Rabbit responded to him (see fig. 5.7). The musical notations are reminders of the oral nature of the story, the fact that it was meant to be performed rather than read. They hint, then, that oral transmission of information central in many African cultures was carried over to African American expressive traditions.

THE LEGACY
OF THE ANCESTRAL ARTS[1]

ALAIN LOCKE

MUSIC and poetry, and to an extent the dance, have been the predominant arts of the American Negro. This is an emphasis quite different from that of the African cultures, where the plastic and craft arts predominate; Africa being one of the great fountain sources of the arts of decoration and design. Except then in his remarkable carry-over of the rhythmic gift, there is little evidence of any direct connection of the American Negro with his ancestral arts. But even with the rude transplanting of slavery, that uprooted the technical elements of his former culture, the American Negro brought over as an emotional inheritance a deep-seated æsthetic endowment. And with a versatility of a very high order, this offshoot of the African spirit blended itself in with entirely different culture elements and blossomed in strange new forms.

There was in this more than a change of art-forms and an exchange of cultural patterns; there was a curious reversal of emotional temper and attitude. The characteristic African art expressions are rigid, controlled, disciplined, abstract, heavily conventionalized; those of the Aframerican,—free, exuberant, emotional, sentimental and human. Only by the misinterpretation of the African spirit, can one claim any emotional kinship between them—for the spirit of African expression, by and large, is disciplined, sophisticated, laconic and fatalistic. The emotional temper of the American Negro is exactly opposite. What we have thought primitive in the American Negro —his naïveté, his sentimentalism, his exuberance and his improvizing spontaneity are then neither characteristically African nor to be explained as an ancestral heritage. They are the result of his peculiar experience in America and the emotional up-

[1] Illustrations are from the Barnes Foundation Collection.

254

THE NEGRO DIGS UP HIS PAST 255

heaval of its trials and ordeals. True, these are now very characteristic traits, and they have their artistic, and perhaps even their moral compensations; but they represent essentially the working of environmental forces rather than the outcropping of a race psychology; they are really the acquired and not the original artistic temperament.

BUSHONGO

A further proof of this is the fact that the American Negro, even when he confronts the various forms of African art expression with a sense of its ethnic claims upon him, meets them in as alienated and misunderstanding an attitude as the average European Westerner. Christianity and all the other European conventions operate to make this inevitable. So there would be little hope of an influence of African art upon the western African descendants if there were not at present a growing in-

Fig. 5.8. The opening pages of Locke's illustrated and expanded essay on African art in *The New Negro. Locke, ed.*, The New Negro, 254–55. Mask, Guro Peoples, BF #A106.

The texts in *The New Negro* that draw attention to African art also imply the significance of the connection between Africa and African Americans. Locke's essay "The Legacy of the Ancestral Arts" is the strongest argument for this connection. It is a greatly expanded version of the one-paragraph comments he offered about African art in the *Survey Graphic* issue. In the book, the essay helps readers understand the significance of the designs throughout the volume; it also emphasizes the social implications of an appreciation for African art. This work, Locke argued, demonstrates that "the Negro is not a cultural foundling without his own inheritance" (256). Accordingly, Locke asserted that there was "a vital connection between this new artistic respect for African idiom and the natural ambition of Negro artists for a racial idiom in their art expression" (262). In turn, he continued, when artists began to reflect racial subjects in their work, they would discover a beauty in them "which prejudice and caricature have overlaid" (264). Revealing that beauty would decrease these results of racism. In other words, respect for African art would lead to respect for African artists, which would lead to an increase in race pride and then an increase in artwork that takes

THE NEGRO DIGS UP HIS PAST

Faint and slow, of anger, rise
To smitten cheek and weary eyes.

Lord, forgive me if my need
Sometimes shapes a human creed.

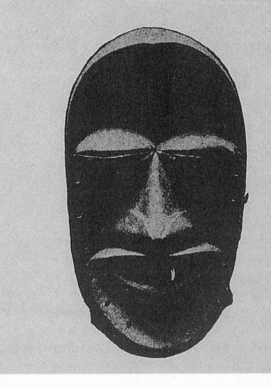

Fig. 5.9. The final page of Countee Cullen's "Heritage" in *The New Negro*.
Locke, ed., The New Negro, *253.*

on racial subjects and styles. Locke set up a cycle of images and social change, asserting that social changes lead to different kinds of images, which then lead to greater social change. Locke encouraged that cycle in this essay by including photographs of works of African art, identified by their place of origin (see fig. 5.8 for an example). These demonstrate the achievements of

African artists; they also allow readers of *The New Negro* to connect these works with the designs they see throughout the book, making the African context even more clear. Locke's argument about the importance and influence of African culture, then, assured that the African context of African American culture is read in a way that contributes to possible reassessments of African American culture.

However, the connections between Africans and African Americans raised in this essay are also questioned within the essay and by the text that immediately precedes it: Countee Cullen's poem "Heritage." Locke opened his essay by differentiating between African and African American culture, going so far as to assert that "there is little evidence of any direct connection of the American Negro with his ancestral arts" (254). If that is the case, the "profound and galvanizing influence" of African arts on African Americans will be in the future (256). Locke's point here, then, was less to describe the existing connection between African art and African Americans and more to encourage the connections he hoped would develop. Cullen's poem, furthermore, works as an example of African Americans' mixed feelings toward Africa, given the speaker's repeated musings of "What is Africa to me?" and the ambiguity with which he answers that question, asserting both his distance from Africa and his inability to separate himself from it. The fact that the speaker of the poem cannot escape Africa's importance—that he sits with his thumbs in his ears but still hears the beating of African drums, for example—implies that Africa is an important part of his identity. But his repeated questioning of this connection asserts that this is a connection to be pondered rather than assumed. In the *Survey Graphic* issue, photographs of African masks and statues had been reproduced with the poem, thus affirming the connection the speaker questions. Here, most of them are moved to the following essay, Locke's "Legacy," leaving Cullen's poem more ambiguous. But one mask is reproduced below the closing lines of Cullen's poem, as if it represents the dark god he calls for (see fig. 5.9). The mask gets the final word, figuratively: the reader leaves the poem with a stronger impression of the connection to Africa than Cullen's poem by itself would have given.

The fiction in the volume also offers mixed messages about African Americans' connection to Africa. Locke argues that the work of the younger black writers shows that they "have instinctive love and pride of race, and, spiritually compensating for the present lacks of America, ardent respect and love for Africa" ("Negro Youth Speaks" 52–53). But most of the stories have little to do with Africa. The first, for example, is Rudolph Fisher's "The City of Refuge," a short story about the experiences of King Solomon Gillis, a black man who flees North Carolina for Harlem. In fact, all of the short stories here are set in the United States, from Harlem to the South, except Bruce Nu-

Fig. 5.10. Douglas's "Meditation" from *The New Negro. Locke, ed.,*
The New Negro, *56.*

gent's "Sahdji," a brief impressionistic sketch of an African girl, and Eric Walrond's "The Palm Porch," a short story set in the Caribbean. Similarly, all but
one of the poems here—Lewis Alexander's rendering of an African dance in
"Enchantment"—speak of black people's experiences in America. They thus
do little to demonstrate Locke's argument. Again, though, they are accompanied by visual texts that assert the connection between African Americans
and Africa: one of Reiss's Africanist designs appears at the end of Locke's
essay, and a drawing by Douglas opens the selection of fiction. Douglas's
"Meditation" offers a peaceful scenario by the banks of a river with African-
looking huts in the background (see fig. 5.10). It faces the opening page of
Fisher's "City of Refuge," establishing an Africanist context for a story set entirely within Harlem. The connection asserted by the visual text, then, is not
apparent in the fiction or the poems.

Most of the essays in the second section of the book, "The New Negro in
a New World," focus, as do the short stories and poems, on black people in
America. They thus do little to assert a connection between African Americans and Africa. In fact, Melville Herskovits's "The Negro's Americanism," a
reprint of his essay from the *Survey Graphic* issue, goes even further than
this. Herskovits argued that black people were so integrated into American
culture that no differences between black and white Americans existed. In
other words, Herskovits asserted that there was no significant connection
between African Americans and Africa. The visual texts reproduced with his

essay tell a different story, though: the essay opens and closes with Reiss's Africanist drawings, which imply a connection between African Americans and Africa that directly contradicts Herskovits's essay. Similar designs appear throughout the section, even though the essays are on topics like the significance of cities like Harlem and Durham as centers for African American life, the importance of African American universities like Howard, Hampton, and Tuskegee, and the challenges that face African Americans as they move from the South to the North and become more upwardly mobile. In short, these are topics that have no explicit connection to Africa.

The visual texts in the book, in sum, run throughout the written texts, implying a link to Africa even when one is not present in the content of the written texts. The effect is a sense that Locke is forcing texts to fit his argument about the link between African Americans and Africa. His use of Africa as a factor that unites African Americans seems imposed; as an aspect of African American identity, the connection to Africa seems far more contested than agreed upon. If there is a unity based on that connection, then, it is a tenuous unity at best.

Furthermore, the extent to which Reiss's portraits define a simple "type" of New Negro is complicated by the book's attention to multiple identities within African American identity. The book shows, for example, the complexity and range of experiences even within the members of the African American elite. Even Reiss's portraits show African Americans in a variety of professions: he depicted editors, writers, activists, educators, musicians, and an actor—and some of his subjects fit into more than one of these categories. The contributors to the volume comprise an expanded group of elites: they reflect the variety within the elite in terms of age, profession, and interests. For example, all of the short stories and most of the poems reproduced here are written by members of the younger generation, including Fisher, Toomer, Cullen, Zora Neale Hurston, Claude McKay, and Langston Hughes. But the essays of the volume are written by the established elders, with William Stanley Braithwaite, Charles Johnson, James Weldon Johnson, Kelly Miller, Moton, and Du Bois being the most notable. The subjects of their contributions range from Harlem to Durham; from the new generation of African American writers to writers from the past; from African art to African American folklore; from "The Negro's Americanism" to "Gift of the Black Tropics" and "Worlds of Color." If the contributors embody through their own identities and interests a definition of the elite of the race, then, that definition is incredibly complex. The contents of the book and the identity of the people who contributed these texts thus demonstrate that even the African American elite cannot be thought of as a simple, homogenous group of people.

In addition, the book also draws attention to the significance of the African American folk. This takes place both through Locke and other contributors' assertions of the importance of black folk culture but also through their comments about the role of the folk in the New Negro movement and through the four portraits by Reiss that focus on folk subjects. These references to "the folk" and to folk culture complicate the overall portrait of the New Negro, but they also allude to many different aspects of the lives of ordinary African Americans, and so they underline the diversity within the folk as well.

Locke himself drew attention to the folk in many of his essays. As early as the first paragraph of his "Foreword," for example, he posited the folk and folk culture as embodying African American identity: "Here in the very heart of the folk-spirit are the essential forces, and folk interpretation is truly vital and representative only in terms of these" (ix). In other words, what is truly characteristic of African American identity is sensed in the folk spirit and expressed through folk culture. Furthermore, Locke argued in "The New Negro" that it was "the masses" who demonstrated the characteristics of the New Negro, particularly the changes in attitude, and he argued that they, in the patterns of their lives, embodied the dramatic changes occurring among African Americans: "The migrant masses," he asserted, "shifting from countryside to city, hurdle several generations of experience at a leap" (4). Later in the same essay, he argued that it was "the rank and file who are leading, and the leaders who are following. A transformed and transforming psychology permeates the masses" (7). In short, it was the folk—the "masses" of ordinary African Americans—who played the primary roles in the transformations that characterized the New Negro movement, and it was their expression of their experiences, in the form of folk culture, that offered particularly clear recordings of those transformations.

Given that emphasis on the importance of the folk in the New Negro movement, it is not surprising that Locke included a good deal of literature that focuses on the folk. Fisher's story about King Solomon Gillis depicts the kinds of experiences that many African American migrants might have shared, while Hurston and Toomer, in the short stories they contributed to *The New Negro*, focused on the lives of African Americans still living in the South. Much of the poetry in the book likewise focuses on folk characters. All are left anonymous: the "brown boy" and "brown girl" who are praised in Cullen's poems could be any young Harlemites; in Hughes's "I Too," the speaker who is sent to the kitchen when company comes but dreams of a future when he will be included at the table could be any domestic worker; the lady who Anne Spencer praises in "Lady, Lady" could be any washerwoman, with her hands bleached white from her work. A more detailed portrayal of the folk appears in Willis Richardson's "Compromise: A Folk Play," which focuses on an African American family in Maryland. The changes in the attitude of the mother, Jane Lee, toward the white man who lives nearby, Ben Carter, demonstrate the increasing self-assertiveness Locke heralded in the New Negro. Seven years prior to the events of the play, Carter had been inadvertently responsible for the deaths of Jane's husband and one son, but at the beginning of the play Jane still is willing to be pleasant to him. However, when it becomes clear that Carter's son, Jack, has gotten Jane's daughter pregnant, and when Carter refuses to honor his promise to send Jane's other two children to school, Jane refuses to compromise with Carter any further. After her youngest son, Alec, breaks Jack's arm, Jane helps Alec escape certain punishment and vows to stand up to Carter herself. Up until that moment, Jane has been far more accommodating than Alec; Richardson thus depicts both the range of attitudes held by various members of the folk and the changes in attitude of some of the folk. These creative texts demonstrate that the folk are not a simple "type"; they also position the folk as demonstrations of Locke's arguments about the changes occurring within that group.

A number of texts in *The New Negro* also emphasize the significance of African American folk culture. In "American Negro Folk Literature," for example, Arthur Huff Fauset identified African American folktales as evidence of the influence of African culture on African Americans, as noted earlier. Fauset warned of the errors in method and content in Joel Chandler Harris's Uncle Remus stories, but he argued that a serious appreciation of folktales was merited by their formal qualities and by the insights they offer into African Americans' experiences and ways of looking at the world. Locke made a similar argument about African American folk music in "The Negro Spirituals." Locke, too, warned of the tendency to not fully understand African American folk culture, in this case because it was too easy to allow "the deceptive simplicity of Negro song" to mask its richness in themes and idioms of rhythm and harmony (200). Locke offered a history of the spirituals and attitudes toward them, and he mentioned their links to other forms of folk music, such as work songs, "shouts," and folk ballads (205). He closed by emphasizing that "it is in the interest of musical development itself that we insist upon a broader conception and a more serious appreciation of Negro folk song, and of the Spiritual which is the very kernel of this distinctive folk art" (210). The importance of these two arguments about African American folk culture is underlined by the fact that both are accompanied by transcriptions of examples of the art form in question. Following Fauset's essays are the transcriptions of the two folktales mentioned earlier; following Locke's essay on the spirituals are transcriptions of two folk songs (see fig. 5.11 for "Listen to de Lambs"). These transcriptions appear nearly at the

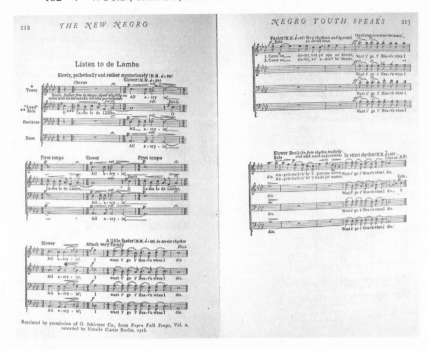

Fig. 5.11. The transcription of "Listen to de Lambs." *Locke, ed.*, The New Negro, 212–13.

center of *The New Negro;* their placement makes "the classical sound of Afro-America" the central element around which the rest of Locke's portrait grows (Baker 73).

With this emphasis on the importance of folk culture in mind, the presence of the folk as subjects for some of Reiss's portraits becomes more apparent and seems more significant. In particular, the importance of that portrait of "The Brown Madonna" should not be overlooked (see fig. 5.4). Like most of Reiss's portraits, it is in full color, on glossy paper stock. The bright blue of the woman's sweater and the clear white of the baby's dress capture the reader's attention. This type study of a mother and child, cast into the genre of religious iconology by the title, immediately asserts the spiritual side of Locke's New Negro. But because this Madonna and child are human figures, the portrait ties that spirituality to the human level. Mary as a historical figure was a poor woman whose child rose to become a lasting symbol of hope and redemption; the portrait hints that this New Negro, like Mary's new child, can bring about a new age. Furthermore, Mary, despite being a figure of adoration for centuries, has little space devoted to her in the New Testament. She is an individual about whom little is known. In some ways, then, she is in the same position as the New Negro: new texts need to be created that will provide information about her.[13] In that sense, the identity of this Madonna and child as black is particularly significant: this portrait is a rewriting of biblical history that casts black people as the central figures. The fact that this mother and child are presented in the same way that the folk are, finally, suggests the important role of the folk in the New Negro movement.

Reiss's portrait series in *The New Negro* also includes four other portraits of the folk. Three are portraits that appeared in the *Survey Graphic* issue: "From the Tropic Isles," "The Librarian," and "The School Teachers" are retitled reprints from the "Portraits of Negro Women" series (see fig. 4.7, 4.8, and 4.9). The fourth type study in *The New Negro* is "Ancestral": a smiling woman, wrapped in a blanket, sits in front of a patterned background (see fig. 5.5). The presence of these five portraits of anonymous African American women adds complexity to Reiss's series of portraits of intellectual and creative leaders: his New Negroes include the folk as well as the elite. The portraits of the folk, though outnumbered, seem significant, particularly because Locke, in his biographical notes on Reiss at the end of the volume, drew attention to Reiss's work with folk types, reprinting the description from the *Survey Graphic* issue that notes his work with "folk types" in Europe and the United States (419). Locke went so far as to describe Reiss as "a folk-lorist of the brush and palette, seeking always the folk character back of the individual" (419–20). This description of Reiss seemed more appropriate when it appeared alongside his work in the *Survey Graphic* issue, but here it allowed Locke to draw attention to an aspect of Reiss's work that he clearly felt was important: Reiss's depiction of the folk.

For readers who consider the portraits in detail, then, they offer a much more complicated definition of African American identity than a first glance might suggest. The fact that these portraits open up so many questions about the importance of the folk as well as the elite suggests the complexity that is embodied in the book as a whole. The effect of the attention to both the elite and the folk in *The New Negro* is that the nature of representativeness is thrown into question; rather than holding a few individuals—or even one class—as representative, Locke's volume offers an assertion that both are important and that they are interrelated. But all of that is masked, to some extent, by the degree to which a reader can flip through this book, locate the portraits of the elite men, and come away with a relatively simple, one-dimensional portrait of the New Negro. Offering a set of visual texts that can be read simplistically allowed Locke to offer a unified image of the New Negro; the fact that those texts also, when read more closely, hint at the complexities inherent in his definition of the New Negro suggests the degree to which Locke was simultaneously undermining the tendency to take such one-dimensional portraits as representative.

While that complexity in some ways undermines or complicates the unity asserted in the book, it in fact plays an important role in Locke's portrait of the New Negro. In fact, Locke drew attention to some of the conflicts within his book, which helped him raise readers' awareness of the complexity of collective identity and the limited perspective any one text might offer.

For instance, there are disagreements about the importance of the elite and the folk even within Locke's own essays. Locke complicated his own assertion of the significance of the folk when he repeatedly emphasized the role of the elite in the New Negro movement. In "The New Negro," for example, he argued that a major shift in thinking had occurred among all African Americans, but that it was only fully appreciated by the elite: "The multitude perhaps feels as yet only a strange relief and a new vague urge, but the thinking few know that in the reaction the vital inner grip of prejudice has been broken" (4). Locke continued to emphasize the importance of the elite when he wrote, a few pages later, that if improved race relations were going to occur, the elites of both races had to come into contact:

> mutual understanding is basic for any subsequent coöperation and adjustment. The effort toward this will at least have the effect of remedying in large part what has been the most unsatisfactory feature of our present stage of race relationships in America, namely the fact that the more intelligent and representative elements of the two race groups have at so many points got quite out of vital touch with one another. (8–9)

These "more intelligent and representative elements" of African Americans in this comment seem to be the African Americans who most demonstrate the characteristics of the New Negro, despite the evidence in other texts that it is the folk who fill that role. Furthermore, Locke's comment that "No sane observer, however sympathetic to the new trend, would contend that the great masses are articulate as yet" reinforces the sense that it was these "new intellectuals" who were the most representative New Negroes (7). This assertion also throws doubt onto the significance posited elsewhere for African American folk culture. In short, even Locke's own comments send multiple—and sometimes conflicting—messages about the role of the folk in relation to the role of the elite. But rather than being evidence of flaws in Locke's thinking or in the coherence of the book, these contradictory messages suggest the complexity of African American identity and the difficulty of pinning down the most distinctive aspects of that collective identity.

Similarly complicated messages are sent by other texts in *The New Negro*. For example, Locke in his essay "The New Negro" emphasizes the changes occurring among African Americans; it is followed by Albert Barnes's primitivist "Negro Art and America," in which the art collector argued that African Americans had inherited certain characteristics from their African ancestors and that these remained unaltered in the 1920s (19). It seems odd that Locke included both essays, and even more odd that he printed them right next to one another. But the juxtaposition sends an important message: it reminds readers that they should not base their assumptions on one portrait of African Americans; instead, they should consult a number of texts—or at least keep in mind that any one text presents only one possible representation of African Americans. If readers apply that message to *The New Negro* as a whole, they might realize that, to the extent that its texts fuse into one coherent, overall portrait of African Americans, they should be skeptical of Locke's definition. Perhaps they too should seek out additional texts, in order to get a fuller understanding of African Americans.

Perhaps surprisingly, rather than denying this possibility and leading readers to assume that *The New Negro* was definitive and accurate, Locke drew readers' attention to other texts that might complement or even complicate his portrayal of African Americans. He made a bibliography the final text of the book, thus encouraging readers to learn more about black people in America and around the world. The *Survey Graphic* had included a short bibliography; this is a much expanded version of that—so expanded, in fact, that it was "the most comprehensive to appear since Du Bois', published by Atlanta University early in the century. It was to remain the best available until Alain Locke's subsequent updating of it in the early Thirties in an American Library Association publication" (Long 19). The bibliography opens with information about the contributors to this volume, including impressive information about the background and accomplishments of these notable African American writers, artists, and intellectuals and the few whites who also contributed. Even more importantly, though, the bibliography continues with a list of sources of information about African Americans and African American culture. Included are "Negro Americana and Africana," early books by black people; "The Negro in Literature," more recent books by black and white writers that feature black characters; "Negro Drama," plays about black life; "Negro Music," a list of collections and arrangements of spirituals and folk songs, as well as commentaries about folk music and a list of American and European music influenced by black themes and idioms; "Negro Folk Lore," collections and analyses of folktales, customs, and so on; and "The Negro Race Problems," a list of sociological, historical, and international studies. These lists allow readers of *The New*

Negro to continue their study of black people; their extensiveness is evidence of the wealth of material produced by black people in the United States and the importance of their cultural contributions. These lists also ensure that *The New Negro* is merely a starting point for readers, the first step in growing knowledge about and understanding of African Americans.

The New Negro, then, has the potential to make readers more critical consumers of images. If readers leave the book armed with an awareness of the constructedness of racial categories and the limits of representation, they might respond differently the next time they are faced with a one-sided depiction of African Americans. Rather than being persuaded by that image, they might be more likely to question its assumptions and be aware of its shortcomings. Raising readers' consciousness makes the project of redefining African Americans more difficult for African Americans, too: they cannot simply present one image and hope it would change minds. But given the prevalence of racist images in the 1920s, they probably never could. Raising readers' awareness of the need to consult many texts, then, was a logical and potentially successful strategy for them. And, as a book like *The New Negro* shows, they certainly were able to produce a plethora of texts depicting African Americans.

It is important to note, though, that there are flaws and shortcomings in the book. It does reflect a number of unfortunate hierarchies and omissions that add problematic dimensions to its portrayal of African Americans. The most significant of these have to do with its treatment of women and of class. While the book's inclusion of texts by women and its attention to the importance of the African American folk are significant, both are undermined by a certain level of elitism and sexism. Furthermore, there are a number of omissions that render the portrait of African Americans incomplete in troubling ways.

On the issue of the representation of women in *The New Negro,* it is particularly significant that most of Reiss's portraits are of the male elite: of Reiss's ten portraits, only two are of women, McDougald and Bethune. The fact that the portraits draw more attention to African American men than women suggests that it was the male elite, and not the female, who played the most important roles in the emergence and the development of the New Negro. This implication is complicated by the fact that it is the Madonna figure who opens the book and by the fact that there are six images of African American women, but there are important differences between how men and women are shown. Each of the male subjects of Reiss's work is identified by name, and their portraits all are reproduced in full color. Of the women, only McDougald and Bethune are identified by name. The other women portrayed are Reiss's "types" and remain anonymous. Furthermore, only McDougald, Bethune, the Madonna figure, and the "ancestral" woman are portrayed in color. The fact that the portraits of the woman from the tropic isles, the librarian, and the teachers appear in black and white implies that they are less important than the other subjects. In addition, if the Madonna in the frontispiece portrait "gives life to succeeding generations" (Baker 79), the woman is relegated to a nurturing role. The child she raises will become the articulate and creative New Negro of the future. Women's work as mothers certainly is important, but to frame women in this way masks the important roles African American women played in the New Negro movement and the importance of their own creative and editorial work.[14]

This sense that certain people play more important roles in the New Negro movement than others also holds true for class, and the implications about class also complicate the implications about gender. While McDougald and Bethune are presented the way the elite men are—named rather than as anonymous types—most of the elite whom Reiss portrays are men. On the other hand, all of his type studies are of women, and the representatives of the folk are likewise female. The implication of these images, then, is that it is men who fill most of the black elite and women who comprise the bulk of the folk. Even with the portraits of African American women, *The New Negro* does not record fully their importance in the renaissance of African American culture or fully register their roles in the changes that the race had gone through and those that the future held in store. The use of exclusively male pronouns to refer to the New Negro throughout the book furthers this impression, as does the fact that women do not receive a great deal of space or attention in its written texts. Locke did include fiction by Hurston; poetry by Spencer, Georgia Johnson, and Angelina Grimke; and essays by McDougald, Jessie Fauset, and Helene Johnson, but these seven women are far outnumbered by the twenty-nine men whose work Locke also included. Furthermore, only McDougald's essay, "The Task of Negro Womanhood," a retitled and expanded version of the one in the *Survey Graphic* issue, focuses specifically on women's issues. The portraits thus send a message about race leadership that is upheld by the selection of texts in the rest of the volume: that elite black men are the leaders of the race, while women and the folk are in secondary roles.

The differences between the portraits of the folk and the elite also raise questions about class hierarchies in *The New Negro*. There are significant differences in Reiss's depictions of the elite and the folk, in terms of their mood and their physical presences. Again, Locke's portrait is typical of

Reiss's presentation of the elite. As are all of the other intellectuals portrayed by Reiss, Locke is solemn, staring out of his portrait with intensity. It is as if the role of these individuals as representatives is a heavy burden, which impresses upon them a certain seriousness. Furthermore, as he does with Locke, Reiss only sketches in their clothes, while he devotes much more detailed attention to their hands and heads. The effect emphasizes their role as intellectuals and as creators of texts. Reiss's "Ancestral" is a marked contrast to this (see fig. 5.5). This woman smiles broadly, as if her connection with her past has brought joy to her. Her mood is much more typical of the spirit that Locke describes as part of the New Negro movement; it is interesting, then, that it is one of the folk, and particularly one of the folk who shows her connection to the past, who demonstrates this characteristic. Furthermore, her body is at least visible behind the blanket she wraps around herself, as is the body of the librarian (see fig. 4.8) and as are those of the public schoolteachers (see fig. 4.9). Although it really is the clothes, rather than the bodies, that Reiss detailed in these portraits, these figures have a physical presence that the elite do not have. If detailing the heads and hands of the elite emphasized their intellectual capabilities, the greater attention to the bodies of the folk suggests the importance of their physical presence. This might be positive: perhaps the folk have their intellectual and their physical presences much more balanced than the elite. But this style of representation might also be more negative, if it identifies the folk as physical, manual laborers without intellectual capabilities. Locke's comment in "The New Negro" that the masses remained inarticulate makes this reading more likely. The portraits of the folk and the elite in *The New Negro*, then, suggest an unfortunate degree of class bias.

The book also reflects a number of omissions. For example, it includes very little attention to the blues. Locke mentioned the blues briefly in his essay on the spirituals, and J. A. Rogers linked the blues to jazz in his essay on the latter. But given the popularity of the blues in the 1920s and the emergence of a number of African American recording companies that specialized in the blues, the relative lack of attention to the blues seems an odd omission.[15] Critics of the book have tended to read this omission as evidence of Locke's elitism. That might be an overstatement, given that it conflicts with Locke's attention to the folk and to other aspects of black folk culture, but it does raise questions about why Locke would have left out the blues. Locke also mentioned Marcus Garvey only in passing. This is another odd omission, particularly given Locke's emphasis on the changes in attitude among African Americans and the link between African Americans and Africa. Certainly Garvey's mass movement could have been used as an example of both. But given that Garvey was serving prison time for mail fraud by the time Locke edited this book, perhaps Locke did not want to associate the New Negro with Garvey.

Locke also failed to address issues of sexuality in *The New Negro*. This implies that sexuality was not an important aspect of African Americans' lives in the 1920s. Perhaps Locke wanted to avoid the association of sexuality with the New Negro as a way of counteracting the emphasis on sexuality in so many portrayals of African Americans and of Harlem in popular culture. But leaving explicit discussions of sexuality out of the book adds another level of incompleteness to Locke's portrayal. It also renders invisible the fact that so many of the participants in the Harlem Renaissance were homosexual, including Locke.[16] The only way in which sexuality is addressed in the book is through the fact that many of the characters in its stories and poems are married, are parents, or give voice to their attraction to members of the opposite sex. In effect, the presence of these heterosexual relationships and the absence of any acknowledgment of homosexual relationships normalize heterosexuality and keep homosexuality hidden.

There are many other omissions in *The New Negro*. For example, there is little attention to economic conditions in Harlem, to racism against African Americans, or to the political and social efforts of African Americans to fight their mistreatment. Certainly each of these omissions can be logically explained; each, somehow, conflicts with Locke's portrayal of African Americans in the 1920s. But realizing that these points are missing from his portrayal is an important step that draws our attention to the fact that, despite the complexity and the scope of Locke's book, his definition of African American identity should be seen as only partial. Furthermore, the omissions reveal that, in order to offer unified and unifying definitions of African American identity, Locke left certain aspects of the complexity of African American identity hidden. Being aware of these omissions, we are more aware of the need to look elsewhere to complete our portrait.

What, then, do we understand about African American identity as we finish *The New Negro*? The answer is complicated, in a number of ways. It is clear that to see African Americans as a race, the category must be understood to be one that contains very different groups of people. While Locke started the book as if it would offer a definitive portrait, he ended it not with a sense of completion but with directions for further study. He drew readers in by apparently offering a simplistic vision of "The New Negro"— as if one such being existed—but through the book he showed the extent to which no such simplistic representation is possible. The irony of the book, then, is that it prevents any easy definitions or simplistic generalizations. And that, in fact, is perhaps the most significant way Locke worked against racism, a belief system that is based on monolithic stereotypes and generalizations.

Locke's inclusion of conflicting representations of African Americans leads to the establishment of the New Negro as a "type" that includes many different types, folk and elite, male and female. Locke's mix of texts obviously is crucial to the demonstration of the complexity of African Americans as a group. His juxtaposition of so many texts and so many kinds of texts allows him to replace simplistic images of African Americans and African American culture with complicated ones that resist easy generalizations. Although Locke demonstrates conflicting aspects of African American identity, those conflicts do not fragment the asserted unity of African Americans but suggest that African American identity has an integral nature despite those conflicts. Locke's ability to show both the unity and the diversity of African American identity is a reminder that identity politics can be practiced in constructive ways. It is possible to define collective identities, *The New Negro* shows, in ways that avoid simple essentializing and instead send "multiple, and often strategic, critical, complex and contradictory" messages about the identity in question—particularly if a work "holds in productive tension both identity and difference" (Franklin 15).

The hierarchies and omissions of the volume do, however, remind us of the difficulty of struggling against one form of oppression without contributing to others—and the need to consult many texts before we begin to assume that we understand the identity in question. The collaborative, multi-genre format of *The New Negro* reveals the usefulness of anthologies for defining collective identities, because even within their pages they include so many different texts. And the degree to which Locke invited us to look beyond its pages, and drew attention to the conflicts within the book, pushes us to look at other representations of African Americans in the 1920s. The editors, writers, and artists who worked in the wake of *The New Negro* in many cases picked up on the aspects of African Americans' lives that were left out of Locke's book and developed alternative or complementary portraits of the race. Their work reveals, even more than *The New Negro* does, the need to look at many definitions of African American identity from the period.

6

The Importance of Multiple Identities: *Fire!!* as an Avant-garde Arts Magazine

In 1926, the younger generation of African American writers, artists, and editors to whom Locke had dedicated *The New Negro* responded to his portrait of the New Negro with a portrait of their own. Led by editor Wallace Thurman, they published what they meant to be the premier issue of a magazine, *Fire!! A Quarterly Devoted to Younger Negro Artists*. The status of *Fire!!* as an independent publication, free of the controlling interests of an organization like the NAACP or the NUL, allowed contributors to launch vicious attacks on their elders and to include controversial subject matter. They used written and visual texts to create a space where African American writers and artists could present images that were dramatically different from the images included in *The Crisis, Opportunity,* the *Survey Graphic* issue, or *The New Negro. Fire!!,* in fact, is a critique of the ideas about African American identity and about representation communicated in these and other collaborative illustrated volumes published during the Harlem Renaissance. Thurman and the other contributors used the written and visual texts of *Fire!!* to break away from the African American "intelligentsia," who they found too conservative in their representations of African Americans, too insistent on the idea of using art as a political and social tool, and too obsessed with the idea of race. Objecting to the oppressive aspects of these beliefs, contributors to *Fire!!* used essays, statements, short stories, poems, plays, and drawings to critique their conservative elders and to offer their own collective definition of African American identity.

Unfortunately, *Fire!!* came to a quick end; its first issue was its last. But *Fire!!* adds significantly to the portrait of African Americans that emerged during the 1920s, and its contributors engaged with the issues of representation and identity in ways not seen in other collaborative illustrated volumes produced as part of the movement. The inclusion in *Fire!!* of texts that draw attention to aspects of African Americans' experiences ignored elsewhere—

most importantly, sexuality—complicates the definition of African American identity offered during the Harlem Renaissance. In addition, the format of *Fire!!* as an independent magazine demonstrates the engagement by African Americans with yet another strategy of representation. Finally, *Fire!!* echoes, in style and content, a number of periodicals published during the 1910s and 1920s that were part of the white American avant-garde, suggesting that the avant-garde became a model for this younger generation of African American writers and artists. The similarities between white avant-garde publications and *Fire!!* also have implications for the concepts of identity suggested by *Fire!!:* contributors' use of these magazines as models implies that racial identity was less important than shared ideologies in their choice of precursors. It suggests that for contributors, their status as artists and their beliefs were as important—if not more so—than their racial identity to their collective self-definition.

At the same time, many of the texts in *Fire!!* do insist on the significance of racial identity to their creators or their characters. In that sense, *Fire!!* is different from most publications of the white avant-garde. The significance of race in the subtitle of the issue and many of its texts suggests that if contributors were linking themselves to the avant-garde, they were establishing an explicitly African American avant-garde. Thus, while the white avant-garde provided a model for this group of younger African American writers and artists, they expanded that model to make it their own. In short, *Fire!!* was an attempt to carve out a wholly independent space for an African American avant-garde, set apart from both the black intelligentsia and the white avant-garde. It demonstrates both the advantages and the difficulties of finding a position between those two movements.

The position of *Fire!!* as both related to and independent from both the New Negro movement and the white avant-garde parallels the messages sent about identity in its pages. Most importantly, the contents of the creative texts in *Fire!!* reflect an ambiguity about the significance of race. The racial identity of characters is significant only in some texts; in others, it is less important than their nationality, gender, sexual orientation, or ideology. On the whole, then, the creative texts in *Fire!!* treat race as one aspect of identity, one that intersects with other aspects. Where other collaborative illustrated volumes published during the Harlem Renaissance tend to privilege one aspect of African Americans' identity—their Americanness in the *Survey Graphic* issue or their racial identity in *The New Negro,* for example—*Fire!!* resists this privileging: it draws attention to race and nationality and gender and sexuality and class and age and location and ideology. In emphasizing so many different aspects of African Americans' identity, it illuminates the limited nature of the definitions of African American identity in other work of the period. Its innovative and unique assertions about the complications of African American identity set it in line with the insights of critical theorists of the 1990s; it demonstrates concepts of identity that would be fully articulated only seventy years after its demise. *Fire!!,* then, demands consideration.

Fire!! is only now beginning to receive regard from scholars of the Harlem Renaissance. Before 1982, few devoted much attention to the magazine, perhaps partly because of the scarcity of copies of its only issue.[1] When the Fire!! Press reprinted the issue in 1982, it became far more easily accessible. Still, it has not received the full analysis it deserves.[2] Furthermore, those scholars who have written about *Fire!!* have not addressed the mix of written and visual texts in the magazine or its relation to white avant-garde magazines of the 1910s or 1920s. A reassessment of the volume, especially of the interactions among the different kinds of texts, recovers its distinctive contributions to the debates of the period about representations of African Americans and about African American identity. *Fire!!* demonstrates the usefulness of strategies of representation used in avant-garde little magazines for communicating ideas about African Americans, raises questions about the importance of race as a category, and suggests benefits and consequences of establishing a collective group identity that reflects the many aspects of identity that might affect the experiences of an individual.

Fire!! also offers insights into the realities of publishing during the Harlem Renaissance. The magazine was both devoted to and produced by the "younger Negro artists." "Artists" here refers both to writers and visual artists: the contents of the magazine comprise both written texts and illustrations. These texts were compiled by an editorial board that included a number of the period's most noteworthy young African American writers and artists: Thurman, Langston Hughes, Gwendolyn Bennett, Richard Bruce Nugent, Zora Neale Hurston, and Aaron Douglas.[3] Nugent, reminiscing about the magazine in 1982, attributed the idea for the magazine to Hughes and asserted that Hughes was "always guiding unobtrusively" at meetings ("Lighting FIRE!!"). But it was Thurman who was identified in the table of contents as the primary editor, and it was Thurman who incurred the bulk of the debt for the printing costs. Thurman also contributed both the short story "Cordelia the Crude" and an editorial about critics' responses to Carl Van Vechten's recently published novel, *Nigger Heaven.* The other editors also contributed creative texts to the forty-eight-page issue: Hughes published two poems in *Fire!!;* Bennett contributed the short story "Wedding Day"; Hurston published the short story "Sweat" and the play "Color Struck";

Nugent added two drawings and "Smoke, Lilies and Jade," the opening section of what was meant to be a novel; and Douglas contributed three drawings, a number of "incidental art decorations," and the cover design. Other contributors included Arthur Huff Fauset, who wrote an attack on the black "intelligentsia" for the magazine, and six other poets whose work appeared with Hughes's in a section of poetry called "Flame from the Dark Tower." Put together, the texts form a vibrant, multi-media, and multi-genre whole. In its inclusion of a mix of texts by African American writers and artists, *Fire!!* is similar to the other collaborative illustrated volumes produced during the Harlem Renaissance, but the texts in *Fire!!* offer a very different picture of African Americans than did the volumes edited by Du Bois, Johnson, or Locke.

That difference in content was part of the point. Two aspects of Thurman's desire to publish *Fire!!* were his skepticism about the idea that art could and should change perceptions of African Americans and his concerns about what he saw as the dangers of such beliefs, particularly in terms of the limits they placed on the creative work of writers and artists. Thurman wrote in *Harlem,* the magazine he published briefly after *Fire!!* folded, that many of the editors of African American magazines were "intoleran[t] of new ideas," which left the artist who did not follow the old ideas "without a journalistic asylum" ("Editorial" 21). His vision for *Fire!!* was that it would be a place where African American writers and artists could publish high-quality work regardless of whether it fit particular social or political criteria.[4] In that sense, the status of *Fire!!* as an independent magazine, one with no connections to a larger governing body, was crucial. That status gave the editors complete control over its contents; they were under no obligation to exclude texts that did not fit a particular notion of what literature or art should be like or what it should show about African Americans.

But the independence of *Fire!!* also had a disadvantage: with no sponsoring organization to offer financial assistance, the editorial board of the magazine had to shoulder the responsibility of securing funds for the magazine. Each editor pledged to contribute $50 toward the cost of the first issue and to provide subscribers and patrons (Hughes, *The Big Sea* 236; van Notten 151). The issue boasts a list of nine sponsors, indicating that they had some success in gathering support. However, the issue includes only two advertisements, one for *The New Masses* and the other for *Opportunity.* Certainly coming up with more ads or more patrons would have been helpful. Instead, the editors of the magazine collectively took on about $700 in debt (van Notten 151). Thurman signed for the delivery of the 500 magazine copies, so he carried the largest share of the financial burden (van Notten 151–52). He hoped to recoup that money through sales of the issue, but when many of the copies of the issue were, ironically, destroyed in a fire before they could be distributed or sold, he lost that opportunity. Few of his collaborators could meet their obligations to him; only three of the editors met their initial $50 pledge (Hughes, *The Big Sea* 236). Hughes and Hurston contributed additional funds, sending the proceeds of some of their work to Thurman (van Notten 154). Despite his own financial loss, Thurman wanted badly to produce a second issue, as he wrote in a letter to Hughes (qtd. in van Notten 153). But the editorial board scattered, both geographically and in interest, and Thurman had a hard time getting the original editors to contribute their time and energy to the magazine (van Notten 153–55). *Fire!!* itself came to an end. A second issue, planned for April 1927, never materialized.

The reception of the magazine cemented its failure. A few critics responded to it in positive terms, including the anonymous writer of "A Challenge to the Negro," who hoped that *Fire!!* would be "the thing [the Negro artist] needs to keep his artistic individuality," and that it would awaken in that artist "some sense of his own inimitable worth" (259). Robert Kerlin wrote that he saw *Fire!!* as "fire new, as the saying goes, and . . . worthy to continue flaming," and he emphasized its originality (284). But there were more negative than positive reviews, and the negative ones were more damning than the positive ones were laudatory. Thurman, in "Negro Artists and the Negro," remembered the vicious reviews in the press rather than the positive ones. He cited "a store of suppressed invective" that was unleashed against the editors of the magazine, quoting one particularly nasty review: "Under the heading 'Writer Brands Fire as Effeminate Tommyrot,' a reviewer in one of the leading Negro weeklies said: 'I have just tossed the first issue of Fire— into the fire, and watched the cackling flames leap and snarl as though they were trying to swallow some repulsive dose'" (37).[5] Benjamin Brawley in his review found *Fire!!* offensive because of its grammar, its vulgarity, and what he saw as a lack of mastery of technique on the part of its contributors; he declared "that if Uncle Sam ever finds out about it, it will be debarred from the mails" (183).

This harsh criticism might have been expected, given that Thurman and his collaborators included equally harsh critiques of the African American elite in their magazine. The worse fate for them was obscurity, which was what other critics seemed to give them. Only a few white publications reviewed *Fire!!*, and a number of African American periodicals denied *Fire!!* their attention. Hurston, Hughes, Bennett, and Thurman were invited to read at a tea at the Civic Club on January 2, 1927 (Hemenway 50; van Notten 151), but a one-paragraph note was the only review of the magazine that was published in *The Crisis.* That note was particularly bland, too: it described the magazine as an example of fine printing and mentioned nothing about its content ("The Looking Glass: Literature" 158). Privately, apparently, Du Bois felt only contempt for the magazine. Journalist Fred Bair wrote to Countee Cullen about Du Bois's reaction to it: "I was so indiscreet as to mention Thurman and Fire!! the first thing out of the box when I went to see Du Bois. It hurt his feelings so much that he would hardly talk to me" (qtd. in van Notten 151). Perhaps Du Bois's strategy was to avoid talking about the issue, in hopes that interest in it would die away quickly.

That seems to be what happened. Thurman turned his attention to his new magazine, *Harlem,* which he determined would be much less controversial than *Fire!!,* open to "everything and everybody regardless of age, race, or ideology" (van Notten 158). Describing it to Claude McKay, he wrote that he meant it to "appeal to all" (qtd. in van Notten 159). But he was able to publish only two issues of *Harlem* before that magazine, too, went out of business. Despite the lessons he had learned from *Fire!!,* Thurman could not get a magazine off the ground. But his publishing efforts, and their failure, illuminate a number of points. First, Thurman's goals for *Fire!!* make clear that he and other young writers and artists were frustrated with the prescriptions of the "intelligentsia." *Fire!!* draws our attention to the negative effect of the optimism of the Harlem Renaissance: the hope that art would contribute to social change resulted in pressures that were strongly felt by writers and artists who had different ideas. Second, *Fire!!* demonstrates the fierce commitment of these writers and artists to publish a magazine that would allow for a wider range of perspectives. They clearly felt a need for such a magazine, and they showed great initiative in attempting to launch it themselves. But the difficulties they encountered underline the financial realities of such an endeavor. It's one thing to announce a commitment to art for art's sake, but it's another thing to be able to pay for it. Editorial freedom, it seems, came with too high a price for the younger generation of African American artists and writers of the Harlem Renaissance.

As the volume in which these younger writers and artists defined themselves, *Fire!!* is the manifestation of their ideas about representation and identity. If the New Negro movement is characterized by the desire to use literature and art to change perceptions of African Americans, *Fire!!* is an attempt to turn the movement in a new direction. Rather than linking the arts to social change, the creators of *Fire!!* used the arts to expand what was shown about African Americans. Similar efforts to change the focus and goals of white American literature were under way among members of the white avant-garde, and the ideological parallels between *Fire!!* and the white avant-garde reveal the distance between its creators and their African American elders, as well as the affinities between them and the white avant-garde.

The contents of *Fire!!* reflect its contributors' rejection of the social and political goals of people like Du Bois or Charles S. Johnson and are in keeping with critiques of the movement they articulated elsewhere. Thurman was particularly critical of the New Negro movement, which he routinely dismissed as a fad for white publishers to make money. In a review of *The New Negro,* for example, he raised the question of "what this Negro literary renaissance has accomplished other than providing white publishers with a new source of revenue, affording the white intellectuals with a 'different' fad and bringing a half dozen Negro artists out of obscurity" (qtd. in West 78–79).[6] In an essay he published in 1927, he mocked the optimism of many in the movement that the texts of the period would undermine racism, writing with characteristic sarcasm, "Everyone was having a grand time. The millennium was about to dawn" ("Negro Artists and the Negro" 37). Clearly, he found the high hopes of the leaders of the New Negro movement foolish.

Thurman also worried that the ideals of the New Negro movement, particularly the link it emphasized between the arts and propaganda, had a negative impact on the quality of work produced by African American writers and artists. In a review of Walter White's novel *Flight,* for example, Thurman categorized White as "one of the most salient users" of art as propaganda and then launched a criticism of the tendency for those who link the two to neglect the demands of art. "All art no doubt is propaganda, but all propaganda is most certainly not art. And a novel must, to earn the name, be more than a mere social service report, more than a thinly disguised dissertation on racial relationships and racial maladjustments" ("A Thrush" 154). Generalizing about the merging of art and propaganda, Thurman wrote in another essay that "critical standards have been ignored" in the assessment of work by African Americans; "the measure of achievement has been racial rather than literary" ("Nephews" 296). He feared, in short, that the need for texts by African Americans meant that work not of the highest quality was being published.

Thurman also was concerned that the tendency during the Harlem Renaissance to encourage art to work as propaganda would lead to the censorship of representations of certain types of African Americans. Thurman believed that expecting art to work as propaganda required that various aspects of African American life be hidden from readers. To Thurman, this meant that the importance of parts of black America was denied. In contrast, Thurman wrote to a friend about the need to recover aspects of African Americans' lives that had been hidden. Describing the period as one of transition, he argued that in such periods people were "eternally discovering things about themselves and about their environment which it seems to them their elders have been at pains to hide" (qtd. in van Notten 141–42). Part of the point of *Fire!!* seems to have been to uncover those hidden things. In that sense, then, the attempt of the editorial board of *Fire!!* to break away from the African American elite was an attempt to bring about a kind of social change—not to undermine racism but to undermine the oppressiveness of conservative ideas about art and politics. Publishing *Fire!!* was an attempt to break away from those ideas and an assertion of the need for freedom in the portrayal of African Americans.

Actually, the most explicit statement of the attempts of the younger writers and artists to define themselves and assert their independence was published in *Nation,* not in *Fire!!*. But it was written in the months the editors worked on *Fire!!*, and it was written by Hughes, who was perhaps as central a figure as Thurman to the new magazine. Like Thurman, Hughes was resistant to the idea of art as propaganda, and he had concisely rejected the duty and responsibility of the artist in his April 1926 contribution to Du Bois's symposium, "The Negro in Art," in *The Crisis.* Hughes's statement begins, "What's the use of saying anything—the true literary artist is going to write about what he chooses anyway regardless of outside opinions" ("The Negro in Art" 278). For Hughes, then, the artist should be free to create, without the pressures of audience or concerns about effect to constrain him. He expanded on this point in an essay he published in *Nation* in June 1926, and his famous closing statement is an assertion of independence for young writers and artists:

> We younger Negro artists who create now intend to express our individual dark-skinned selves without fear or shame. If white people are pleased we are glad. If they are not, it doesn't matter. We know that we are beautiful. And ugly too. The tom-tom cries and the tom-tom laughs. If colored people are pleased we are glad. If they are not, their displeasure doesn't matter either. We build our temples for tomorrow, strong as we know how, and we stand on top of the mountain, free within ourselves. ("The Negro Artist and the Racial Mountain" 1271)

Hughes's proclamation put into words the beliefs reflected in *Fire!!*, that artists should create out of their own experiences, with full freedom of expression, and that art should not be held to social or political responsibilities. The creative texts in the magazine are similar declarations of independence from the previous generation.

The attitudes expressed in such texts echo the beliefs of the white avant-garde and hint at the role of that movement as a model for the creators of *Fire!!*. A group of young white writers and artists had defied "the genteel tradition" in American literature in the 1920s: their work is characterized by its iconoclasm, its aesthetic and political radicalism, and its rejection of the values of its predecessors. Their revolt was against the conservative and, to them, repressive elements of the genteel tradition that demanded that writers and artists glorify America; they insisted that writers portray the bad as well as the good of the nation's social and cultural life (Cowley 5–9). Members of the avant-garde included in their work frank sensuality, a justification of drunkenness, and "a revolt of the lower middle classes against the conventions that . . . prevented them from telling the truth about their world" (Cowley 16). With subtle differences, this description fits the protest against the African American elites in *Fire!!*. If the conservative elders in effect denied that certain aspects of African Americans' lives existed, Thurman and his collaborators proved them wrong by focusing on sensuality, but also sexuality—and homosexuality and bisexuality as well as heterosexuality. This revelation and description of proscribed activities is a version of the justification of drunkenness featured in the white avant-garde, and the insistence on the realities of such activities—as well as the focus on the folk, which had not so much been proscribed as eclipsed by the focus on the elite—became the way that the creators of *Fire!!* asserted the truths about African American lives that they refused to keep hidden.

The contributors to *Fire!!* may have seen these principles put into action in a number of avant-garde magazines published between the 1890s and the early 1920s.[7] Some of the most well known of these were published in England. One of the first was *The Yellow Book,* launched in 1894, about which one of the founders, Aubrey Beardsley, declared, "Our idea is that many brilliant story painters and picture writers cannot get their best stuff accepted in the conventional magazine, either because they are not topical or perhaps a little risqué" (qtd. in Bishop 288). Beardsley, who is most famous as a visual artist who illustrated a number of magazines, plays, and novels in the 1890s, emphasized that the criteria for inclusion in this magazine would be simply "the absolute rule of workmanship—value from the literary point of view" (qtd. in Bishop 288). This emphasis on quality—rather than content or adherence to a political or social ideology—was echoed in the statements of principles of many other avant-garde little magazines (Bishop 288). The role of such magazines as outlets for non-conformist work can also be seen in *BLAST,* which demonstrates other features that would be found in *Fire!!*. Published in London in 1914 and 1915, *BLAST* is striking for the violence it directs against the status quo, its long lists of things to either "blast" or "bless," and its use of typography as a graphic element (see fig. 6.1). Another significant feature of avant-garde magazines is a focus on topics that would have been quite shocking in the late 1800s and the early 1900s, such as lust, masturbation, and homosexuality. In the United States, avant-garde maga-

1

BLAST First (from politeness) **ENGLAND**

CURSE ITS CLIMATE FOR ITS SINS AND INFECTIONS

DISMAL SYMBOL, SET round our bodies,
of effeminate lout within.
VICTORIAN VAMPIRE, the LONDON cloud sucks
the TOWN'S heart.

A 1000 MILE LONG, 2 KILOMETER Deep

BODY OF WATER even, is pushed against us

from the Floridas, **TO MAKE US MILD.**

OFFICIOUS MOUNTAINS keep back DRASTIC WINDS

SO MUCH VAST MACHINERY TO PRODUCE

THE CURATE of "Eltham"
BRITANNIC ÆSTHETE
WILD NATURE CRANK
DOMESTICATED
POLICEMAN
LONDON COLISEUM
SOCIALIST-PLAYWRIGHT
DALY'S MUSICAL COMEDY
GAIETY CHORUS GIRL
TONKS

11

Fig. 6.1. A sample of the kind of typographical design typical of avant-garde arts journals like *BLAST.*

zines that followed these trends included *The Little Review,* edited by Margaret Anderson beginning in Chicago in 1914, and *The Quill,* a monthly magazine published in Greenwich Village starting in 1917 and touching on topics including free love, psychoanalysis, and socialism (Hoffman, Allen, and Ulrich 245, 252).

Fire!! is similar in many ways to these avant-garde journals, which also are often referred to as "little magazines." One definition of them could apply with no changes to *Fire!!*:

> Little magazines are by definition magazines that do not make money; they are trying to promote new ideas or forms of art, rather than sales. They are usually funded by a small group of supporters, and a few paying subscribers, and are created to provide an outlet for work that would not appear otherwise. The little magazine is always in an adversarial position with regard to the dominant culture, and when it loses that adversarial edge, or the enthusiasm of its backers, it dies. Thus most little magazines have a very short run. (Bishop 287)

Alain Locke, in his review of *Fire!!*, picked up on the links between such little magazines and *Fire!!* when he wrote that the "obvious artistic cousins" of the magazine included *The Little Review, The Quill,* and *This Quarter* ("Fire: A Negro Magazine" 563).[8]

In fact, Nugent, in his comments about the genesis of *Fire!!*, hinted at the influence of the white avant-garde on its contents: "Wally and I thought that the magazine would get bigger sales if it was banned in Boston. So we flipped a coin to see who wrote bannable material. The only two things we could think of that were bannable were a story about prostitution or about homosexuality" (qtd. in Kalaidjian 91). In the end, Thurman wrote a short story about a prostitute—"Cordelia the Crude"—and Nugent wrote a story about homosexuality—"Smoke, Lilies and Jade." Nugent may have mentioned Boston because that was where a vendor had been arrested for selling the April 1926 issue of H. L. Mencken's *The American Mercury*—significantly, because it included a story about a prostitute. Mencken got himself arrested in protest, and his widely publicized trial drew much attention to his magazine (van Notten 138). Thurman and Nugent hoped for similar attention, with the idea that it might boost sales. This recollection indicates that figures like Mencken provided particularly relevant models for the younger generation of African American intellectuals. In fact, younger black writers "saw a connection between [Mencken's] attack on the genteel tradition in American literature and their own warfare against genteel Negro culture" (Scruggs, *Sage in Harlem* 133). Mencken's iconoclasm, the contents of his magazine, and his response to efforts to censor *The American Mercury* provided the creators of *Fire!!* with strategies that they used to demonstrate the distance between themselves and the African American elite.

In fact, the avant-garde tone and contents of the texts in *Fire!!* are particularly clear signals of the distance between contributors and the leaders of the New Negro movement. The issue opens with a number of non-fiction texts that indicate contributors' revolt against the ideas of their elders and include obvious visual and rhetorical echoes of avant-garde publications.

Foreword

FIRE . . . *flaming, burning, searing, and penetrating far beneath the superficial items of the flesh to boil the sluggish blood.*

FIRE . . . *a cry of conquest in the night, warning those who sleep and revitalizing those who linger in the quiet places dozing.*

FIRE . . . *melting steel and iron bars, poking livid tongues between stone apertures and burning wooden opposition with a cackling chuckle of contempt.*

FIRE . . . *weaving vivid, hot designs upon an ebon bordered loom and satisfying pagan thirst for beauty unadorned . . . the flesh is sweet and real . . . the soul an inward flush of fire. . . . Beauty? . . . flesh on fire—on fire in the furnace of life blazing. . . .*

> *"Fy-ah,*
> *Fy-ah, Lawd,*
> *Fy-ah gonna burn ma soul!"*

Fig. 6.2. The foreword of *Fire!!* (1).

The written text on the "Foreword" page is the first to link the magazine to the avant-garde. It clearly establishes the revolutionary goals of the contributors to *Fire!!*, using the metaphor of fire to establish the destructive but invigorating ideals of its creators. Crucial among these is stirring those who had become lethargic to action, as is indicated in the first description of fire "flaming, burning, searing, and penetrating far beneath the superficial items of the flesh to boil the sluggish blood" (1). The opening repetition of gerunds is a call to action that is made even more clear in the second point, which sounds "a cry of conquest in the night, warning those who sleep and revitalizing those who linger in the quiet places dozing" (1). The next point includes the kind of destructive imagery typical of the military language of the avant-garde: it describes fire "melting steel and iron bars, poking livid tongues between stone apertures and burning wooden opposition with a cackling chuckle of contempt" (1). The language echoes avant-garde calls for violent challenges to the status quo and the destruction of existing ideologies. But in this case, what will be destroyed is the complacency of conservative African American elders like Du Bois; once their mental framework is in cinders, greater artistic freedom will be possible.

The foreword also echoes the avant-garde visually. Wavy lines scroll across the top and bottom of the page; the words are arranged on the page in a way that turns them into graphic elements (see fig. 6.2). The word "FIRE," followed by ellipses and repeated four times, is the only word that is set flush against the left margin. The words describing fire's violent actions are set in italics with a hanging indent, and the final three lines, the words from a spiritual, are set near the center of the page. On the following page, an appeal for financial support is presented in a more conservative layout, but it identifies the goals of the magazine in typical avant-garde fashion, calling it "a noncommercial product interested only in the arts" (2). This language implies a distancing of art from politics that both echoes the interests of the avant-garde and distances the editors from those like Du Bois, with his insistence that the arts should serve the purposes of propaganda.

The two essays that close the issue, Fauset's "Intelligentsia" and Thurman's "Fire Burns," use rhetoric that parallels that of the avant-garde. Fauset offered a scathing critique of the African American elite, particularly its ideas about leadership and representation. The half-brother of Jessie Fauset, he opened by labeling the intelligentsia one of the "doughty societies" of the era—others including the "Kluxers and Beavers"—from which "we all suffer" (45). He mocked the attitude of these self-appointed intellectual leaders:

> According to the ultra-advanced notions of the great majority of this secret order if it were not for the Intelligentsia this crippled old world would be compelled to kick up its toes and die on the spot. Were it not for these super-men all the brilliance of the ages and the inheritance which is so vital to the maintenance of the spark of progress would vanish and pass away. In other words if the Intelligentsia were to stick their divinely appointed noses a little higher into the ethereal regions and withdraw themselves completely from the tawdry field of life that field would soon become a burial ground for the rest of humanity. (45)

Fauset never identified his targets explicitly as the African American elite, but certainly his comments could be taken as criticism of the Talented Tenth mentality of people like Du Bois and Locke. To Fauset, it was high time to put an end to these "snobbish sycophantish highbrow hero-worshippers" (46). Significantly, Fauset's rhetoric echoes that of Mencken and his crowd, particularly in the title of "Ku Kluxers," a term that Mencken often used. Making the connection even more clear is the fact that Fauset mentioned Mencken as one of the "truly intellectual types . . . who are in every respect creative critics and thinkers" (46), in contrast to the sham intellectuals who merely read and take on the ideas of those true intellectuals.

Thurman's commentary on the reception of *Nigger Heaven* continues this attack. Du Bois and a number of other critics had responded to the book with various amounts of dismay or anger, believing that Van Vechten's portrayal of what Du Bois called the African American underworld would be taken as realistic by white readers and would reinforce their belief in stereotypes of African Americans. Thurman dismissed any such connection between literary representation and assumptions about African Americans, arguing that the response of critics like Du Bois had exposed their "inherent stupidity" ("Fire Burns" 47). Thurman emphasized that critics who panned the book did so because they felt it portrayed African Americans as "debased, lecherous creatures," instead of showing more representative types (47). Their fear, then, at least according to Thurman, was that white readers would assume that all blacks in Harlem were like Van Vechten's worst characters. Thurman found that ridiculous: "It is obvious that these excited folk do not realize that any white person who would believe such poppy-cock probably believes it anyway, without any additional aid from Mr. Van Vechten" (47). Furthermore, he cast doubt on the power of other kinds of images to change a reader's perceptions of African Americans: he argued that if a person were to read a novel with the more prescribed

> non-cabareting, church-going Negroes, presented in all their virtue and glory and with their human traits, their human hypocrisy and their human perversities glossed over, written, say, by Jessie Fauset, said person would laugh derisively and allege that Miss Fauset had not told the truth. . . . It really makes no difference to the race's welfare what such ignoramuses think. (47–48)

Such an attack parallels the satiric barbs Mencken so often published in *The American Mercury* and *The Smart Set*. Mencken began to work as a co-editor of *The Smart Set* in 1914, and its motto is typical of the tone he often took in his book reviews and columns: "One civilized reader is worth a thousand boneheads" (Fitzpatrick, "The Smart Set" 335). Mencken left *The Smart Set* and began to edit *The American Mercury* in 1924, and he filled the latter even more than the former with "irreverent commentary upon the American scene" (Fitzpatrick, "The American Mercury" 8). As had *The Smart Set, The American Mercury* included a feature called "Americana," in which the editors "reprinted items gleaned from magazines and newspapers published all across the land" and which was "[d]esigned to prove the imbecility of the American mind" (Fitzpatrick, "The Smart Set" 336; see also "The American Mercury" 9). In fact, satire and attacks became the prominent characteristic of *The American Mercury:* "more than one-third of the essays published between 1924 and 1929 lampooned some aspect of the American scene" (Fitzpatrick, "The American Mercury" 9). In effect, then, Mencken, through the rhetoric and tone he so often used, offered examples of social critique that the creators of *Fire!!* mimicked. The types of texts and the rhetoric modeled by Mencken and other avant-gardes proved to be useful tools with which they could distance themselves from the African American intelligentsia.

The link between *Fire!!* and the avant-garde and the break between the magazine and the New Negro leadership also is clear in the content of the creative texts in the magazine. The most obvious avant-garde element is the focus on sex and sexuality. Written and visual texts combine to draw attention to this aspect of black culture—an aspect that had been completely left out of other representations of the New Negro. Issues of sexuality appear nowhere in *The Crisis, Opportunity,* the *Survey Graphic* issue, or *The New Negro,* and homosexuality is unmentioned. The creators of *Fire!!* did much to bring it back into focus and to implicitly expose the limitations of the definition of African American identity that had been offered.

While sexuality plays a key role in a number of the texts throughout *Fire!!,* it is especially obvious in the magazine's opening texts. Sexuality is the first thing readers encounter when they move beyond the table of contents. It is visually announced on the page facing the opening of "Cordelia": Nugent's black-and-white drawing of a full-breasted woman, completely naked, languishing in front of a coconut tree, confronts the reader with nudity and sensuality (see fig. 6.3). Her short braids and the designs on the side of the picture give this a slightly Africanist focus; the effect of the Africanisms and the nudity is to draw the two together, to establish a connection between Africa and sensual pleasures. Another drawing follows the section of poetry. This is more of a side view, but the woman's nakedness again seems to be the point (see fig. 6.4). The contrast is stunning between these texts and the portraits by Winold Reiss in *The New Negro,* with their subjects clad in business suits and with their formal poses.

Thurman's story "Cordelia" also draws attention to sexuality. The story opens just after Cordelia and her family move to New York City from the rural South. In the South, Cordelia seemed innocent enough; she wanted

Fig. 6.3. The first of two drawings by "Richard Bruce Nugent" in *Fire!!* (4).

only to marry her boyfriend. But once in Harlem, where her parents are unable to control her and where temptations abound, she soon finds a place in what Du Bois would have called the underworld. Thurman offered his readers detailed descriptions of the setting and the characters of these places, as the narrator relates Cordelia's turn from a Harlem theater "chippie" into a prostitute. Thurman languished in the details of his characters, describing them in depth. For example, he gave a long portrait of the "embryo avenue sweetbacks," the men who prowl the aisles of the theaters in search of single women:

> with their well modeled heads, stickily plastered hair, flaming cravats, silken or broadcloth shirts, dirty underwear, low cut vests, form fitting coats, bell-bottom trousers and shiny shoes with metal cornered heels clicking with a brave, brazen rhythm upon the bare concrete floor as their owners angled and searched for prey. (5)

Further immersing his reader in the details of the scene, Thurman used a narrator who is both the distanced reporter of these details and a participant in this pick-up scene. Walking in behind Cordelia one night, he is drawn to her by the "conscious sway of invitation" of her hips, and he slides into the seat behind her (6). When he takes her out after the movies and heads for

Fig. 6.4. The second of Nugent's drawings in *Fire!!* (24).

sexual favors, climbing the run-down stairs of her tenement building with her, Thurman hinted at barely repressed sensuality in his description of their "animal kiss" at each landing (6). But on the last landing the narrator suddenly panics, throws two dollar bills at Cordelia, and flees. The final scene of the story completes the sexual implications, though: six months later, the narrator sees Cordelia at a party at a whore house, "savagely careening in a drunken abortion of the Charleston" (6). The scene is rich with details: the "chaotic riot of raucous noise and clashing color," the smoke hanging overhead, the "perspiring circle of handclapping enthusiasts," the languid slow drag Cordelia starts when she sees the narrator (6). It is clear that she has become a prostitute.

The story's focus on Cordelia's sexual activities marks its link to the avant-garde and its refusal to follow Du Bois's call for art as propaganda. Furthermore, the narrator's identity and his role in Cordelia's transformation reverse the idea that the elite are uplifting the masses. When the narrator appears at the whore house, one of the other girls asks Cordelia, "Who's the dicty kid?" and she replies, "The guy who gimme ma' firs' two bucks . . ." (6). The narrator, then, who with his sophisticated language could be one of Du Bois's talented tenth, is implicated as the perpetrator of her shift from a "potential prostitute" to a real one—he has initiated not her social rise but her downfall. But Thurman even criticized him in that role, leaving him the demasculinized "dicty kid" who was unable to carry through on his sexual pursuit. Cordelia faces him "without the least trace of emotion" (6); clearly he has become irrelevant to her life. In addition to showing aspects of African American life that Du Bois wanted to keep hidden, then, Thurman in this story implied that the African American elite is leading the masses in the opposite direction than what Du Bois might have asserted, if they have any impact on the lower classes of African Americans at all.

Sexuality also is the focus of Nugent's story "Smoke, Lilies and Jade." The story, "considered the first one to deal with black homosexuality" (Smith 214), is told in a fragmented form, full of ellipses that leave much to the reader's imagination. The central element of the story is Alex's relationship with Adrian, who he calls Beauty. They meet on the street, when Alex is walking home from a party, and the story includes descriptions of a number of their encounters.[9] Nugent's description of their first kiss is detailed and vivid, full of Alex's resistance and his pleasure. While Alex pretends to sleep, repressing his desires, Beauty wakes and hovers over him:

> Alex could feel Beauty's hair on his forehead . . . breathe normally . . . breathe normally . . . could feel Beauty's breath on his nostrils and lips . . . and it was clean and faintly colored with tobacco . . . breathe normally Alex . . . Beauty's lips were nearer . . . Alex closed his eyes . . . how did one act . . . his pulse was hammering . . . from wrists to finger tip . . . wrist to finger tip . . . Beauty's lips touched his . . . his temples throbbed . . . throbbed . . . his pulse hammered from wrist to finger tip . . . Beauty's breath came short now . . . softly staccato . . . breathe normally Alex . . . you are asleep . . . Beauty's lips touched his . . . breathe normally . . . and pressed . . . pressed hard . . . (37)

This long description is typical of the attention Nugent drew to his characters' homosexual intimacy and indicative of the magazine's emphasis on what would have been shocking material. Later in the story, Alex can admit his love of Beauty—although perhaps only to himself—but he also realizes that he does still love Melva, his girlfriend, and the story ends with his relieved realization that "one *can* love two at the same time," as, in his imagination and in his dreams, Melva and Beauty melt into one androgynous figure (39). Of course, this exploration of and languishing in sexual desire— and, in particular, homosexual and bisexual desire—was a direct affront to the conservative notions of propriety that governed ideas about socially and culturally responsible portrayals of African Americans. Du Bois had complained about the emphasis on heterosexual sexuality in portrayals of African Americans; bisexuality or homosexuality was an issue that he never even acknowledged. *Fire!!* answered that silence with a clear proclamation of acceptance.

The focus on sexuality here and in other creative texts also illuminates the links between the editors of *Fire!!* and white avant-gardes, given the attention among the avant-gardes to topics that would have broken out of the mold of respectability. Specific references to Mencken and other figures in the avant-garde make these connections even more clear. In "Smoke, Lilies and Jade," Alex repeatedly mentions Mencken as one of the people he knows. Oscar Wilde also is identified as someone whose work Alex's friends all have read and whom they discuss at length (34). When Alex's mother discredits his ambition to be an artist, he wonders if "Wildes' [*sic*] parents or Shelly's or Goya's talk to them like that" (34). Alex also repeatedly muses on the pleasure of smoking, on his absolute satisfaction with being "young and hungry and an artist" and doing nothing but blowing "blue smoke from an ivory holder" (35). Lying on his bed smoking becomes a symbol of Alex's decadence, which is even more clearly tied to Wilde when Alex wonders "was it Wilde who had said . . . a cigarette is the most perfect pleasure because it leaves one unsatisfied" (35). Wilde's commitment to art for art's sake probably resonated with the creators of *Fire!!*. For example, when he was asked about the controversial aspects of *The Picture of Dorian Gray,* he emphasized that literature should be judged according to its quality; he believed the question of morality was irrelevant (Foldy 10). The creators of *Fire!!* also may have admired him for his focus on controversial topics, in texts like *Dorian Gray* and the play *Salome.* Wilde's personal conduct also was controversial: he was accused of sodomy in 1895 and convicted of "acts of gross indecency between men," for which he served a two-year prison term (Foldy ix). His trials drew an enormous amount of attention, and, again, the creators of *Fire!!* may have hoped to achieve similar notoriety.

Nugent's illustrations also suggest the importance of the white avant-garde to the creators of *Fire!!*. Their sexual nature, of course, is again an echo of that focus in the avant-garde. Beardsley's illustrations are significant precursors: although he worked in a different style than Nugent, Beardsley stirred up a good deal of controversy with his emphasis on eroticism, which was considered by many to be pornographic and certainly shocking. Many of his illustrations of Wilde's *Salome,* for example, include naked men or women with bare breasts; his illustrations for other texts feature men with enormously exaggerated genitals.[10] Beardsley's use of female nudes is echoed in Nugent's depictions of naked figures. Nugent's illustrations, furthermore, are woodcuts, with large heavy areas of solid black. This style of illustration was popular among avant-garde little magazines of the 1920s. The cover of the February 1922 issue of *Broom,* a short-lived "international magazine of the arts" that published parts of Jean Toomer's *Cane* in 1923, is particularly telling: the figure thumbing his nose at tradition could easily be a metaphor for the attitude of the creators of *Fire!!* toward their elders.[11] The color scheme of the cover of *Fire!!* also is a visual echo of the avant-garde: the cover, with its title and designs in bright red and its black background, echoes the bright colors used so often on the covers of magazines like *BLAST*.[12] Even the type style used for the title on the cover, on the title page, and on the first page of "Cordelia" gives the magazine an avant-garde look, which is further reinforced by the wavy lines emanating from the title.

In short, then, there are many parallels between *Fire!!* and the white avant-garde and many breaks between *Fire!!* and the New Negro leaders. The creators of *Fire!!* certainly were familiar with Mencken and Wilde, as their explicit references make clear. Their consciousness of other white avant-gardes is less easy to establish, but the rhetoric, content, and visual texts in *Fire!!* are so similar to those found in white little magazines of the 1920s that it seems likely that these young Negro writers, artists, and editors knew the work of their white counterparts. In any case, *Fire!!* demonstrates how helpful the rhetoric and kinds of texts found in the avant-garde were for the articulation by these young African American writers, artists, and editors of a new identity for themselves, one that is independent from their African American elders.

But the contributors to *Fire!!* also moved beyond the usual focus of the white avant-garde in at least one important way: few of the publications of the white avant-garde addressed issues of racial identity. In the two issues of *BLAST*, for example, only one text—a short story by Rebecca West—refers at all to race. That text, furthermore, is full of essentializing comments about its black female character; it is hardly insightful or enlightening about black identity.[13] *The American Mercury* was an exception: Mencken opened its pages to African Americans, and it included discussions of "[e]very possible aspect of Negro culture" (Scruggs, *Sage in Harlem* 7). Otherwise, though, the contributors to *Fire!!* were breaking new ground when they used the techniques of the avant-garde to enter the discourse about racial identity. In addition, the contributors to *Fire!!* seem to have wanted to avoid the appearance of assimilation. They established themselves as independent of the New Negro movement, but they also specified that *Fire!!* was a distinctly black publication—so much so that the work of one potential contributor, Harvey Carson Crumbine, was dropped when it was discovered that he was white (van Notten 152–53). The identification of *Fire!!* as devoted to the Negro artist became an important part of the contributors' resistance to white American culture—a resistance they felt was lacking among the African American elite. In "Negro Artists and the Negro," for example, Thurman used Hughes's work to demonstrate the importance of focusing on the folk, "those people who had been the least absorbed by the quagmire of American Kultur" (37). Thurman's admiration for the folk, and his belief in the importance of literature focused on the folk, is clear in the contents of *Fire!!*. This publication may have been influenced by the example of white avant-garde little magazines, then, but it went beyond the typical content of those magazines to record African Americans' experiences and to offer texts that reflected African American identity.

Ideologically, then, *Fire!!* can be linked to the white avant-garde, but its attention to race as an important aspect of identity means that, in effect, *Fire!!* claims a place between the two poles of the New Negro movement and the white avant-garde. The fact that the magazine is both tied to and distanced from both movements is hinted at in its subtitle, its dedication to the "younger Negro artists." The three terms of this dedication suggest three different affiliations for contributors. Their status as artists, committed to art for art's sake and not for the sake of politics or social change, links them to the avant-garde on the basis of ideology. Their status as part of a younger generation suggests the split between them and their elders, the African American intelligentsia. But the status of contributors as "Negro artists" simultaneously links them to the New Negro movement on the basis of racial identity. If the identity of contributors to *Fire!!* includes all three of these elements, it seems logical to assume that at any given moment, any one of the three might take precedence. In effect, the multiple affiliations claimed by the creators of this magazine suggest an understanding of identity that incorporates various aspects of identity and that understands that the relations between those different aspects shifts according to circumstances. Decades before critical and cultural theorists would articulate concepts of identity as positional, as shaped by multiple elements, the creators of *Fire!!* communicated exactly that understanding of African American identity.

The texts in *Fire!!* suggest many different arguments about the importance of racial identity to African Americans. In some of its texts, racial identity is explicitly emphasized or implicitly marked as crucial. For example, the Africanist aesthetics of some of Douglas's illustrations implicitly emphasize the importance of race to the magazine. The most striking of these is his cover illustration, which takes as its central focus a lion; its reclining posture with head held high calls to mind the familiar image of the Egyptian sphinx, particularly given the beard that grows from its chin (see fig. 6.5). At the edges of the drawing, Douglas depicted the silhouette of a human head,

Fig. 6.5. Douglas's cover for *Fire!!*. In the original, the background was red.

Fig. 6.6. An untitled design by Douglas in *Fire!!* (28).

using the conventional presentation of features to suggest the black identity of this person: a slit eye and exaggerated, protruding lips. Similar features can be seen in a drawing that closes Bennett's "Wedding Day"; it shows a man next to a stream stretching back a bow and arrow (see fig. 6.6). Douglas's depiction of the man's features, particularly the slanted slit he used to suggest the man's eye, suggests the style of representation seen in African Dan masks of the Ivory Coast (Kirschke 83). Douglas's depiction of the man's torso, flattened and shown in silhouette, echoes the depiction of the

Three Drawings

Aaron Douglas

Fig. 6.7. Another untitled design by Douglas in *Fire!!* (29).

human form in Egyptian tomb paintings (Kirschke 98). Another drawing, this one appearing on the opening page of Douglas's series of three portraits, is of a mask that looks like those that inspired the work of Winold Reiss (see fig. 6.7). Douglas's use of Africanist aesthetics in these illustrations suggests the importance of racial identity to the magazine.

But other aspects of Douglas's contributions suggest different messages. For one thing, the importance of the drawings like the ones that accompanied "Wedding Day" is downplayed, both by their relatively small size and by the fact that they are called "incidental" in the table of contents. Where the Africanist designs had been one of the unifying forces in *The New Negro*, here they are presented as merely decorations. In addition, Douglas also contributed three portraits to *Fire!!* that are strikingly different in style and content. These three drawings are printed near the center of the issue, as if to suggest that they have a central position in the issue's definition of African American identity. The first is of a preacher, looking down at the open Bible on the podium (see fig. 6.8). The second is of an artist, brush in hand, working at his easel (see fig. 6.9). The third is of a waitress, her stockings curled below her knees, carrying dishes away from a table (see fig. 6.10). In these pen-and-ink drawings, Douglas merely outlined his figures, and he suggested rather than explicitly identified their racial identity. The features and hair of these three subjects hint that they are African American, but it seems as if their professions are far more important than their racial identity. Each

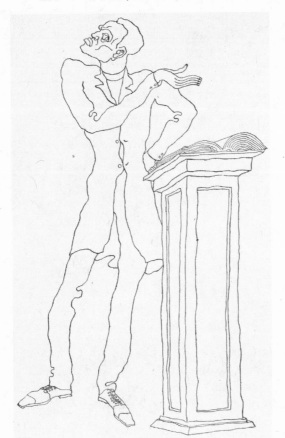

Fig. 6.8. Douglas's preacher in *Fire!!* (30).

of the portraits depicts its subject at work, in the clothes—such as aprons and smocks—that mark their professions. Furthermore, the style of these portraits marks a significant departure from the African Americanist aesthetics Douglas was developing in other work. Here, he used only wavy lines to outline his figures, and none of the heavy blocks of black that characterize his more Africanist illustrations, particularly those he contributed to *The New Negro*. In *Fire!!*, his drawings suggest none of the "love of Africa" for which Locke called; they suggest merely the outline of these three humans. These drawings contrast with the cover illustration; these imply that racial identity is less important than class.

The written texts in the magazine also make a range of arguments about the importance of racial identity. For example, race is the central term in the subtitle of the magazine, which is reproduced on the cover as well as on the appeal for funds, on the title page, and on the opening page of "Cordelia"; it draws the reader's attention repeatedly to the magazine's dedication to

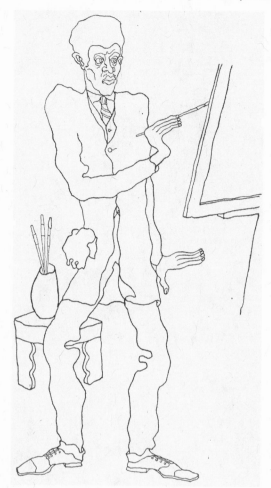

Fig. 6.9. Douglas's artist in *Fire!!* (31).

younger Negro artists. The racial identity of a number of characters in the creative texts in the issue also seems significant. Hurston first introduced the cast of her play "Color Struck" in the Jim Crow car of the train taking them to St. Augustine to compete in a cake walk; she described the group in the stage directions as "a happy lot of Negroes" (7). Even the skin tone of the characters is significant, particularly since the main female character, Emma, is horribly jealous of African Americans who have lighter skin than she does. Colorism plays a key role in Emma's breakup with her boyfriend, John, and in the death of her daughter twenty years later. In Bennett's story, racism from white Americans plays a key role. Bennett identified her main character, Paul Watson, as a "Negro of enormous height and size" in her first sentence; his race is among the first things readers learn about him (25). His ha-

Fig. 6.10. Douglas's waitress in *Fire!!* (32).

tred of the racism of white Americans is his most well-known characteristic. But he cannot escape racism, even in Paris, where he lives. His life is full of fights with racist whites, and he spends time in jail after shooting two white men who insulted him. When he falls in love with Mary, a white American expatriate, then, their relationship represents a major change in his attitude toward white Americans. But it proves unwarranted: she calls off their marriage at the end of the story, fleeing on the day of their wedding and leaving him a note in which she explains that she "'just couldn't go through with it,' white women just don't marry colored men" (28). The story ends with Paul, dazed, confused, and in pain, stumbling into the subway. His experience is a warning that the possibility of seeing people as people, rather than as defined by race, is only illusionary or temporary.

In other texts, though, the racial identity of the characters is hinted at but not explicitly identified. For example, Thurman set "Cordelia" in Harlem but did not immediately identify his characters as black. Only when the narrator, near the end of the story, describes Cordelia's "light brown complexion" and her hair does the reader know that she is black (6). The narrator, furthermore, is identified as black only in the question that labels him a "dicty kid" (6)—and even that question marks him as black only if the reader knows that "dicty" is a mocking term used to refer to African Americans who considered themselves members of the elite. In Hurston's story, "Sweat," the reader finds out that Delia is black when Sykes uses a racial insult to refer to her (40). But Hurston did not specifically identify the race of the other characters; the reader is left to assume that they are black given their use of the same dialect Delia speaks and given Sykes's frustration with the fact that Delia washes white folks' clothes (40). Nugent also was relatively vague about the racial identity of his characters in "Smoke, Lilies and Jade": he never identified Alex as black or white, and in Alex's dream he imagines two white legs that turn out to be Beauty's. It seems, then, that Beauty is white: if Alex is black, theirs is an interracial as well as a homosexual relationship.

In many of the other texts, racial identity is never mentioned. In the section of poems, for example, only in "Jungle Taste" by Edward Silvera is racial identity specified. Silvera's focus is on black men's songs and black women's beauty. But this poem is printed on the same page as another poem by Silvera, "Finality," in which racial identity is unspecified. Here, racial identity seems irrelevant to the subject of the poem: the rising of souls to God after death. In a number of the other poems, racial identity can be assumed from suggestive details, such as the apparently lynched figure dangling from a tree in Helene Johnson's "A Southern Road" or the girl with "purple powdered skin" in Hughes's "Railroad Avenue." But the dying man in Waring Cuney's "The Death Bed" is not identified as black or white; nor is Hughes's main character in "Elevator Boy" or Lewis Alexander's "Little Cinderella." Race also seems irrelevant in Alexander's "Streets" and Arna Bontemps's "Length of Moon." Overall, then, the poems collected in the magazine send very different messages about the importance of racial identity—which is also true of the other texts in the magazine. Though their creators are all black, their racial identity is only sometimes reflected in the content of their work or in the characters they portray.

Fire!! also demonstrates that there are a number of other aspects of identity that are crucial to its African American subjects, and that their experiences often are shaped by or emerge from the intersections of these factors. For example, Cordelia's identity as black may be somehow relevant, but her turn to prostitution seems more influenced by her family's move to Harlem and the poverty that necessitates that both her mother and father have to work and have too little time or energy to "try to control [their] recalcitrant child" (6). The types of people with whom she interacts also have a decided influence on her interests. She initially goes to the Roosevelt Theatre simply because it is close to her home; it is there that she is "almost immediately initiated into the ways of a Harlem theatre chippie" and there that she begins to associate with the "embryo avenue sweetbacks" (5). But it is her chance encounter with the narrator that turns her from a "potential prostitute" to an active one (5, 6). For Cordelia, then, location, money, family situation, and associations with other people all impact the identity she assumes by the end of the story.

In Hurston's "Sweat," Delia's experiences are likewise shaped by a number of factors. Class is one of them: Delia, like the other characters in the story, is a member of the folk. Her identity as an African American also is significant, particularly given Sykes's frustration with the fact that Delia washes white people's laundry. Her experiences also are affected by the economic and patriarchal systems that oppress African American women. Delia's job of washing laundry for a living dominates the story. Hurston opened with a description of Delia hard at work sorting clothes at 11 P.M. on a Sunday night, and in other scenes Hurston described her collecting and delivering clothes. The house is full of piles of clothes and laundry tubs. Delia's marriage to Sykes also is a crucial element of her life. Their relationship has disintegrated to constant fights—over her work, his mistress, which of them owns the house. Sykes is hateful to Delia: he flaunts his relationship with another woman, Bertha, for example, and he uses Delia's fear of snakes to torment her, namely by bringing home a huge rattlesnake that he leaves in their house. The other residents of their small town are well aware of Sykes's mistreatment, but they do nothing. They comment on the fact that Delia has been "ruined" by hard work and abuse from Sykes, reflecting that she used to be "a right pritty lil trick" but has now become a skinny, work-worn woman (41, 42). But though they know how hard she works and watch Sykes spend the money she earns on Bertha, they merely declare "we oughter kill 'im" (42) and do nothing to help change the situation.

Delia's identity, then, is shaped by race, gender, marriage, abuse, economics, and the attitude of others in her community. Other characters see her in different ways: to Sykes, she is the obstacle to his relationship with

Bertha; he defines Delia according to her race and her stubbornness. The men on the porch see her as Sykes's wife. She sees herself as a hard worker. The story, then, offers in Delia an illustration of how many aspects of experience shape one person's life, and of the ways those factors take on different levels of importance, depending on who is defining the individual in question. This point is true, indeed, of many of the texts in *Fire!!*. "Wedding Day" shows nationality to be an issue, as well as race and gender: Paul's hatred of racism is particularly directed at white Americans, and he is quick to fight white men. When he first meets Mary, he sends her away, telling her "I don't like your kind!": he might be referring to her identity as "'merican" or as female, given that he "never knew the companionship of a woman" and that the other characters tease him about being "scared to death of one woman" (26). Nugent's "Smoke, Lilies and Jade" features characters who define themselves according to their age and their sexuality as well as their ideology. Alex is nineteen years old and still has to deal with the disapproval of his mother (34). It is his status as an artist and his interest in artists like Wilde and Mencken, though, that most connects him to the group of people with whom he associates (34). Finally, it is his attraction to both Beauty and Melva that creates the tension in the story. Each of these texts, then, focuses on a main character whose identity is shaped around multiple factors, which exist in shifting and changing relationships to one another.

Furthermore, each of the texts in *Fire!!* adds different elements to the overall portrait of African Americans in the magazine. Readers see a very different definition of African American identity in "Smoke, Lilies and Jade," for example, than they do in "Sweat." Readers who peruse only selected texts in the magazine are given glimpses of certain aspects of African Americans' identity; those who read the entire magazine are offered a complex portrait of African Americans. The same could be said about the other collaborative illustrated volumes produced during the Harlem Renaissance, of course. For instance, class, age, and gender are all relevant to the portrayal of African Americans in the *Survey Graphic* issue and *The New Negro,* and the individual texts in these volumes draw different amounts of attention to these different factors. But in those two volumes, one element of identity is given precedence over these others: nationality and race, respectively. In *Fire!!*, on the other hand, even the defining statements always reflect a number of different aspects of identity. As a result, the magazine more clearly shows that there are many elements that must be taken into account if the identity of any individual or group is to be understood.

On that point, the creators of *Fire!!* presented a definition of African American identity that precedes by decades the insights of cultural theorists. The understanding of identity as shaped around many different elements has been emphasized by a number of scholars in the fields of cultural studies, feminist studies, and ethnic studies in the 1990s. Stuart Hall, for example, argues that identities are "multiply constructed across different, often intersecting and antagonistic, discourses, practices and positions" ("Who Needs 'Identity'?" 4). Susan Stanford Friedman applies such insights to feminist theory in her exploration of what she calls "the new geographics of identity" (13), a concept of identity as "the product of complex intersections and locations" (16). Certain critics of African American literature note the same understanding of identity in the work they study: Martin Favor asserts about James Weldon Johnson's Ex-Colored Man that his identity "forms from an amalgam of positions—color, class, gender, sexuality, geography— that refuse to be neatly aligned, that are always in negotiation and contestation" (52). Black feminist theorists such as Mae Gwendolyn Henderson similarly emphasize the importance of this concept of identity and its application to African American subjects. Henderson, for example, warns against "privileging one category of analysis at the expense of the other" and emphasizes the need to recognize "the plural aspects of the self" ("Speaking in Tongues" 17, 18). The creators of *Fire!!* were doing exactly that: they put into practice ideas about the complexity of identity that have become the focus of a wealth of analysis from literary and cultural theorists in the past few decades.

These insights point to the truly innovative aspects of *Fire!!*. Its creators experimented with strategies of representation more frequently used, at the time, by the white avant-garde, and they made those kinds of texts their own by altering their contents to reflect the experiences of their African American subjects. They also found new ways to define African American identity, in contrast to the emphases and prescriptions offered by the leaders of the New Negro movement. As they did so, they developed constructions of African American identity that demonstrate insights articulated by cultural theorists seventy years later. Truly, then, these writers and artists were on the cutting edge of ideas about representation and identity.

The failure of *Fire!!*, however, suggests the difficulty of creating an independent, avant-garde magazine, and of carving out a unique and independent position from which the complexities of African American identity can be fully comprehended. While the magazine succeeded in breaking out of categories, in resisting the ossification of the black elite, and in avoiding simply following a pattern laid out by white avant-gardes, it was unable to maintain that position. Its failure can be read as a rejoinder to Hughes's hopes that the "Negro artist" would be able to write without concern for his or her audience, solely out of experience and interest. The creators of the magazine distanced themselves from the African American elite, thus losing that audience; they reached toward the white American avant-garde but could not stir up sufficient interest there; and they failed to establish a strong group of subscribers among other African American populations. In a telling statement, Thurman wrote a year after *Fire!!* folded that the black artist "will receive little aid from his own people unless he spends his time spouting sociological jeremiads or exhausts his talent in building rosy castles around Negro society" ("Negro Artists and the Negro" 38). His conclusion may have been extreme, but his experience with *Fire!!* suggests that there was a grain of truth in it. The demise of the magazine reflects how difficult it was for an African American avant-garde to establish an independent position for itself, to draw in readers, and to earn the support of African American patrons. Failing the latter two, the contributors to *Fire!!* were able to do the first only for a brief moment.

But the insights offered through the magazine are notable, in terms of the contexts in which we read it. First, its links to the white avant-garde demonstrate that ideas about representation and identity traveled across racial lines during the 1920s. It seems logical to assume that African American writers and artists would have been influenced by what their white counterparts were doing, and that the work of the Harlem Renaissance would have impacted in turn other artists and intellectuals in the 1920s. But little of the scholarship on the Harlem Renaissance sets it in the context of broader movements of the period. *Fire!!*, by demonstrating the engagement of African Americans with ideas and representational techniques practiced by white as well as black Americans, suggests that to fully understand the complexity and the significance of the Harlem Renaissance, we need to study it in the context of other cultural and intellectual movements of the 1920s. Second, the differences between *Fire!!* and other collaborative illustrated volumes produced during the Harlem Renaissance impresses upon us the need to see the movement as a dynamic one, one in which ideas about representation and identity were fruitfully explored and actively developed.

Fire!! also demonstrates a few crucial points about the accomplishments of its contributors. *Fire!!* demonstrates their masterful appropriation of the form of the avant-garde little magazine to serve their interests and needs. The magazine's creators used it to insert themselves into an avant-garde discourse that, very often, reflected little awareness of race as an important aspect of identity. Simultaneously, they used their magazine to insert themselves into a discourse about African American identity that reflected only some of the many aspects of African Americans' experiences in the 1920s.

Their claiming of an independent position, free of the controlling efforts of a governing body and of ideas about the social responsibility of art, allowed for experiments in content and style and a more complicated definition of African American identity than was offered elsewhere. *Fire!!* communicated with particular clarity the complexities of African American identity: it showed the many relevant aspects of an individual's identity and the changing relations among those factors. That message would have been even more clear if *Fire!!* had continued beyond its first issue, for additional issues certainly would have added other elements of African Americans' identities and depicted different situations in which the relevance of these factors varied. That issue, though, remains a dramatic demonstration of the independent spirit of these young African American writers and artists—a spirit that, as Kerlin argued in his review, was "worthy to continue flaming" (284).

Conclusion:
The Evolving Portrait

Perhaps the most obvious goal of the work produced during the New Negro movement was to replace derogatory images of African Americans with ones that draw attention to their achievements and their contributions to American society and culture. The desire to do so is most likely behind much of the criticism of the kinds of images in *Fire!!*. But if another goal of the movement was to break Americans out of the habit of stereotyping, the images in *Fire!!* might have been just as helpful as those in *The New Negro*. The portraits of African Americans in *Fire!!* and in *The New Negro* have little in common, but African Americans in the 1920s would have seen aspects of their lives reflected in both volumes. Taken together, the two volumes offer dramatically different visions of African Americans and the New Negro. To-gether, they underline the diversity within the race, which certainly was an important point at a time when, as Sterling Brown concluded, too many people had decided that knowing a few African Americans allowed them to draw conclusions about "*the* Negro" ("Negro Character" 150). The contrast between the images in these two volumes is a reminder that, as Brown put it, what one really would discover, should one truly study African Americans, is that "*the* Negro is more difficult to find than the countless beings called Ne-groes" (150; emphasis Brown's).

That point is made particularly clear by the differences between these collaborative illustrated volumes. The contrasts between Locke's portrait in *The New Negro* and the very different arguments about African American identity in *Fire!!* are perhaps the most obvious evidence of the variety of def-initions offered during the Harlem Renaissance. But that range also is evi-dent in other significant differences between the volumes. For example, Du Bois's depiction in *The Crisis* of African Americans as victims of racist vio-lence is quite different than Charles Johnson's emphasis on their contribu-tions to American industries and institutions in *Opportunity*. Likewise, the focus on African Americans' integration and contributions to American culture in the *Survey Graphic* issue is quite different from the emphasis on the development of a unified racial identity in *The New Negro*. And, of course, the portraits of "Harlem Types" and other representatives of the African American folk in that issue contrast with the portraits of the elite that shape the first impression of the New Negro in Locke's anthology. If the presentation of competing definitions of African American identity helps make readers aware of the constructed nature of identity, these volumes work remarkably well toward that goal.

Even beyond that, the range of images available in these volumes is a challenge to the process of stereotyping, the process of reducing individuals and groups of people to simplified, homogenous entities. The collaborative volumes of the Harlem Renaissance push against that process, individually and collectively. Despite the fact that, on some level, each presents generalizations about African Americans, they also make clear the diversity of African Americans' experiences, ideas, and identities. Two texts in any given volume may offer completely different arguments about their subjects. When those subjects are people, that range of messages is a reminder that human beings are complex, that they have inner and outer selves, that they may fit into types in some ways, but that those types also fail to communicate the complexity of human identity. The range of messages in these volumes also is a reminder that, while group affiliations can be important and helpful, those affiliations occur despite differences among individuals, not because those individuals are all the same.

Perhaps the complexity of the images in these volumes should not be surprising. After all, *The Crisis* and *Opportunity* were ongoing projects, presenting month after month of images. Certainly, then, it would be almost impossible to not include some diversity in those images. Similarly, the sheer number of contributors to the *Survey Graphic* issue and, especially, to *The New Negro* makes diverse perspectives likely. And the desire of the contributors to *Fire!!* to offer a greater range of images than they saw in *The New Negro* and the two magazines makes it likely that they would have included some variety in their publication. But the circumstances of the production of each of these volumes might have led to much more simplistic portraits. After all, the very project of representing and defining African Americans and African American identity implies a certain degree of simplification. Furthermore, the emergence of the concept of the New Negro—particularly as "he" was identified as a single type, even a single individual—could have led to exactly the kind of simplification and stereotyping that Brown warned against. Falling into the trap of simply replacing one stereotype of African Americans with a new one would have been easy. The fact that *The Crisis*,

Opportunity, and the *Survey Graphic* issue were produced under the direction of organizations that had relatively uniform ideologies would have added to the likelihood that these volumes would have offered homogenous images of African Americans and African American culture, as would the fact that *The New Negro* was conceived of as a defining text. These realities make the diversity of images within each volume all the more striking.

Any reader who encountered these volumes upon their production in the 1920s surely would have been struck by the complexity of the portrait that emerges. But scholars of the Harlem Renaissance, without considering these collaborative volumes and others like them, too often offer easy generalizations about the Harlem Renaissance. Various critics have concluded that the movement failed because it was too elitist, or too folk centered, or too integrationist, or too conservative. Each of these conclusions has merit when applied to a particular aspect of the Harlem Renaissance, but when a scholar offers only one of these points, he or she offers a too-simplistic assessment of *the* Harlem Renaissance. What we learn from these volumes is that the movement was a little of each—and instead of being a fault or a shortcoming, that can be seen as a strength. The fact that participants were sometimes elitist, sometimes folk centered, sometimes integrationist, and sometimes conservative can help us appreciate the complexity of the movement; it helps us realize that participants defined African American identity in ways that were constantly developing and changing.

These volumes, in effect, provoke a reconsideration of the Harlem Renaissance, enhancing our appreciation of the complexity of the arguments about African American identity asserted by participants. In addition, though, these volumes demonstrate the degree to which the Harlem Renaissance was a broad cultural movement. Far too often, we study the literature or the essays of the movement without enough of a sense of the relations between the written work produced in the 1920s and its counterparts in other media. These volumes allow us to recover the context in which some of the most famous written texts of the Harlem Renaissance appeared. To offer just one example: the fact that Du Bois's call for texts that work as propaganda in "Criteria of Negro Art" appeared in *The Crisis* amongst pages and pages of photographs of beautiful African American children turns the essay into a demonstration rather than merely a discussion of the affirmative possibilities of texts. In such cases—and the collaborative illustrated volumes of the movement are full of them—the messages sent by any one text are multiplied, reinforced, and sometimes challenged in ways that reveal complex ideas about representation and African American identity.

Furthermore, these volumes help us appreciate that the participants of the Harlem Renaissance were remarkably adept at the processes of representation. African Americans working during the 1910s and 1920s mastered the techniques of protest journalism, of objective reporting, of literature and visual arts, of ethnographic representation, of anthologizing, and of creating independent journals. Such range and such achievement deserve appreciation and respect. Their work also enhances our own understanding of the ways that, in collaborative volumes, different texts work together. In some cases, individual texts fuse into complex arguments; in other cases, different texts complement one another by offering various types of evidence for a particular assessment; in still other cases, the mix of texts in a volume reveals the complexity of the ideas presented. In all cases, the whole can have an impact that any of the parts would have failed to achieve on its own.

In truth, though, these collaborative illustrated volumes constitute only a slice of the Harlem Renaissance. The work of representation seen here continued for years after the publication of *Fire!!*—and it took place in many different kinds of texts. *The Crisis* and *Opportunity* went on, though their focus changed and their attention to the arts diminished after the resignations of Charles Johnson and Du Bois in 1928 and 1934, respectively. *The New Negro* was complemented by other multi-genre, illustrated anthologies like Johnson's *Ebony and Topaz,* published in 1927, and Nancy Cunard's *Negro: An Anthology,* published in 1934, each of which emphasized different aspects of African American identity and used a range of texts to do so. The work of anthologies also was carried on by collectors including Countee Cullen, who published *Caroling Dusk* in 1927; James Weldon Johnson, who published two collections of *American Negro Spirituals* in the mid-1920s and revised *The Book of American Negro Poetry* in 1931; and V. F. Calverton, who published his *Anthology of American Negro Literature* in 1929. Wallace Thurman continued his editorial efforts in the magazine *Harlem* in 1928, but he put the avant-garde orientation of *Fire!!* behind him. There are more collaborative illustrated volumes that could be mentioned; the point is that the proliferation of images seen in the volumes analyzed in this study continued in similar works published in the following years. The scope and the range of these works is an extension of the rich efforts at representation carried out during the early years of the Harlem Renaissance.

The volumes studied here draw our attention to the awareness of participants in the movement of the significance of work in many media, and that, too, is continued in different kinds of texts published both alongside and after these collaborative illustrated volumes. Langston Hughes's incorporation of the blues into his poetry is the best-known example of the fusion of music and literature; *The Weary Blues* and *Fine Clothes to the Jew,* published in 1926 and 1927, provide numerous examples of blues poems and blues-influenced poems. Many of Sterling Brown's poems reflect a similar fusion of blues and poetry; those in *Southern Road,* published in 1932, are particularly notable. James Weldon Johnson's use of poetry to draw attention to the artistry of African American preachers in *God's Trombones* exemplifies attention to another aspect of African American oral culture. And Zora Neale Hurston's collections of African American folklore, in books like *Mules and Men,* add yet another dimension to this picture. Even the contents of some of the novels published during the 1920s highlight the work being done by African Americans in many media. In Jessie Fauset's *There Is Confusion,* for example, the main character, Joanna Marshall, is both a dancer and an actress. The fact that books like *The Weary Blues, Southern Road,* and *God's Trombones* were illustrated or included cover art by the most significant visual artists of the 1920s draws the work of painters and illustrators to our attention, too. Again, there are many more examples that could be offered; the point is that the attention to many different kinds of texts in the collaborative illustrated volumes of the Harlem Renaissance is typical of much more of the work of the period.

Other texts produced during the 1920s and 1930s draw attention to what was left out of these volumes. Fauset's focus on the experiences of her female protagonist is echoed by the novels of Nella Larsen. *Quicksand,* in particular, as an exploration of the limited possibilities open to African American women during the 1920s, does much to complement the masculinist focus of books like *The New Negro.* So, too, does Hurston's *Their Eyes Were Watching God.* Larsen's *Passing* adds even more evidence of the flexibility of African American identity to other definitions, with the book's depiction of African Americans passing as white. Its suggestions of homosexual desire between the two main female characters, furthermore, illuminate the issues of sexuality and sexual desire, hidden in so many other of the works of the period. Cullen's *Home to Harlem,* focusing as it does on its main characters' sexual pursuits, openly celebrates heterosexual desire. And, finally, the optimism of much of the work of the Harlem Renaissance gives way to the mockery of that hopefulness in Wallace Thurman's *Infants of the Spring,* with its final image of the crumbling Niggerati Manor, and George Schuyler's lampooning of the American obsession with skin color in *Black No More.* The bitter satire of these two books, in only a few years, was replaced, in turn, by the anger and frustration articulated in protest novels like Richard Wright's *Native Son* and Chester Himes's *If He Hollers Let Him Go.*

The texts analyzed in this study, then, were published in just one moment in a long tradition of African American cultural production. In that sense, these volumes embody merely one step in a long process of defining African American identity, and they present only one possible set of arguments about that identity. Indeed, the volumes themselves encourage us to see them that way: they push us to think beyond their boundaries. Their techniques and implications are still relevant to our understanding of the processes of representation—both in their limitations and in their achievements. The racism and the discrimination they reflect—and the problematic representation of minority groups that made them necessary—has not disappeared from American society; the oppression that motivated African Americans to redefine themselves still permeates our media and our culture. When one considers, for example, the ongoing protests of the NAACP and other organizations of the limited roles for African Americans or actors of other ethnic backgrounds on television, the continuing problems of representation are clear. We might still use the collaborative illustrated volumes of the Harlem Renaissance to push our own thinking about the texts published today, about the messages they send, and about how we ourselves might engage in the processes of representation and identity formation.

NOTES

Introduction

1. My page numbers are from the 1925 edition. In the 1992 version, Locke's foreword is on pages xxv–xxvii.

2. These and other questions have been suggested to me by scholars in cultural studies, such as Mieke Bal, Stuart Hall, Richard Dyer, Roland Barthes, and W. J. T. Mitchell. Readers familiar with their work will recognize that I am applying their insights about the processes of representation to the work of the Harlem Renaissance.

3. Fredrickson's *The Black Image in the White Mind* remains the most extensive analysis of such ideas about African Americans. Fredrickson focuses on the years 1817–1914, with his last two chapters covering the last decades of the late nineteenth century and the first decades of the twentieth century (256–319).

4. Campbell 55–56n27. Page's description of African Americans was part of a series of essays published in *McClure's* in 1904 in which he presented his assessment of the causes and prevention of lynching; Campbell also discusses Mary Church Terrell's answer to Page's arguments (41–50).

5. Petesch, in *A Spy in the Enemy's Country,* discusses many of these kinds of texts (3–20 and 79–131), and Gates reproduces examples at the end of "The Trope" (149–55). The video *Ethnic Notions,* directed by Marlon Riggs, also offers a survey of such images, from clips of *The Birth of a Nation* to images in cartoons and newspapers.

6. Miller and Miller reproduce and discuss a sampling of postcards from the turn of the century in *Picture Postcards in the United States.* Many of their examples are benign or even humorous. *Without Sanctuary,* a collection of photographs of lynching victims, includes postcards that served as celebratory souvenirs of the horrifying and dehumanizing treatment of African Americans.

7. The portrait of Wheatley raises questions about the extent to which portraits of authors were printed as frontispieces to their books. They seem to have been common. Trachtenberg, for example, indicates that the portrait of Walt Whitman that appeared as the frontispiece to the 1855 version of *Leaves of Grass* violated clearly established conventions for authors' portraits (61–63). But I have been unable to find more specific details, like the percentage of books that included portraits.

8. Other than Olney's descriptions, I could find no extensive discussion of the photographs and portraits that appeared with slave narratives or of the image of Douglass that was included with his *Narrative.* The only reference to Douglass's portrait that I could find was in the "Note on the Texts" in *Frederick Douglass: Autobiographies,* which describes a number of promotional materials, including the "notice" that mentions the portrait (1078–79). The portrait in fig. I.2 appears in Quarles's edition of Douglass's *Narrative,* across from the title page of the original text. Though it is not identified here, it seems likely that it is the original portrait

that appeared with the work. A more tightly cropped version of the same portrait appears as the frontispiece of Preston's *Young Frederick Douglass,* identified only as "ca. 1845, shortly after he left Maryland" (n.pag.). Quarles includes a similar portrait in *Frederick Douglass,* which he dates 1845 (page facing 82).

9. Helpful surveys of the black press in the nineteenth and early twentieth century include Wolseley (24–78), Jordan (10–35), Simmons (9–68), and Dann. On black magazines in particular, see studies by Daniel and by Johnson and Johnson.

10. For brief overviews of the rise of illustrations in newspapers, see Sloan and Parcell 316–49. In Hutt's *The Changing Newspaper,* reproductions of hundreds of pages from early newspapers visually demonstrate these changing tendencies. Magazines followed similar patterns in the late nineteenth and early twentieth centuries; see Johnson and Prijatel 62–67. By 1910, some were heavily illustrated, but many kept the older look: flipping through the pages of magazines like the *Nation* or the *New Republic,* for example, one finds few if any illustrations in the 1900s or the 1910s.

11. The need for such an approach is asserted by Nelson in terms of modern American poetry. Part of Nelson's argument in *Repression and Recovery* is that much of the poetry published in the early twentieth century appeared with visual texts that contributed to its impact. Against the tendency to trivialize the visual components of the work, Nelson includes many of these illustrations in his book as a way of demonstrating "that the material presentation of texts can significantly increase the kinds of meaning they can be used to produce" (218).

1. Protest and Affirmation

1. The mixes of texts in *The Crisis* are preserved in microfilm reproductions of the original editions and in a reprint of the early issues that was published in 1969 by the Negro Universities Press. The reprint edition includes the covers of the magazines, as well as the entire contents, as far as the press was able to determine, and it seems to be complete. One notable difference between the original issues and the reprint, though, is that the reprint version is entirely in black and white, while the originals included some color, as Du Bois's comments indicate ("Editing *The Crisis*" xxviii).

2. Scholars do offer important insights into the magazine's political role. In his biography of Du Bois, for example, Lewis offers an illuminating discussion of the events of the 1910s and Du Bois's response to those events in the pages of *The Crisis* (*Du Bois* I: 386–580). Lewis's biography is the most recent in a number of books on Du Bois that offer insights into his work on *The Crisis.* See, for instance, Rampersad, *Art and Imagination* 133–69 and 184–201; Rudwick, *W. E. B. Du Bois;* and DeMarco 63–103. Kornweibel's studies also shed light on *The Crisis* in its first decade; see *"Investigate Everything"* 132–48 and *"Seeing Red"* 54–75.

The Crisis included fiction, poetry, and essays on the arts from its first issues, but they became much more common in the magazine's second decade. The magazine's attention to the arts, particularly in the 1920s, will be analyzed in chapter 3 of this book.

3. The series includes *Writings in Periodicals Edited by W.E.B. Du Bois;* the first volume comprises work from *The Crisis* from 1911 to 1925. Other collections include those edited by Lester and Moon.

4. None of the scholars mentioned above include any illustrations from *The Crisis* or extended discussion of its visual texts or its layout. But they are not alone: Barnhurst notes the lack of attention to layout and visual elements in studies of newspapers (164), and the tendency holds true for analyses of magazines as well.

5. Du Bois, *Correspondence* 108. Du Bois detailed his criticism of the existing periodicals in notes he sent to the same person, the banker Jacob Schiff; see "A Proposed Negro Journal" 78.

6. See Daniel 248–51 on *Moon* and 207–10 on *Horizon. Horizon* was the organ for the Niagara movement, and Du Bois shared ownership and editorial duties with Freeman Murray and La Fayette Henshaw (Daniel 207).

7. Lewis, *Du Bois* I: 409–10. Du Bois often asserted, with pride, the magazine's financial independence from the organization. For him, the magazine's editorial freedom depended on its ability to support itself. When circulation fell in the 1930s and *The Crisis* needed the support of the NAACP—and when Du Bois's ideas were again coming into conflict with the board's—he resigned (Du Bois, *Autobiography* 291–99).

8. On the tensions between Du Bois and the NAACP board in the 1910s, see Lewis, *Du Bois* I: 466–500 and Rudwick, "W. E. B. Du Bois in the Role of *Crisis* Editor" 218–25. In the first years of the publication of *The Crisis,* few of its editorials were signed. Most scholars assume that Du Bois wrote most of them and identify him as the author of individual texts, whether or not he is named—a practice that makes sense in light of the board's criticism of Du Bois for the editorial pronouncements in the magazine. Aptheker, for example, includes articles signed or initialed by Du Bois but also articles "unsigned but certainly by him" in his *Complete Published Works* (Introduction 1: xix).

Du Bois often refused to mince words, even when his pronouncements caused tension with the board. He considered the magazine a vehicle for the expression of his own ideas and not the board's, particularly because, he believed, "no organization can express definite and clear-cut opinions" (*Autobiography* 261). Perhaps to ease some of this tension, in November 1918 the editorial column was renamed "Opinion of W. E. B. Du Bois," thus making explicit his authorship of these pieces.

Circulation of *The Crisis* peaked at one hundred thousand subscribers in 1919 (Du Bois, "Editing *The Crisis*" xxix–xxxi). The longevity of *The Crisis* also is significant: the NAACP continues to publish a version of *The Crisis* today.

9. The organization sometimes had to go out of its way to attract white members. Readership of the magazine was estimated to be only 20 percent white in 1912 and 1916, which led to efforts to bring in more white readers (Kellogg, *NAACP* 1: 117–19, 1: 150–51).

10. "The Crisis: A Business Proposition" 3. Calls for pictures were repeated in many of the announcements of forthcoming special issues, especially the children's and education issues, which depended on submissions of photographs and information from readers.

11. Du Bois, "Editing *The Crisis*" xxix. The affirmative photographs in *The Crisis* must have contributed to its popularity; it seems probable that African American readers, hungry for positive visual images of themselves, would have been more likely to subscribe to the magazine if they knew it contained such photographs.

12. For descriptions of the written and visual contents of these and other magazines, see Frank Luther Mott. For *Harper's Weekly*, see 2: 469–87. For *Collier's*, see 4: 453–79.

13. For instance, an editorial in February 1911 singled out the *Charleston News and Courier* as, "on most matters," a "sane and able newspaper," but one whose coverage of "the Negro problem" was tragic ("Southern Papers" 21). The magazine also reproduced or critiqued examples of racist and potentially violence-provoking news coverage in May ("The Manufacture of Prejudice" 35–37), September ("Promotion of Prejudice" 196–97), and November ("Some Headlines" 31–32). On the second anniversary of the founding of *The Crisis*, an editorial emphasized its importance, given the difficulty of getting "publicity on the Negro problem in the regular periodical press unless the black man is vilified and traduced" ("Editorial: The Second Birthday" 28).

Media historians who discuss the presence of African Americans in white periodicals tend to agree with Du Bois's assessment. Campbell—in just one of many such claims—notes that many newspapers and magazines of the period "ridiculed, derided, and stereotyped [African Americans], consistently reinforcing ideas of white superiority" (38).

14. It is difficult to tell how much attention *Harper's Weekly* or *Collier's* gave to African Americans; neither magazine included an index. If they are anything like two other influential national weekly magazines, though, their articles about African Americans would have been few and far between. The indexes of the *Nation* and the *New Republic* list only occasional references to "Negroes" in the first decades of the twentieth century, perhaps between five and twenty per year.

15. *McClure's* has been called the magazine that "sparked a golden age of investigative reporting" (Aucoin 212) and "the leader of the muckraking magazines" (Frank Luther Mott 4: 599).

16. Du Bois, *Correspondence* 128–29. Du Bois's experience with *McClure's* parallels Mary Church Terrell's; she was never able to publish there, although *North American Review* did print her response to Page's essays (Campbell 39).

17. For discussion of this trend, see Johnson and Johnson 3–4 and Hutton 8–9. Simmons goes so far as to say that many black papers published from 1877 to 1915 were "virtually mute on race issues" (16). He attributes this growing silence about the violence and discrimination against African Americans, ironically, to the increase in brutality against African Americans; that brutality, he posits, made many African American publishers cautious (16). On Wells's exceptional protest journalism, see Simmons 17–20. Trotter's critique of Booker T. Washington also is particularly noteworthy; see Jordan 25–27.

18. The circulation of the *Defender* grew rapidly starting in about 1910, and it extended into the South during World War I (Simmons 28–32). By 1920, its regular circulation was nearly one hundred thousand, and at its peak, it reached as high as two hundred thirty thousand (Jordan 8; Wolseley 54).

19. For example, Du Bois bemoaned the changes in editorial policy at the *Colored American Magazine* between 1904 and 1909, when it came under the control of Washington and became "conciliatory, innocuous, and uninteresting" ("The Colored Magazine in America" 33).

Du Bois was quite vocal in his criticism of the black press. In fact, his critiques of black newspapers led to one of the many clashes between him and the NAACP board (Rudwick, "W.E.B. Du Bois in the Role of *Crisis* Editor" 220–21).

20. Du Bois was frustrated by the degree to which Washington and Tuskegee "filled the horizon so far as national magazines and the great newspapers were concerned" (*Autobiography* 241). The result, he felt, was that agitation and open discussion were stifled. Du Bois wrote that he "resented the practical buying up of the Negro press and choking off even mild and reasonable opposition to Mr. Washington in both the Negro press and the white" (*Autobiography* 242). Lewis describes Washington's initial opposition to the NAACP; see *Du Bois* I: 391–407 and I: 427–29.

21. Gates includes reproductions of illustrations from *Voice of the Negro* in "The Trope" 140–46. *Voice of the Negro* was published by Jesse Max Barber and J. W. E. Bowen from 1904 to 1906 and by Barber as *Voice* from 1906 to 1907. Its militance earned it such criticism from white Southerners that Barber was forced to move its offices from Atlanta to Chicago following the riots in Atlanta in 1906. On the move, see Daniel 373–75; for the history of the magazine, see 369–77.

22. There are, of course, exceptions. One of the more extensive analyses is Gates's "The Trope." Brief mentions of illustrations in black periodicals can be found, for example, in DeSantis 65 and Strother 94 and 97.

23. "Editing *The Crisis*" is a typical statement. Du Bois offered a brief history of the founding of the magazine and its contents, circulation, income, and relationship to the NAACP, but no comment on the process by which each issue was created (xxvii–xxxii). He gave similar commentary about *The Crisis*, for example, in his *Autobiography*, 256–61 and 291–99.

24. I have found only hints about who might have been responsible for the layout of the magazine. For example, Ovington recalled herself and Mary Maclean preparing the "dummy" of a pamphlet against lynching for the printer; she described the women cutting and pasting headlines and photographs onto the pages (*The Walls Came Tumbling Down* 113; "Early Years of the NAACP and the Urban League" 69). Perhaps, then, they took a similar role in the magazine. Maclean was a feature writer for the *New York Times* who volunteered at *The Crisis* and worked as its managing editor until her death in 1912 (Kellogg 151). In her obituary, Ovington noted that Maclean's "judgment was appealed to many times in the making up of the magazine. In the busy days of proofreading and dummying she did her full share" ("Mary Dunlap Maclean" 184). Lewis describes Du Bois and Maclean rushing the December 1911 issue to press, but again, it is not clear who actually would have arranged the texts on the pages (*Du Bois* I: 437). Madeline G. Allison may have played a part in layout after Maclean's death: in 1923, an announcement that she was leaving the staff mentioned that she had "recently" played a role in the makeup of the magazine, where she had worked since 1911 ("The Horizon" 175).

25. Bagehot makes the comment in reference to Charles Dickens's use of juxtaposition in his novels ("Charles Dickens" 2: 87).

26. In fact, Eisenstein used the novels of Dickens and Gustave Flaubert to explain his concept of montage, for both writers often switched abruptly between incongruent scenes, in the way Eisenstein did in his films. For example, he described Dickens's portrait of London as a "dynamic (montage) picture" ("Dickens, Griffith, and the Film Today" 217) and traced montage back to Flaubert ("Through Theater to Cinema" 12–13).

27. Two other similar forms are pastiches and assemblages, but pastiche usually refers to purely written texts, and assemblages are three dimensional. For more detailed explanations of these types of composite texts, in literature or the visual arts, see Weingrod, par. 3–10, or the entries in, for example, Harmon and Holman or Chilvers.

The juxtapositions that characterize montages and collages can be found in many different kinds of composite texts. For discussions of montage in painting and photography, posters, magazine illustrations, dust jackets, caricatures, and music, see Teitelbaum. Wettlaufer discusses montage as a feature of modernist literature but also of art criticism, letters, and prose poems written in the nineteenth century (514–35). Doherty offers an extensive discussion of montage as practiced by dada visual artists in Berlin in the 1910s and 1920s. This attention to the practice of montage in a range of media supports Wettlaufer's argument that "we must expand our vision of montage" (533–34).

28. For a discussion of one such event, see Lewis, *Du Bois* I: 551–54. For discussion of ongoing persecution of *The Crisis,* see Kornweibel, *"Investigate Everything"* 132–48 and *"Seeing Red"* 54–75.

29. This is a significant effect, given the rise of sensationalism in journalism in the 1890s and the 1900s. Joseph Pulitzer and William Randolph Hearst's newspapers are particularly known for exaggerating or even fabricating news (Olasky 109–14). But the *Defender* also is not immune to the charge of sensationalism (Strother 93; DeSantis 65).

30. See "The Looking Glass: The Riot in East St. Louis" 175–78 and "NAACP: The Massacre of East St. Louis" 219–38. The horrible violence left more than six thousand people homeless, almost $400,000 worth of property destroyed, and thirty-nine blacks and eight whites dead. The events and President Woodrow Wilson's silence about them were the catalyst for the famous silent protest parade in New York City on July 28. As many as ten thousand African Americans participated (Lewis, *Du Bois* I: 536–40).

31. Theorists often argue that visual texts are comprehended more quickly than written texts, and that a visual text can be perceived as a simultaneous whole by readers. If so, a visual text may be "supreme" at arousing the emotions of the reader (Fleming 14). Mirzoeff refers to the "undeniable impact" a visual text may have on first sight as its "sensual immediacy" (15).

32. "NAACP: Holmes on Lynching" 110. Ovington credited this card as having "started our lynching campaign" (*The Walls Came Tumbling Down* 295). For her and others at *The Crisis,* the fact that such a card could be sent through the mail was stunning, as was "the men's confidence that no one would dream of prosecuting them" (113).

33. Lewis indicates that a photograph of Washington's corpse was on the cover of the June issue, and that the board was stunned by this placement of an image of charred bones (*Du Bois* I: 514). However, the cover in the Negro Universities Press edition is a photograph of a bride, and that is the image described in the table of contents.

34. Allen 205. The brutality against Washington and the photographs of his corpse were typical, not unique (Litwack 8–28).

35. Although debates about photography's status as an art had occurred since its development in the mid-1800s, at the turn of the century photography was still most often valued for its apparent ability to reproduce the subject objectively, with minimal need of human intervention. In contrast to paintings or drawings, which were the creation of individuals and thus obviously reflected that person's interpretations, photographs were usually assumed to be objective records of reality. See Newhall 67–80.

36. "Editorial: The Gall of Bitterness" 153. Even Booker T. Washington added to this perception: "Although [he] condemned lynching, for many years he was inclined to downplay it, or to suggest it befell mostly vagrants or lowlifes" (Dray viii).

37. Despite the title, both men and women were included. Occasionally the column included a white individual who had made significant contributions to the status of African Americans. The layout changed slightly over the years, but it always included portrait photographs and written descriptions.

38. Such features are similar to a series of essays, "These United States," which were published in the *Nation* from 1922 to 1925. Du Bois contributed an essay about Georgia; he was the only writer to mention the presence of African Americans in the states described. The editors of *The Messenger* responded to this failure to acknowledge African Americans with their own series, "These 'Colored' United States," which ran from 1923 to 1926 (Tom Lutz 6–11).

39. "Colored California" 193–94. Again, as is typical, Du Bois was not explicitly identified as the author of this story, but it seems reasonable to assume that he was. The story includes mention of "my coming to Los Angeles" and speeches delivered by the writer on the trip (193). The activities described are typical of those Du Bois undertook when he traveled, and it is hard to imagine that, if this first-person narrator were not Du Bois, he or she would not be identified.

40. The exceptions are 1920 and 1921, when Du Bois and Jessie Fauset edited the *Brownies' Book*, a magazine geared explicitly for African American children.

41. Du Bois defined the top 10 percent of African Americans as "the Best of this race." These exceptional men—and a few women—showed the potential of African Americans, and Du Bois gave them the responsibility of guiding the masses ("The Talented Tenth" 382 ff).

42. These images bear a notable resemblance to the photographs of the "Gibson Girls" of the 1910s, and the ways *The Crisis* appropriated this style of depicting women to show African American women would be worth exploring further. On popular images of women, see Kitch. Du Bois was a champion of women's rights, and he worked with and clearly admired many professional, socially active women. See, for example, Lewis's commentary on the support of *The Crisis* for women's suffrage in 1911–1913 (*Du Bois* 1: 417–19).

43. The possibility that lynching happened because of African Americans' success was suggested elsewhere; see, for example, Walter White's report on the murder of a black man in Tennessee in 1918. One white woman claimed that part of the reason for the man's murder was that his family was successful enough to drive a big buggy (White, "The Burning of Jim McIlherron" 17). The fact that such success contributed to retaliatory violence demonstrates the absolute failure of American ideals for African Americans.

44. Lewis discusses the treatment of African Americans during and after the war in the opening chapter of *When Harlem Was in Vogue* (3–24).

2. Objectivity and Social Change

1. Three books on the NUL shed at least some light on *Opportunity*, but they give only brief accounts of the magazine, noting how and why the NUL founded it and mentioning the kinds of articles and essays it included. See Weiss 220–33, Parris and Brooks 171–77, and Moore 71–72. A number of studies that focus on Johnson himself devote some attention to his work with the publication. Gilpin, for example, emphasizes the importance of Johnson's attention to black culture in *Opportunity*, as well as his ability to connect African American writers with white publishers (220–42). Pearson explores Johnson's ideas about the role this emphasis on black culture and those contacts would serve, but uses texts from *Opportunity* only briefly in his discussion (123–34). Robbins devotes a chapter of his biography of Johnson to the editor's work on *Opportunity* in the 1920s, briefly discussing the kinds of essays he published in the magazine and how they demonstrate Johnson's goals and his method of working for social change (40–63). The most recent study of *Opportunity* is a chapter of Hutchinson's *The Harlem Renaissance in Black and White* (170–208).

A few of these writers discuss the attention to the arts in *Opportunity*, which will be discussed in the following chapter. None spend much time, if any, doing close readings of the texts in *Opportunity*; none analyze the visual texts that appeared in the magazine.

2. While the NAACP tended to emphasize direct action as a response to discrimination, the NUL emphasized "investigation and diplomatic persuasion," and leaders of the two organizations, including Joel Spingarn and John R. Shillady, saw these efforts as complementary (Weiss 67). Mary White Ovington later wrote of the two organizations that they "divided the field, working together from time to time as action demanded" (*The Walls Came Tumbling Down* 112).

3. At its height in 1927, *Opportunity* had a press run of eleven thousand copies per month (Johnson and Johnson 48). *Opportunity* depended on sales of individual magazines and on subscriptions; the NUL did not have the membership base of the NAACP, and thus *Opportunity* had a more limited audience than did *The Crisis* (Weiss 221). It is estimated that as many as one-third to 40 percent of *Opportunity*'s readers in the 1920s were white (Robbins 47; Weiss 221).

4. For details about the beginning of Johnson's career, including his work on the Chicago Commission on Race Relations, see Lewis, *When Harlem Was in Vogue*

47–49; Robbins ix–63; Gilpin 215–23; Parris and Brooks 167–75; and Hutchinson 173–80.

5. Weiss points out that "considerable correspondence and printed material" was destroyed when the league headquarters moved in the 1950s, that the papers of the Chicago Urban League were destroyed by fire, and that Charles Johnson's papers are "exceptionally unrevealing about his role in the Urban League" (viii).

6. Most of the editorials in the magazine are unsigned. Robbins identifies their writers as Johnson, Ira Reid, "and others" (47); it remains unclear who might have written any individual editorial, although many of them reflect the opinions Johnson expressed in signed pieces. Reid was the industrial secretary of the New York League while Johnson was its research director (Parris and Brooks 195); he succeeded Johnson as research director of the NUL when Johnson left for Fisk University in 1928 (Robbins 46).

7. This argument that the media fanned tension also had been leveled at Du Bois and *The Crisis* on other occasions. Lewis points out that the "thunder and lightning" of the magazine seemed "dangerously inflammatory" to the white philanthropists who supported the NAACP (*Du Bois* I: 477). Lewis also notes that during World War I, criticism of *The Crisis* for this reason became particularly pronounced, and the magazine was seen by officials in the U.S. government and military intelligence as "a major force in creating African-American unrest" (*Du Bois* I: 559). Kornweibel offers a more detailed discussion of these charges in *"Seeing Red"* 54–75 and, especially, *"Investigate Everything"* 132–48.

8. *Autobiography* 222. The lynching of the farmer Sam Hose in Georgia in 1906 seems to have been the catalyst for this shift. Du Bois was working at Atlanta University at the time he heard about Hose's murder. He wrote "a careful and reasoned statement concerning the evident facts," but found out on the way to the office of the Atlanta *Constitution* that Hose's knuckles were on display in a grocery store. In response to the news, Du Bois wrote, "I began to turn aside from my work," with the understanding that detached objectivity was an insufficient response to such violence (*Autobiography* 222)—and, implicitly, to the extreme racism that allows for the celebration of murder manifested in such gruesome displays.

9. Park became a longtime friend for Johnson. When they first met, Johnson was impressed by the fact that Park treated him without the "condescension or oily patronization" to which he had become accustomed (qtd. in Robbins 195n17). However, Park thought about African Americans in sometimes limited and limiting ways, and some of his work on African Americans reflected "pseudo-biological theories" and primitivist generalizations about African Americans (Robbins 31–32; Ladner xxi–xxii).

10. For a discussion of Park's research and influence, see Matthews 157–93. Some of Park's most well-known work is on integration. The conclusions he drew can be applied to African Americans, but he studied integration primarily among immigrants. When Johnson and other African American sociologists used Park's methods to study African Americans, they added to Park's focus in important ways.

11. The links between Park, Johnson, and *Opportunity* are most extensively explored by Hutchinson (50–58, 174–76).

12. Social work, too, was a developing field in these years, as the changes at the University of Chicago hint. Originally, social welfare courses were taught in the sociology department, but in 1920 an independent department of social service administration was established at the school (Bulmer 39).

13. Trachtenberg 171. The field of social work can also be linked to reform efforts supported by investigative journalism and muckraking. But *Opportunity*'s concern with being non-inflammatory makes this field a less obvious precursor for the magazine than other kinds of social work.

14. One example is a poster that demonstrates the process of "making human junk" out of children. It includes photographs by Hine and captions that emphasize that the failure to protect children from harsh labor conditions turned them from "good material at first" to workers with "no future and low wages" (Stange 70).

15. *Opportunity*'s writers often abbreviated "thru" and "tho." In the interest of accuracy, I am preserving their spelling.

16. Johnson does not mention the role of campaigns, like those in the *Chicago Defender* from 1916 to 1919, to encourage African Americans to migrate north. The *Defender* used the positive aspects of life in Chicago but also the racism of the South to convince African Americans to move. The influx of migrants and the concurrent return of soldiers from World War I are seen as contributing to the tension that led to the riots in Chicago in 1919. See DeSantis 66–69. Perhaps Johnson did not mention campaigns like this because he did not want to associate migrants with the violence in readers' minds.

17. On the Tenement House Exhibition, see Stange 28–45. On Riis, see Leviatin 1–50.

18. Du Bois was often similarly critical of philanthropy, arguing along the same lines that the philosophy of simply giving to or working for people was implicitly patronizing. See, for example, Lewis, *Du Bois* I: 470, 494, and 545.

19. Lewis, *Du Bois* I: 419–20, 536–37, and 546. Du Bois's frustration with the unions' discriminatory practices continued in the 1920s, as Lewis shows (*Du Bois* II: 250–53).

20. See, for example, Lewis's discussion of the controversy around Fayette A. McKenzie, a white man who was president of Fisk University in the early 1920s, as well as Du Bois's criticism of policies at other historically black colleges and universities (*Du Bois* II: 136–48).

21. Washington, in fact, was made a member of the NUL's executive board in 1915. On the connections between Washington and the NUL, see Weiss 60–64.

3. The Arts as a Social Tool

1. The idea that literature and the visual arts could serve an important role in changing perceptions of African Americans was not new in the 1920s or unique to *The Crisis* or *Opportunity*; it was relatively widely accepted by African American intellectuals during the period and before, as I discuss in my introduction. But the attention to the possibilities of the arts during the Harlem Renaissance was much more widespread than it had been before the 1920s. *The Crisis* and *Opportunity* were the most important outlets for the work of African American artists and writers, as

well as the vehicles for the most extensive discussions of the arts. But other magazines participated in this discussion of the arts, too, including national African
American periodicals like *The Messenger* and smaller publications like *Black Opals*
or *Saturday Evening Quill*. In addition, a number of African American writers and
artists published their work in predominantly white magazines, like *Seven Arts* and
Liberator.

2. The most extensive commentaries on the attention Johnson and Du Bois
paid to the arts in *Opportunity* and *The Crisis* are offered by Ikonné (90–106), Johnson and Johnson (31–63), and Hutchinson in two chapters of *The Harlem Renaissance in Black and White* (137–208). All three studies also include *The Messenger*, as
does Kornweibel's *No Crystal Stair* (105–31). For comparisons among the three
magazines, see also Robbins (50) and Gilpin (223). Other helpful commentaries on
the use of the arts in either *The Crisis* or *Opportunity* include Pearson's discussion of
the arts in *Opportunity* and Rampersad's description of Du Bois's inclusion of literature in *The Crisis* (*Art and Imagination* 184–201). Yellin's list of literary materials in
The Crisis is enormously helpful for searches of the magazine.

3. Fabre and Feith's *Temples for Tomorrow* is one of the critical studies that reflects the range of media in the movement, particularly in its section on "Criteria of
Renaissance Art," which includes essays on art, music, film, and literature (51–141).
But the various media are discussed in separate essays; only one essay explicitly addresses the connections among different media. This separation also occurs in
Rhapsodies in Black, in which discussions of different arts and media remain sepa-
rated into different chapters. This tendency to focus on one medium at a time holds
true, too, of scholarship on creative texts in *The Crisis* and *Opportunity,* which focuses primarily on literature in the two magazines. None of the scholars mentioned
in note 2, for example, discuss the connections established among the arts in *The
Crisis* or *Opportunity.*

4. Although it lies outside of my focus here, a comparison could be made between the use of the arts in the Harlem Renaissance to shape public opinion about
African Americans and the use of the arts in the early twentieth century to nurture
and define American identity. See, for example, Munson or Charles Alexander.

5. Lewis, *Du Bois* I: 461. See also 459–61. For one of Du Bois's descriptions, see
"The Star of Ethiopia." Du Bois's development of this pageant fits with his support
for the development of "Negro theater"; see Hutchinson 158–66. Johnson also emphasized the importance of drama in *Opportunity;* see Hutchinson 189–97.

6. This editorial also underscores the importance of *The Crisis* as an outlet for
black writers and artists: it includes a list of important writers whose work had been
published in the magazine. In the next few years, *The Crisis* published early work by
poets who would become major figures in the Harlem Renaissance: Claude McKay,
Langston Hughes, Jean Toomer, and many others.

7. The inclusion of the arts as part of the social and political struggles of *The
Crisis* also reflects Du Bois's own work. He was, after all, a sociologist, historian, and
activist who also wrote poems, short stories, and novels. For discussions of his many
kinds of writing, see Rampersad, *Art and Imagination,* and Byerman. Jessie Fauset
also certainly played an important role in directing the magazine's attention to the
arts, as Wall emphasizes (33–84). Fauset was director of the "What to Read" depart-

ment beginning in 1912; she was hired as literary editor in 1919, and she kept that position until 1926 (Hutchinson 153).

8. Gilpin suggests that "reporting and promoting black *culture* in the United States and the world at large" became more pronounced in *Opportunity* than in *The Crisis* by the mid-1920s (222–23). But the arts did have a prominent place in *The Crisis*—so much so, in fact, that the writers in *The Messenger* criticized Du Bois's magazine for paying too much attention to the arts. An essay titled "W. E. B. Du Bois" in the July 1918 issue noted that items about "Music and Art" often were the leading entries in the "Horizon" column in *The Crisis* and that literary events were prominent under "Meetings." In *The Messenger*, the writer noted, "Economics and Politics" were first in order and importance (27). By the mid-1920s, though, *The Messenger* too came to pay more attention to the arts.

9. Information about the announcements, financing, judging, celebrations, and suspension of the contests in both magazines is available in Austin (235–46) and Ikonné (91–106); Gilpin discusses the *Opportunity* contests in depth (226–36).

10. Du Bois's ideas about the arts changed over time, though. See Rampersad, *Art and Imagination* 190–92. Furthermore, he sometimes gave conflicting advice. For example, Christopher Mott characterizes Du Bois's invitation to entrants for the 1926 Krigwa contest as "fraught with the tension of maintaining an open mind against the impulse to push the program he felt most capable of destroying racism" (260–61).

11. For further discussion of the symposium, see Lewis, *Du Bois* II: 176–82, and Rampersad, *Art and Imagination* 194–96. The contributors' resistance to Du Bois's calls for socially responsible art perhaps was a sign of the magazine's "wavering power over black writing" (Hutchinson 166–67).

12. For a much more in-depth discussion of *Opportunity*'s inclusion of literature and contributors' opinions about criteria for literature, see Hutchinson 197–208.

13. Comments about the essential differences between black and white Americans are extensive and frequent in the texts of the period. For discussion, see Coles and Isaacs.

14. For a more wide-ranging discussion of the attention to African art in *Opportunity*, see Hutchinson 182–86.

4. *Survey Graphic*'s Harlem Issue

1. Despite these insights, very little critical attention has been paid to the Harlem issue; critics interested in Locke's work, for example, have focused almost exclusively on *The New Negro*, mentioning the *Survey Graphic* issue only briefly if at all. The lack of attention to the *Survey Graphic* issue may in part be due to the fact that few copies of the original remain. Scholars of the period, therefore, had only limited access to it until, in 1980, Black Classic Press in Baltimore reprinted the issue. In 1995–1996, a hypermedia edition of the issue was prepared by Kirchenbaum and Tousignant, which makes it even more available to scholars.

A number of studies of the Harlem Renaissance mention the *Survey Graphic* issue; these are mostly historical accounts of how the magazine came about and how it later grew into *The New Negro.* See, for example, Hutchinson 392–95, Lewis, *When Harlem Was in Vogue* 115–17, and Long 15–18. Lewis and Long give brief descriptions of the contents of the magazine issue, but neither offers any sort of detailed analysis of the magazine or the messages it sends about African Americans. Baker's discussion of the national dimensions of race in *The New Negro* is relevant to my discussion of the *Survey Graphic* issue, but Baker does not mention the issue (71–89).

2. The dynamics of this subject/reader relationship also can be found in Kellogg's work on the Pittsburgh Survey in 1909–1914. For discussion, see chapter 2.

3. The difference between being displayed and being a viewer of a display is discussed, for example, in studies like John Urry's analysis of the importance of who is doing the looking and who is being seen in *The Tourist Gaze,* Catherine Lutz and Jane Collins's discussion of how American readers see the Third World through photographs in *Reading "National Geographic,"* John and Jean Comaroff's consideration of how ethnographers and anthropologists present their subjects in *Ethnography and the Historical Imagination,* and Meike Bal's discussion of the relation between museum visitors and the subjects of the exhibits in *Double Exposures,* particularly her introduction and chapter 1. Feminist film critics beginning with Laura Mulvey in *Visual and Other Pleasures* and art critics, notably John Berger in *Ways of Seeing,* also focus on the dynamics of representation and the gaze.

4. There are a few discrepancies in the accounts of the evening. Lewis records, on one hand, that Kellogg approached Johnson, who turned the project over to Locke to edit (*When Harlem Was in Vogue* 94–95); on the other hand, Hutchinson reports that Kellogg approached Locke directly (392).

5. Long reports of the discussion between Locke and Kellogg: "At some point in late 1923, . . . Dr. Locke had a conversation with Paul Underwood Kellogg. . . . In January 1924, there was a letter from Kellogg to Locke asking for a list of topics for a special issue of Survey Graphic based upon their earlier conversation. In the next few months such a list was discussed and consideration of persons who might be helpful was made" (15).

6. These and Locke's other publications are listed in Martin's bibliography of Locke's work (89–96).

7. In fact, while the readership of the *Survey Graphic* was predominantly white, the issue also had a significant number of African American readers. The Harlem issue had much higher circulation than other issues of the magazine did. Usual circulation for the magazine at this point was about twenty-one thousand; this issue was published in an initial run of thirty thousand copies and "was an immediate sensation" (Long 16). Given that response, a second run of twelve thousand copies was arranged, paid for in part by Barnes, George Foster Peabody, and Joel and Amy Spingarn. The three thousand copies commissioned by them were distributed free to black students and organizations (Long 16). These black readers seem to have been expected: many of the small ads toward the back of the issue are directed at African Americans. These include, for example, ads for the real estate company of Nail and Parker, identified as "Specialists in Harlem and Colored Tenement Properties" (712); in ads for Howard University and a number of other black colleges and schools, the institutions emphasized that they served African American students.

However, the fact that these ads are found in the back of the issue, as opposed to the ads aimed at white readers that opened the issue, implies that black readers were the secondary rather than the primary intended audience. The question of how the *Survey Graphic* issue appealed to its African American readers is worthy of exploration but lies outside of my focus here.

8. Qtd. in Stewart 50. Stewart offers a more extensive account of these reactions. He also notes that Locke defended his use of Reiss's portraits in "To Certain of Our Phillistines," published in *Opportunity* in May 1925. Locke argued that the reactions against the portraits were simply examples of color prejudice among African Americans; in other words, he believed that African American viewers of the portraits did not like them because the subjects were too dark skinned (Stewart 50–51).

9. The failure of this pageant to materialize is, of course, an ironic contrast to the success of Du Bois's pageant focusing on African American history, which he wrote and staged a number of times in the mid-1910s. See my discussion in chapter 3.

10. The story also exposes a number of other aspects of white Americans' biases. The committee's response to the professor, for example, reveals their antisemitism: another committee member remarks to the narrator about him, "I bet he's a Jew. I've got nothing against Jews but I just don't like them. They're too pushing" (655). The committee's xenophobia, reflected in their worries about the arguments of immigrants, is another of their prejudices. If this committee is representative of white Americans, it reveals the country as plagued with discriminatory ideas.

11. Locke is not actually identified as the writer of this text here, but an only slightly revised version of these comments appears in the "Who's Who of the Contributors" in *The New Negro*, which is signed "A.L." (419–20).

12. Lewis describes McKay's status by the early 1920s in *When Harlem Was in Vogue* (50–58).

5. Collective Identity in the Anthology

1. Locke's decisions about which texts to include in *The New Negro* may have had much to do with outside pressures. For example, he was pushed to produce the volume by December of 1925, only nine months after the *Survey Graphic* issue had appeared, and he felt obliged to include particular pieces in order to meet the demands of his contributors and editors. For a discussion of this process, see Hutchinson 395–400.

2. Julia Wright offers one such example in her discussion of the use of anthologies to construct unified, political identities for residents of Great Britain at the end of the eighteenth and beginning of the nineteenth centuries. Such analyses of anthologies are relatively rare: as Franklin argued in 1997, there is not much sustained, in-depth analysis of anthologies, particularly in terms of their roles in defining collective identities. However, Franklin did note that there were perhaps signs of increased attention to such texts (4, 203n3), and searches of the MLA bibliography turn up a growing number of essays published since the mid-1990s on the use of anthologies to define collective identities.

3. See, for example, Rampersad's characterization of the book as the "definitive text" of the Harlem Renaissance ("Introduction" ix), or Baker's reference to the book as "an intensely successful act of national self-definition" (72).

4. Franklin offers a concise discussion of this tendency among white feminists in the 1970s and early 1980s, as well as the critique of these practices, particularly by feminists of color (11–13).

5. Such considerations are made more difficult, though, when the creators of anthologies mask their selection criteria, naturalizing their criteria and their construction of the identity in question. Editors who present their anthologies as objective and self-sufficient, arguing that they offer complete and accurate portrayals of the work and the groups in question, make it difficult for readers to search out who and what has been excluded. For discussions and examples, see Franklin 6–8 and Gates, *Loose Canons* 33.

6. See, for example, Paul Lauter's comments about the revised *Heath Anthology of American Literature* (327–30) and Henry Louis Gates's discussion of the *Norton Anthology of African American Literature* (*Loose Canons* 31–33).

7. Two important analyses of *The New Negro* are by Baker (72–81, 83–89) and Hutchinson (387–433). Baker is one of the few scholars of the book who considers its visual texts as well as its written texts. There are other helpful essays about *The New Negro*, notably introductions to reprints of the volume by Hayden and Rampersad. Otherwise, though, insights about the book must be drawn from broader studies of Locke's work. See, for example, Scruggs, "Alain Locke and Walter White"; Lott; Akam; Irek; and Mason. There also are insights scattered through *The New Negro Thirty Years Afterward* (Logan, Holmes, and Edwards, eds.) and Johnny Washington's *Alain Locke and Philosophy*. None of these, however, offer a close reading of the texts in the book.

8. Oddly, Rampersad in the introduction to the 1992 edition emphasizes in strong language the importance of Reiss's work; Rampersad neglects to mention that the portraits he describes as serving a role that "cannot be underestimated" do not appear in this edition (xviii).

9. Identifying the differences between these editions is made even more difficult by the fact that Locke made a number of changes between the 1925 first edition and a 1927 reprint. Most importantly, he increased the number of drawings by Douglas from six in the original to eleven in the reprint. He also changed the title of Douglas's drawing "Ancestral" to "Rebirth," dropped two illustrations by Covarrubias, and added a poem by Gwendolyn Bennett. These differences have rarely been laid out by historians, though; in fact, they often are obscured when the 1927 version is used as the basis for contemporary reprints, such as the 1992 Atheneum edition, which includes all eleven of Douglas's drawings without noting which ones were not originally in the book. The 1968 Arno edition is a reprint of the 1925 edition; it includes all of the texts in the original. I am grateful to Martha Jane Nadell for pointing out these changes to me; for further discussion, see her *Enter the New Negroes*.

10. This title is worth considering, given that the same portrait appeared as "A Woman from the Virgin Islands" in the *Survey Graphic* issue. The second title, even more than the first, strips the woman of her identity, given that the second implies

that all that is important is where she is from. Interestingly, the portrait of Robeson is identified only by his name both in the *Survey Graphic* issue and in the caption in *The New Negro*, but on the title page of the latter it is identified as "Study: Paul Robeson as 'Emperor Jones.'" The caption positions Robeson as himself; the title page clarifies that he is in his role.

11. I use the first edition as my primary text; pagination is the same as in subsequent editions, except for the foreword. It runs from ix to xi in the first edition and from xxv to xxvii in the Atheneum/Macmillan edition, the only edition currently in print and widely available.

12. The implicit link here also draws attention to the slippage between the terms "race" and "nation" in the 1920s. The Irish Renaissance and the American Renaissance both were nationalist movements, whereas the New Negro Movement was explicitly a renaissance centered around racial identity. In the rhetoric of the 1920s, "nation" and "race" were thought of in many of the same ways. For a comparison of the Irish and Harlem renaissance movements, see Mishkin.

13. Ruether offers the reading of Mary as a model for the oppressed in her consideration of Mary's meaning in American Catholic culture; Van Biema points out the dearth of references to Mary in his review of two recent studies of her legacy, as does Sullivan in his discussion of her mystery.

14. It seems particularly significant, for example, that Jessie Fauset is not one of the intellectuals portrayed by Reiss in the book. Surely her work as an editor for *The Crisis* and the publication of her first novel, *There Is Confusion*, in 1924 would have made her a suitable representative individual. *The New Negro* does include her essay on work by African American playwrights, but her significance to the literary movement is obscured by the fact that it does not include her portrait. For extended discussions of African American women's work during the Harlem Renaissance, see Wall; Hull; and McDowell (61–97).

15. For a discussion of the growth in black music companies and the popularity of the blues and other types of music in the 1920s, see Spencer.

16. Watson identifies the homosexual participants of the Harlem Renaissance and describes the gay and lesbian nightlife in the area; see 134–37. Schwarz has decoded the veiled language participants used in correspondence with one another; see her *Gay Voices in the Harlem Renaissance*.

6. The Importance of Multiple Identities

1. Very few original copies of the magazine remain. It was reprinted in 1968 by Kraus-Thomson in Switzerland, and Henry refers to a reprint by the Negro Universities Press in 1970 (52n9), but commentary on the issue before the mid-1980s is generally limited to relatively brief descriptions of its publication, rather than analyses of its contents. See Lewis, *When Harlem Was in Vogue* 193–97, Huggins 240–41, Haslam 54, and Perkins 32–34. Only Lewis even mentions the illustrations. In his autobiography, *The Big Sea*, Langston Hughes offered insights into the publishing of the magazine, the goals its creators had for it, and its reception (235–38).

2. Even since 1982, critical attention to *Fire!!* has been scant. The most extended discussion of the volume is van Notten's chapter on *Fire!!* and *Harlem* in her biographical and critical study of Thurman (131–67). Henry also devotes considerable attention to the magazine (40–52). Otherwise, though, insights into *Fire!!* must be gained through brief discussions of it. Some of these appear in works by critics writing about the Harlem Renaissance: see, for example, Kalaidjian 90–92, Hutchinson 129, Wall 147, and Smith 214. Others appear in biographical or critical studies of Thurman and his writing: see Henderson, "Portrait" 151–55, Walden 200–11, and dissertations by McIver and Shirley Haynes Wright. Few of these references offer much in the way of analysis of the texts in the magazine, and most mention the illustrations briefly, if at all.

3. On the table of contents and on his illustrations, Nugent is identified as Richard Bruce, a pen name he used in order to not embarrass his mother with the controversial material in the illustrations and in his story "Smoke, Lilies and Jade" (Lewis, *When Harlem Was in Vogue* 196).

4. Hughes echoed that idea in *The Big Sea* when he described the editors' hope that *Fire!!* would "provide us [the younger Negro writers and artists] with an outlet for publication not available in the limited pages of the small Negro magazines then existing, the *Crisis, Opportunity,* and the *Messenger*" (235–36).

5. Hughes attributes this comment to a writer for the Baltimore *Afro-American* (*The Big Sea* 237).

6. That attitude toward the movement is one that colors many of Thurman's comments on it. See, for example, his reference in "A Stranger at the Gates," his laudatory review of Carl Van Vechten's *Nigger Heaven*, to "the current faddistic interest in things Negroid" (279), as well as his opening complaint in "Nephews of Uncle Remus" that "negro literature and literary material have had to be exploited by fad finders and sentimentalists" (296).

7. *The Little Magazine: A History and a Bibliography,* by Hoffman, Allen, and Ulrich, remains an extremely useful source of information about hundreds of little magazines published in the early twentieth century. See also David Bennet.

8. *This Quarter* was first published in Paris in the spring of 1925; its editors identified themselves as "against literary politics and literary politicians" (Hoffman, Allen, and Ulrich 279).

9. Nugent, in his opening statement for the 1982 reprint of *Fire!!,* described nostalgically how he met Langston Hughes at Georgia Douglas Johnson's Washington, D.C., home, and how they walked back and forth in the streets between their houses all night, with much the same emotion—and with the same elliptical style—that he used to describe Alex's meeting with Beauty ("Lighting *FIRE!!*").

10. For reproductions of the illustrations to *Salome,* see Simon Wilson, plates 11–16. Beardsley's depictions of characters from Aristophanes's *Lysistrata* likewise have ridiculously huge penises; see Wilson, plate 38 and fig. 30. Nugent's drawings are tame in comparison.

11. For commentary on *Broom,* see Hoffman et al. (101–108, 261) and Major (46–52). Nelson reproduces the February 1922 cover in *Repression and Recovery* (225). He also reproduces the cover of the Spring–Summer 1924 cover of *The Little*

Review, which demonstrates both this technique of woodcuts and the use of type as a visual element (228).

12. Perloff reproduces the cover of the first issue of *BLAST* in *The Futurist Moment;* the black type is set on a hot pink background (plate 5). Nelson reproduces two covers of *Broom* in color in *Repression and Recovery;* these two are blue and burnt orange (plates D and E).

13. A close study of little magazines may uncover additional texts that deal with racial identity. But critics who have published analyses of little magazines do not mention such texts, if they exist.

WORKS CITED

Adams, John Henry. "The National Pastime." Cartoon. *The Crisis* (Jan. 1911): 18–19.

Akam, Everett H. "Community and Cultural Crisis: The 'Transfiguring Imagination' of Alain Locke." *American Literary History* 3.2 (Summer 1991): 255–76.

Alexander, Charles C. *Here the Country Lies: Nationalism and the Arts in Twentieth-Century America.* Bloomington: Indiana University Press, 1980.

Alexander, Lewis G. "Africa." *Opportunity* (May 1924): 142.

———. "Enchantment." Locke, ed., *The New Negro,* 149–50.

———. "Little Cinderella." *Fire!!* 23.

———. "Streets." *Fire!!* 23.

Allen, James. Afterword. *Without Sanctuary* 203–205.

"Along the Color Line: Crime." *Crisis* (July 1911): 99–100.

Aucoin, James. "Investigative Journalism." Sloan and Parcell, eds., 209–18.

Austin, Addell. "The *Opportunity* and *Crisis* Literary Contests, 1924–27." *CLA Journal* 32.2 (Dec. 1988): 235–46.

Bagehot, Walter. "Charles Dickens." 1858. *The Collected Works of Walter Bagehot.* Ed. Norman St. John-Stevas. 8 vols. Cambridge, Mass.: Harvard University Press, 1965. 77–107.

Bagnall, Robert W. "The Spirit of the Ku Klux Klan." *Opportunity* (Sept. 1923): 265–67.

Baker, Houston A., Jr. *Modernism and the Harlem Renaissance.* Chicago: University of Chicago Press, 1987.

Bal, Mieke. *Double Exposures: The Subject of Cultural Analysis.* With Das Gesicht an der Wand and Edwin Janssen. New York: Routledge, 1996.

Barnes, Albert C. "Negro Art and America." Locke, ed., "Harlem," 668–69. Rpt. in Locke, ed., *The New Negro,* 19–25.

———. "The Temple." *Opportunity* (May 1924): 138–40.

Barnhurst, Kevin G. *Seeing the Newspaper.* New York: St. Martin's, 1994.

Barthes, Roland. *Image, Music, Text.* Trans. Stephen Heath. New York: Hill and Wang—Farrar, Straus and Giroux, 1977.

Battey, C. M. "Compensation." Photograph. *Opportunity* (Sept. 1923): 272–73.

Bennett, David. "Periodical Fragments and Organic Culture: Modernism, the Avant-Garde, and the Little Magazine." *Contemporary Literature* 30.4 (1989): 480–502.

Bennett, Gwendolyn. "Wedding Day." *Fire!!* 25–28.

Berger, John. *Ways of Seeing.* 1972. London: British Broadcasting Corporation and Penguin, 1977.

Bishop, Edward. "Re:Covering Modernism—Format and Function in the Little Magazines." *Modernist Writers and the Marketplace.* Ed. Ian Willison, Warwick Gould, and Warren Chernaic. New York: St. Martin's, 1996. 287–319.

Bontemps, Arna. "Length of Moon." *Fire!!* 22.

———, ed. *The Harlem Renaissance Remembered.* New York: Dodd, Mead and Co., 1972.

Bracey, John, August Meier, and Elliott Rudwick. "The Black Sociologists: The First Half Century." Ladner, ed., 3–22.

Brawley, Benjamin. "The Negro Literary Renaissance." *Southern Workman* (Apr. 1927): 177–84.

"B'rer Rabbit Fools Buzzard." Locke, ed., *The New Negro*, 248–49.

Brown, Sterling. "Negro Character As Seen by White Authors." *Journal of Negro Education* 2 (Apr. 1933): 179–203. Rpt. in *A Son's Return: Selected Essays of Sterling A. Brown*. Ed. Mark A. Sanders. The Northeastern Library of Black Literature. Ed. Richard Yarborough. Boston: Northeastern University Press, 1996. 148–83.

———. *Southern Road*. Illustrated by E. Simms Campbell. Harcourt, 1932. Boston: Beacon Press, 1974.

Bulmer, Martin. *The Chicago School of Sociology: Institutionalization, Diversity, and the Rise of Sociological Research*. The Heritage of Sociology. Ed. Morris Janowitz. Chicago: University of Chicago Press, 1984.

Byerman, Keith E. *Seizing the Word: History, Art, and Self in the Work of W. E. B. Du Bois*. Athens: University of Georgia Press, 1994.

Call and Response: The Riverside Anthology of the African American Literary Tradition. Ed. Patricia Liggins Hill et al. Boston: Houghton Mifflin, 1998.

Calverton, V. F., ed. *Anthology of American Negro Literature*. New York: Modern Library, 1929.

Campbell, Karlyn Kohrs. "The Power of Hegemony: Capitalism and Racism in the 'Nadir of Negro History.'" *Rhetoric and Community: Studies in Unity and Fragmentation*. Ed. J. Michael Hogan. Studies in Rhetoric and Communication. Columbia: University of South Carolina Press, 1998. 36–74.

"A Challenge to the Negro." Rev. of *Fire!!. Bookman* (Nov. 1926): 258–59.

Chambers, Clarke A. *Paul U. Kellogg and the Survey: Voices for Social Welfare and Social Justice*. Minneapolis: University of Minnesota Press, 1971.

Chesnutt, Charles Waddell. "The Doll." Illustrated. *The Crisis* (Apr. 1912): 248–52.

Chielens, Edward E., ed. *American Literary Magazines: The Twentieth Century*. Historical Guides to the World's Periodicals and Newspapers. Westport, Conn.: Greenwood, 1992.

Chilvers, Ian. *A Dictionary of Twentieth-Century Art*. Oxford: Oxford University Press, 1998.

Chinitz, David. "Literacy and Authenticity: The Blues Poems of Langston Hughes." *Callaloo* 19.1 (1996): 177–92.

Coles, Robert A., and Diane Isaacs. "Primitivism as a Therapeutic Pursuit: Notes Toward a Reassessment of Harlem Renaissance Literature." Singh, Shiver, and Brodwin, eds., 3–12.

The Colored American Magazine. Washington, D.C. 1900–1909.

Comaroff, John and Jean. *Ethnography and the Historical Imagination*. Studies in the Ethnographic Imagination. Ed. John Comaroff, Pierre Bourdieu, and Maurice Bloch. Boulder: Westview Press, 1992.

"The Contest." *Opportunity* (May 1925): 130–31.

"The Contest." *Opportunity* (Oct. 1925): 291–92.

"A Contest Number." *Opportunity* (June 1926): 173.

Cowley, Malcolm. "Foreword: The Revolt Against Gentility." *After the Genteel Tradition: American Writers 1910–1930*. Ed. Malcolm Cowley. 1936. Carbondale: Southern Illinois University Press, 1964. 3–20.

"The Creative Art of Negroes." *Opportunity* (Aug. 1923): 240–45.

The Crisis. New York: National Association for the Advancement of Colored People. 1910–.

Cullen, Countee. *Color*. Illustrated by Charles Cullen. New York: Harper & Brothers, 1925.

———. "The Dark Tower." *Opportunity* (Mar. 1928): 90.

———. "Heritage." Locke, ed., "Harlem," 674–75. Rpt. in Locke, ed., *The New Negro*, 250–53.

———. "To a Brown Boy." Locke, ed., *The New Negro*, 129.

———. "To a Brown Girl." Locke, ed., *The New Negro*, 129.

Cunard, Nancy. *Negro: An Anthology*. Illustrated. London: Nancy Cunard, 1934.

Cuney, Waring. "The Death Bed." *Fire!!* 19.

Daniel, Walter C. *Black Journals of the United States*. Historical Guides to the World's Periodicals and Newspapers. Westport, Conn.: Greenwood, 1982.

Dann, Martin E. Introduction. *The Black Press, 1827–1890: The Quest for National Identity*. Ed. Dann. New York: Putnam's, 1971. 11–31.

De Jongh, James. *Vicious Modernism: Black Harlem and the Literary Imagination*. Cambridge: Cambridge University Press, 1990.

DeMarco, Joseph P. *The Social Thought of W.E.B. DuBois*. Lanham, Md.: University Press of America, 1983.

"Democracy in Boston." *Opportunity* (Sept. 1923): 285–86.

DeSantis, Alan D. "A Forgotten Leader: Robert S. Abbott and the Chicago *Defender* from 1910–1920." *Journalism History* 23.2 (Summer 1997): 63–71.

Doherty, Brigid. "'See: "We are all Neurasthenics! "'": or, the Trauma of Dada Montage." *Critical Inquiry* 24.1 (Autumn 1997). *Expanded Academic ASAP*. InfoTrac. Wichita State University Libraries, Wichita, Kan. 5 Feb. 2002. http://web5.infotrac.galegroup.com/.

Domingo, W. A. "The Tropics in New York." Locke, ed., "Harlem," 648–50. Rpt. as "Gift of the Black Tropics" in Locke, ed., *The New Negro*, 341–49.

Douglas, Aaron. "Ancestral." Locke, ed., *The New Negro*, 268. Rpt. as "Rebirth" in Locke, ed., *The New Negro* (1927), 56.

———. Cover. *Fire!!*.

———. "I Couldn't Hear Nobody Pray." *Opportunity* (Nov. 1925): 333.

———. "I Needs a Dime for Beer." "Two Artists," 314.

———. "Ma Bad Luck Card." "Two Artists," 315.

———. "Meditation." Locke, ed., *The New Negro*, 56.

———. "On De No'thern Road." "Two Artists," 315.

———. "Play de Blues." "Two Artists," 315.

———. "Three drawings." *Fire!!* 30–32.

———. Untitled. ("The Black Runner.") *Opportunity* (Sept. 1925): frontispiece.

———. Untitled. ("Feet o' Jesus.") *Opportunity* (Oct. 1926): cover.

———. Untitled. ("Incidental art decorations.") *Fire!!*.

———. Untitled. ("To Midnight Nan at Leroy's.") *Opportunity* (Jan. 1926): 23.

———. "Weary as I Can Be." "Two Artists," 314.

Douglass, Frederick. *Frederick Douglass: Autobiographies*. New York: Library of America, 1994.

———. *The Narrative of the Life of Frederick Douglass, An American Slave, Written by Himself*. 1845. New York: Dover, 1995.

———. *The Narrative of the Life of Frederick Douglass, an American Slave*. Ed. Benjamin Quarles. 1960. Cambridge, Mass.: Belknap—Harvard University Press, 1996.

Dray, Philip. *At the Hands of Persons Unknown: The Lynching of Black America*. New York: Random House, 2002.

"Dr. Barnes." *Opportunity* (May 1924): 133.

Du Bois, W. E. B. *The Autobiography of W. E. B. Du Bois: A Soliloquy on Viewing My Life from the Last Decade of Its First Century*. 1968. N.p.: International Publishers, 1997.

———. "The Black Man Brings His Gifts." Locke, ed., "Harlem," 655–57, 710.

———. *The Correspondence of W.E.B. Du Bois*. Vol. 1: *Selections, 1877–1934*. Ed. Herbert Aptheker. Amherst: University of Massachusetts Press, 1973.

———. "Criteria of Negro Art." *The Crisis* (Oct. 1926): 290–97.

———. *Dusk of Dawn: An Essay Toward an Autobiography of a Race Concept*. 1940. New York: Schocken Books, 1968.

———. "Editing *The Crisis*." March 1951. *The Crisis Reader: Stories, Poetry, and Essays from the N.A.A.C.P.'s Crisis Magazine*. Ed. Sondra Kathryn Wilson. New York: Modern Library—Random House, 1999. xxvii–xxxii.

———. "Editorial: Close Ranks." *The Crisis* (July 1918): 111.

———. "Editorial: Returning Soldiers." *The Crisis* (May 1919): 13–14.

———. "The Immediate Program of the American Negro." *The Crisis* (Apr. 1915): 310–12.

———. "An Institute of Negro Literature and Art." *The Crisis* (June 1922): 58–59.

———. "The Negro in Literature and Art." 1913. Rpt. in *The Emergence of the Harlem Renaissance*. Ed. Cary D. Wintz. New York: Garland, 1996. 2–7.

———. "Negro Writers." *The Crisis* (Apr. 1920): 298–99.

———. "A Proposed Negro Journal." 1905. *Against Racism: Unpublished Essays, Papers, Addresses, 1887–1961, by W.E.B. Du Bois*. Ed. Herbert Aptheker. Amherst: University of Massachusetts Press, 1985. 77–81.

———. "The Star of Ethiopia." *The Crisis* (Dec. 1915): 90–93.

———. "The Talented Tenth." 1903. *Crossing the Danger Water: Three Hundred Years of African-American Writing*. Ed. Deirdre Mullane. New York: Anchor—Random House, 1993. 382–92.

———. *Writings in Periodicals Edited by W.E.B. Du Bois: Selections from THE CRISIS, Vol. 1, 1911–1925*. Ed. Herbert Aptheker. The Complete Published Works of W.E.B. Du Bois. Millwood, N.Y.: Kraus-Thomson, 1983.

[Du Bois, W. E. B.] "The Amy Spingarn Prizes in Literature and Art." *The Crisis* (Oct. 1924): 247.

———. "Anthony Crawford." *The Crisis* (Dec. 1916): 67.

———. "The Burden: Another Southern Idyl." *The Crisis* (Mar. 1913): 246.

———. "Colored California." *The Crisis* (Aug. 1913): 192–96.

———. "The Colored Magazine in America." *The Crisis* (Nov. 1912): 33–35.

———. "The Crisis: A Business Proposition." *The Crisis* (Feb. 1911): 3.

———. "Editorial." [Two Italians] *The Crisis* (Nov. 1910): 11.

———. "Editorial: Awake America." *The Crisis* (Sept. 1917): 216–17.

———. "Editorial: The Crisis." *The Crisis* (Nov. 1910): 10.

———. "Editorial: East St. Louis." *The Crisis* (Sept. 1917): 215–16.

———. "Editorial: The Gall of Bitterness." *The Crisis* (Feb. 1912): 153.

———. "Editorial: Lynching." *The Crisis* (Aug. 1911): 158–59.

———. "Editorial: N.A.A.C.P." *The Crisis* (Dec. 1910): 16–17.

———. "Editorial: Of the Shielding Arm." *The Crisis* (Oct. 1912): 287–88.

———. "Editorial: The Second Birthday." *The Crisis* (Nov. 1912): 27–28.

———. "Editorial: Starvation and Prejudice." *The Crisis* (June 1911): 62–64.

———. "Editorial: The Truth." *The Crisis* (Apr. 1911): 21–22.

———. "KRIGWA 1926." *The Crisis* (Dec. 1925): 67–68.

———. "Krigwa, 1927." *The Crisis* (Feb. 1927): 191–93.

———. "The Manufacture of Prejudice." *The Crisis* (May 1911): 35–37.

———. "Our Baby Pictures." *The Crisis* (Oct. 1914): 298–300.

———. "Promotion of Prejudice." *The Crisis* (Sept. 1911): 196–97.

———. "A Questionnaire." *The Crisis* (Feb. 1926): 165.

———. "Short Story Competiton." *The Crisis* (Aug. 1912): 189.

———. "Some Headlines." *The Crisis* (Nov. 1911): 31–32.

———. "Southern Papers." *The Crisis* (Feb. 1911): 21.

———. "The Year in Colored Colleges." *The Crisis* (July 1912): 133–36.

———, and Alain Locke. "The Younger Literary Movement." *The Crisis* (Feb. 1924): 161–63.

Dyer, Richard. *The Matter of Images: Essays on Representations.* London: Routledge, 1993.

Eisenstein, Sergei. "Dickens, Griffith, and the Film Today." *Film Form: Essays in Film Theory.* 1949. Ed. and trans. Jay Leyda. New York: Harvest—Harcourt Brace Jovanovich, 1977. 195–255.

———. "Through Theater to Cinema." *Film Form: Essays in Film Theory.* 1949. Ed. and trans. Jay Leyda. New York: Harvest—Harcourt Brace Jovanovich, 1977. 3–17.

———. "Word and Image." *The Film Sense.* 1942. Ed. and trans. Jay Leyda. New York: Harvest/HBJ—Harcourt Brace Jovanovich, 1975. 3–65.

Ethnic Notions. Dir. Marlon Riggs. Videocassette. San Francisco: California Newsreel, 1986. 58 minutes.

Fabre, Geneviève, and Michel Feith, eds. *Temples for Tomorrow: Looking Back at the Harlem Renaissance.* Bloomington: Indiana University Press, 2001.

Faris, Robert E. L. *Chicago Sociology 1920–1932.* 1967. The Heritage of Sociology. Ed. Morris Janowitz. Chicago: University of Chicago Press, 1970.

Fauset, Arthur Huff. "American Negro Folk Literature." Locke, ed., *The New Negro,* 238–44.

———. "Intelligentsia." *Fire!!* 45–46.

———. "The Negro's Cycle of Song—A Review." *Opportunity* (Nov. 1925): 333–35, 348.

Fauset, Jessie. "Emmy." Illustrated. *The Crisis* (Dec. 1912): 79–87; (Jan. 1913): 134–42.

———. "The Prize Story Competition." *The Crisis* (June 1923): 57–58.

———. "The Sleeper Wakes." Illustrated by Laura Wheeler. *The Crisis* (Aug. 1920): 168–73; (Sept. 1920): 226–29; (Oct. 1920): 267–74.

———. *There Is Confusion.* New York: Boni & Liveright, 1924.

Favor, J. Martin. *Authentic Blackness: The Folk in the New Negro Renaissance.* New Americanists. Ed. Donald E. Pease. Durham, N.C.: Duke University Press, 1999.

Fire!! 1926. Metuchen, N.J.: Fire Press, 1982.

Fisher, Rudolph. "The City of Refuge." Locke, ed., *The New Negro,* 57–74.

Fitzpatrick, Vincent. "The American Mercury." Chielens, ed., 7–16.

———. "The Smart Set." Chielens, ed., 333–41.

Fleming, David. "Can Pictures Be Arguments?" *Argumentation and Advocacy* (Summer 1996): 11–22.

Foldy, Michael S. *The Trials of Oscar Wilde: Deviance, Morality, and Late-Victorian Society.* New Haven, Conn.: Yale University Press, 1997.

"Foreword." *Fire!!* 1.

Franklin, Cynthia. *Writing Women's Communities: The Politics and Poetics of Contemporary Multi-Genre Anthologies.* Madison: University of Wisconsin Press, 1997.

Fredrickson, George M. *The Black Image in the White Mind: The Debate on Afro-American Character and Destiny, 1817–1914.* 1971. Hanover, N.H.: Wesleyan University Press, 1987.

Friedman, Susan Stanford. "'Beyond' Gynocriticism and Gynesis: The Geographics of Identity and the Future of Feminist Criticism." *Tulsa Studies in Women's Literature* 15.1 (Spring 1996): 13–40.

Gates, Henry Louis, Jr. *Loose Canons: Notes on the Culture Wars.* New York: Oxford University Press, 1992.

———. "The Trope of a New Negro and the Reconstruction of the Image of the Black." *Representations* 24 (Fall 1988): 129–55.

———, and Nellie Y. McKay, eds. *The Norton Anthology of African American Literature.* New York: Norton, 1997.

Gelburd, Gail. *A Blossoming of New Promises: Art in the Spirit of the Harlem Renaissance.* Hempstead, N.Y.: Hofstra University, Emily Lowe Gallery, 1984.

Gilpin, Patrick J. "Charles S. Johnson: Entrepreneur of the Harlem Renaissance." Bontemps, ed., 215–46.

Goin, Chelsea Miller. "Malinowski's Ethnographic Photography: Image, Text and Authority." *History of Photography* 21 (Spring 1997): 67–72.

Golding, John. "Cubism." *Concepts of Modern Art.* Ed. Tony Richardson and Nikos Stangos. New York: Icon Editions—Harper & Row, 1974. 53–81.

Green, Dan S., and Edwin D. Driver, eds. *W. E. B. Du Bois on Sociology and the Black Community.* The Heritage of Sociology. Ed. Morris Janowitz. Chicago: University of Chicago Press, 1978.

Gregory, Montgomery. Rev. of *Cane,* by Jean Toomer. *Opportunity* (Dec. 1923): 374–75.

————. "The Spirit of Phyllis [*sic*] Wheatley: A Review of *There Is Confusion,* by Jessie Redmon Fauset." *Opportunity* (June 1924): 181–82.

Guillaume, Paul. "African Art at the Barnes Foundation." *Opportunity* (May 1924): 140–42.

Hall, Stuart. "Introduction: Who Needs 'Identity'?" *Questions of Cultural Identity.* Ed. Stuart Hall and Paul Du Gay. London: Sage, 1996. 1–17.

————, ed. *Representation: Cultural Representations and Signifying Practices.* Culture, Media and Identities. London: Sage and Open University, 1997.

Harmon, William, and Hugh Holman. *A Handbook to Literature.* 9th ed. Upper Saddle River, N.J.: Prentice Hall, 2003.

Harthan, John. *The History of the Illustrated Book: The Western Tradition.* London: Thames and Hudson, 1981.

Haslam, Gerald. "Wallace Thurman: A Western Renaissance Man." *Western American Literature* 6 (Spring 1971): 53–59.

Hayden, Robert. "Preface to the Atheneum Edition." 1968. Locke, ed., *The New Negro,* 1969. ix–xiv.

Haynes, George E. "The Church and the Negro Spirit." Locke, ed., "Harlem," 695–97, 708–709.

Hemenway, Robert E. *Zora Neale Hurston: A Literary Biography.* Urbana: University of Illinois Press, 1977.

Henderson, Mae Gwendolyn. "Portrait of Wallace Thurman." Bontemps, ed., 147–70.

————. "Speaking in Tongues: Dialogics, Dialectics, and the Black Woman Writer's Literary Tradition." *Changing Our Own Words: Essays on Criticism, Theory, and Writing by Black Women.* Ed. Cheryl A. Wall. New Brunswick, N.J.: Rutgers University Press, 1989. 16–37.

Henry, Matthew. "Playing with *Fire!!:* Manifesto of the Harlem Niggerati." *Griot* 10.2 (Fall 1992): 40–52.

Herskovits, Melville J. "The Dilemma of Social Pattern." Locke, ed., "Harlem," 676–78. Rpt. as "The Negro's Americanism" in Locke, ed., *The New Negro,* 353–60.

Hill, Leslie Pinckney. "The Teacher." *The Crisis* (Jan. 1911): 23.

Himes, Chester. *If He Hollers Let Him Go.* 1945. New York: Thunder's Mouth Press, 1991.

Hoffman, Frederick J., Charles Allen, and Carolyn F. Ulrich. *The Little Magazine: A History and a Bibliography.* Princeton, N.J.: Princeton University Press, 1946.

Holmes, D. O. W. "Our Negro Colleges: Howard University." *Opportunity* (Mar. 1923): 10–13.

"The Holstein Prizes." *Opportunity* (Oct. 1926): 318–19.

hooks, bell. *Black Looks: Race and Representation.* Boston: South End Press, 1992.

"The Horizon." *The Crisis* (Feb. 1923): 175–80.

Horne, Frank S. "Black Verse." Illustrated by Francis C. Holbrook. *Opportunity* (Nov. 1924): 330–32.

Houze, J. O. "The National Malleable Casting Co., Cleveland, Ohio." *Opportunity* (Jan. 1923): 20–22.

Huggins, Nathan Irvin. *Harlem Renaissance.* 1971. New York: Oxford University Press, 1973.

Hughes, Langston. *The Big Sea: An Autobiography.* 1940. New York: Hill and Wang—Farrar, Straus and Giroux, 1993.

———. "Bound No'th Blues." "Two Artists," 315.

———. "Down an' Out." "Two Artists," 314.

———. *The Dream Keeper and Other Poems.* Illustrated by Helen Sewell. New York: Knopf, 1932.

———. "Elevator Boy." *Fire!!* 20.

———. "Feet o' Jesus." *Opportunity* (Oct. 1926): cover.

———. *Fine Clothes to the Jew.* New York: Knopf, 1927.

———. "Hard Luck." "Two Artists," 315.

———. "I Too." Locke, ed., *The New Negro,* 145.

———. "Lonesome Place." "Two Artists," 314.

———. "Misery." "Two Artists," 315.

———. "The Negro Artist and the Racial Mountain." *Nation* (June 1926). Rpt. in Gates and McKay, eds., 1267–71.

———. "Our Land." *Opportunity* (May 1924): 142. Rpt. in Locke, ed., "Harlem," 678.

———. "Railroad Avenue." *Fire!!* 21.

———. "To Midnight Nan at Leroy's." *Opportunity* (Jan. 1926): 23.

———. Untitled. "The Negro in Art: How Shall He Be Portrayed." Symposium. *The Crisis* (Apr. 1926): 278.

———. *The Weary Blues.* Cover illustration by Aaron Douglas. New York: Knopf, 1926.

Hull, Gloria T. *Color, Sex, & Poetry: Three Women Writers of the Harlem Renaissance.* Everywoman: Studies in Culture and Literature. Ed. Susan Gubar and Joan Hoff-Wilson. Blacks in the Diaspora. Ed. Darlene Clark Hine and John Mc-Clusky, Jr. Bloomington: Indiana University Press, 1987.

Hurston, Zora Neale. "Color Struck: A Play in Four Scenes." *Fire!!* 7–14.

———. *Mules and Men.* 1935. New York: HarperCollins, 1990.

———. "Spunk." Locke, ed., *The New Negro,* 105–11.

———. "Sweat." *Fire!!* 40–45.

Hutchinson, George. *The Harlem Renaissance in Black and White.* Cambridge: Belknap—Harvard University Press, 1995.

Hutt, Allen. *The Changing Newspaper: Typographic Trends in Britain and America, 1622–1972.* London: Gordon Fraser, 1973.

Hutton, Frankie. "Democratic Idealism in the Black Press." *Outsiders in 19th-Century Press History: Multicultural Perspectives.* Ed. Frankie Hutton and Barbara Straus Reed. Bowling Green, Ohio: Bowling Green State University Popular Press, 1995. 5–20.

Ikonné, Chidi. *From Du Bois to Van Vechten: The Early New Negro Literature, 1903–1926.* Contributions in Afro-American and African Studies 60. Westport, Conn.: Greenwood Press, 1981.

Irek, Matgorzata. "From Berlin to Harlem: Felix von Luschan, Alain Locke, and the New Negro." *The Black Columbiad: Defining Moments in African American Literature and Culture.* Ed. Werner Sollers and Maria Diedrich. Cambridge, Mass.: Harvard University Press, 1994. 174–84.

Johnson, Abby Arthur, and Ronald Maberry Johnson. *Propaganda and Aesthetics: The Literary Politics of Afro-American Magazines in the Twentieth Century.* Amherst: University of Massachusetts Press, 1979.

Johnson, Charles S. "Black Workers and the City." Locke, ed., "Harlem," 641–43, 718–19, 721. Rpt. as "The New Frontage on American Life," in Locke, ed., *The New Negro,* 278–98.

———. "How Much is the Migration a Flight from Persecution?" *Opportunity* (Sept. 1923): 272–74.

———. "The Negro Renaissance and Its Significance." Logan, Holmes, and Edwards, eds., 80–88.

———. [C. S. J.] "Nigger—A Novel by Clement Wood." *Opportunity* (Jan. 1923): 30.

———. "Public Opinion and The Negro." *Opportunity* (July 1923): 201–206.

———, ed. *Ebony and Topaz: A Collectanea.* Illustrated. New York: Opportunity, 1927. Rpt. in *The Politics and Aesthetics of "New Negro" Literature.* Ed. Cary D. Wintz. New York: Garland, 1996. 1–163.

Johnson, Georgia Douglas. "The Black Runner." Illustrated by Aaron Douglas. *Opportunity* (Sept. 1925): frontispiece.

Johnson, Guy B. "The Race Philosophy of the Ku Klux Klan." *Opportunity* (Sept. 1923): 268–70.

Johnson, Helene. "A Southern Road." *Fire!!* 17.

Johnson, James Weldon. *God's Trombones: Seven Negro Sermons in Verse.* 1927. Illustrated by Aaron Douglas. Lettering by C. B. Falls. New York: Penguin, 1990.

———. "The Making of Harlem." Locke, ed., "Harlem," 635–39. Rpt. as "Harlem: The Culture Capital" in Locke, ed., *The New Negro,* 301–11.

———. "To America." Illustrated by Laura Wheeler. *The Crisis* (Nov. 1917): 13.

———, ed. *The Book of American Negro Poetry.* 1922. Rev. ed. 1931. San Diego: Harvest—Harcourt Brace, 1959.

———, and J. Rosamond Johnson, eds. *The Book of American Negro Spirituals.* New York: Viking, 1925.

———, and J. Rosamond Johnson, eds. *The Second Book of American Negro Spirituals.* New York: Viking, 1927.

Johnson, Sammye, and Patricia Prijatel. *Magazine Publishing.* Lincolnwood, Ill.: NTC/Contemporary Publishing Group, 2000.

Johnson, V. D. Rev. of *The Negro in Chicago. Opportunity* (Jan. 1923): 27–28.

Jones, Eugene Kinckle. "'Cooperation' and 'Opportunity.'" *Opportunity* (Jan. 1923): 4–5.

———. "Dear Survey Reader." Locke, ed., "Harlem," 623.

———. "Social Work among Negroes." *The Messenger* (Nov. 1917): 26–27.

Jordan, William G. *Black Newspapers and America's War for Democracy, 1914–1920.* Chapel Hill: University of North Carolina Press, 2001.

Kalaidjian, Walter. *American Culture Between the Wars: Revisionary Modernism and Postmodern Critique.* New York: Columbia University Press, 1993.

Kellogg, Charles Flint. *NAACP: A History of The National Association for the Advancement of Colored People, Vol. 1: 1909–1920.* Baltimore: Johns Hopkins Press, 1967.

Kerlin, Robert T. "Conquest by Poetry." *Southern Workman* 56.6 (June 1927): 282–84.

Kirschke, Amy Helene. *Aaron Douglas: Art, Race, and the Harlem Renaissance.* Jackson: University Press of Mississippi, 1995.

Kitch, Carolyn. *The Girl on the Magazine Cover: The Origins of Visual Stereotypes in American Mass Media.* Chapel Hill: University of North Carolina Press, 2001.

Koepnick, Lutz P. "Allegory and Power: Walter Benjamin and the Politics of Representation." *Soundings* 79.1–2 (Spring/Summer 1996): 59–78.

Kooistra, Lorraine Janzen. *The Artist as Critic: Bitextuality in Fin-de-Siècle Illustrated Books.* Hants, UK: Scolar Press and Brookfield, Vt.: Ashgate, 1995.

Kornweibel, Theodore, Jr. *"Investigate Everything": Federal Efforts to Compel Black Loyalty during World War I.* Bloomington: Indiana University Press, 2002.

———. *No Crystal Stair: Black Life and the Messenger, 1917–1928.* Contributions in Afro-American and African Studies 20. Westport, Conn.: Greenwood, 1975.

———. *"Seeing Red": Federal Campaigns against Black Militancy, 1919–1925.* 1998. Blacks in the Diaspora. Ed. Darlene Clark Hine, John McClusky, Jr., and David Barry Gaspar. Bloomington: Indiana University Press, 1999.

Ladner, Joyce A. Introduction. Ladner, ed., xix–xxix.

———, ed. *The Death of White Sociology.* New York: Random House, 1973.

Larsen, Nella. *Passing.* New York: Knopf, 1929.

———. *Quicksand.* New York: Knopf, 1928.

Lauter, Paul. "On Revising the *Heath Anthology of American Literature.*" In "What Do We Need to Teach?" Forum. *American Literature* 65.2 (June 1993): 327–30.

Lester, Julius, ed. *The Seventh Son: The Thought and Writings of W. E. B. Du Bois.* 2 vols. New York: Random House, 1971.

Leviatin, David. "Framing the Poor: The Irresistibility of How the Other Half Lives." Riis 1–50.

Lewis, David Levering. *W. E. B. Du Bois.* Vol. I: *Biography of a Race, 1868–1919.* 1993. New York: Henry Holt, 1994.

———. *W. E. B. Du Bois.* Vol. II: *The Fight for Equality and the American Century, 1919–1963.* New York: Henry Holt, 2000.

———. *When Harlem Was in Vogue.* 1981. New York: Oxford University Press, 1989.

"Listen to de Lambs." Locke, ed., *The New Negro,* 212–13.

Litwack, Leon F. "Hellhounds." *Without Sanctuary,* 8–37.

Locke, Alain. "The Colonial Literature of France." *Opportunity* (Nov. 1923): 331–35.

———. "Enter the New Negro." Locke, ed., "Harlem," 631–34. Rpt. with "Harlem" as "The New Negro."

———. "Fire: A Negro Magazine." Rev. of *Fire!!. Survey* (15 Aug.–15 Sept. 1927): 563.

———. "Foreword." Locke, ed., *The New Negro,* ix–xi.

———. [A. L.] "Harlem." Locke, ed., "Harlem," 629–30. Rpt. with "Enter the New Negro" as "The New Negro."

———. "The Legacy of the Ancestral Arts." Locke, ed., *The New Negro,* 254–67.

———. "The Negro Spirituals." Locke, ed., *The New Negro,* 199–210.

———. "Negro Youth Speaks." Locke, ed., *The New Negro,* 47–53.

———. "The New Negro." Locke, ed., *The New Negro,* 3–16.

———. "A Note on African Art." *Opportunity* (May 1924): 134–38.

———. "To Certain of Our Phillistines." *Opportunity* (May 1925): 155–56.

———. [A. L.] "Youth Speaks." Locke, ed., "Harlem," 659–60. Rpt. as "Negro Youth Speaks."

———, ed. "Harlem: Mecca of the New Negro." *Survey Graphic* (1 March 1925): 621–724. Baltimore: Black Classic Press, 1980.

———. "Harlem: Mecca of the New Negro: A Hypermedia Edition of the March 1925 *Survey Graphic* Harlem Number." Prepared by Matthew G. Kirschenbaum and Catherine Tousignant. 3 November 1996. University of Virginia, Electronic Text Center. http://etext.lib.virginia.edu/harlem/index/html. 25 March 1998.

———. *The New Negro: An Interpretation.* New York: Albert and Charles Boni, 1925.

———. *The New Negro: An Interpretation.* New York: Albert and Charles Boni, 1927.

———. *The New Negro: An Interpretation.* New York: Arno Press and The New York Times, 1968.

———. *The New Negro: Voices of the Harlem Renaissance.* Studies in American Negro Life. Ed. August Meier. New York: Atheneum, 1969.

———. *The New Negro: Voices of the Harlem Renaissance.* New York: Atheneum—Macmillan, 1992.

Logan, Rayford W., Eugene C. Holmes, and G. Franklin Edwards, eds. *The New Negro Thirty Years Afterward.* Papers Contributed to the Sixteenth Annual Spring Conference of the Division of the Social Sciences. April 1955. Howard University Graduate School. Washington, D.C.: Howard University Press, 1955.

Long, Richard A. "The Genesis of Locke's *The New Negro.*" *Black World* 25.4 (Feb. 1976): 14–20.

"The Looking Glass: Literature." *The Crisis* (Jan. 1927): 158.

"The Looking Glass: Memphis." *The Crisis* (July 1917): 133–35.

"The Looking Glass: The Riot in East St. Louis." *The Crisis* (Aug. 1917): 175–78.

Lott, Tommy Lee. "Nationalism and Pluralism in Alain Locke's Social Philosophy." *Defending Diversity: Contemporary Philosophical Perspectives on Pluralism and Multiculturalism.* Ed. Lawrence Foster and Patricia Herzog. Amherst: University of Massachusetts Press, 1994. 103–19.

Lutz, Catherine A., and Jane L. Collins. *Reading "National Geographic."* Chicago: University of Chicago Press, 1993.

Lutz, Tom. Introduction. *These "Colored" United States: African American Essays from the 1920s.* Ed. Tom Lutz and Susanna Ashton. New Brunswick, N.J.: Rutgers University Press, 1996. 1–12.

M. A. H. "NAACP: Another Lynching." *The Crisis* (Oct. 1916): 275–76.

Maclean, M. D. "African Civilization." *The Crisis* (Mar. 1911): 23–25.

Major, Clarence. "Broom." Chielens, ed., 46–52.

Manly, A. L. "Where Negroes Live In Philadelphia." *Opportunity* (May 1923): 10–15.

Mason, Earnest Douglas. "Alain Locke and Social Realism." *Obsidian: Black Literature in Review* 5.3 (1979): 22–32.

Matthews, Fred H. *Quest for an American Sociology: Robert E. Park and the Chicago School.* Montreal and London: McGill-Queen's University Press, 1977.

McClelland, Edward S. "Negro Labor in the Westinghouse Electric and Manufacturing Corporation." *Opportunity* (Jan. 1923): 22–23.

McDougald, Elise Johnson. "The Double Task: The Struggle of Negro Women for Sex and Race Emancipation." Locke, ed., "Harlem," 689–91. Rpt. as "The Task of Negro Womanhood" in Locke, ed., *The New Negro,* 369–82.

McDowell, Deborah E. *"The Changing Same": Black Women's Literature, Criticism, and Theory.* Bloomington: Indiana University Press, 1995.

McIver, Dorothy Jean Palmer. "Stepchild in Harlem: The Literary Career of Wallace Thurman." Diss. University of Alabama, 1983. *DAI* 44.8 (Feb. 1984): 2473–74-A.

McKay, Claude. "Africa." *Opportunity* (May 1924): 142.

———. *Home to Harlem.* 1928. Boston: Northeastern University Press, 1987.

———. "White Houses." Locke, ed., "Harlem," 662.

Miller, George, and Dorothy Miller. *Picture Postcards in the United States, 1893–1918.* New York: Clarkson N. Potter, 1976.

Miller, Kelly. "The Harvest of Race Prejudice." Locke, ed., "Harlem," 682–83, 711–12.

Mills, Charles M. "Shop Representation." *Opportunity* (Apr. 1923): 25.

Mirzoeff, Nicholas. *An Introduction to Visual Culture.* London: Routledge—Taylor & Francis, 1999.

Mishkin, Tracy. *The Harlem and Irish Renaissances: Language, Identity, and Representation.* Gainesville: University Press of Florida, 1998.

Mitchell, W. J. T. *Picture Theory: Essays on Verbal and Visual Representation.* Chicago: University of Chicago Press, 1994.

Moon, Henry Lee. *The Emerging Thought of W. E. B. Du Bois: Essays and Editorials from "The Crisis."* New York: Simon and Schuster, 1972.

Moore, Jesse Thomas, Jr. *A Search for Equality: The National Urban League, 1910–1961.* University Park: Pennsylvania State University Press, 1981.

Mott, Christopher. "The Art of Self-Promotion; or, Which Self to Sell? The Proliferation and Disintegration of the Harlem Renaissance." *Marketing Modernisms: Self-Promotion, Canonization, Rereading.* Ed. Kevin J. H. Dettmar and Stephen Watt. Ann Arbor: University of Michigan Press, 1996. 253–74.

Mott, Frank Luther. *A History of American Magazines.* 5 vols. Cambridge, Mass.: Harvard University Press, 1938–1957.

Mulvey, Laura. *Visual and Other Pleasures.* Theories of Representation and Difference. Ed. Teresa de Lauretis. Bloomington: Indiana University Press, 1989.

Munson, Gorham. *The Awakening Twenties: A Memoir-History of a Literary Period.* Baton Rouge: Louisiana State University Press, 1985.

"NAACP: Holmes on Lynching." *The Crisis* (Jan. 1912): 109–12.

"NAACP: The Massacre of East St. Louis." *The Crisis* (Sept. 1917): 219–38.

Nadell, Martha Jane. *Enter the New Negroes: Images of Race in American Culture.* Cambridge: Harvard University Press, 2004.

"The Negro in Art: How Shall He Be Portrayed." Symposium. *The Crisis* (Mar.–Nov. 1926).

Nelson, Cary. *Repression and Recovery: Modern American Poetry and the Politics of Cultural Memory, 1910–1945.* Madison: University of Wisconsin Press, 1989.

"The New Generation." *Opportunity* (Mar. 1924): 68.

Newhall, Beaumont. *The History of Photography: From 1839 to the Present Day.* 4th ed. New York: Museum of Modern Art; Rochester, N.Y.: George Eastman House, 1964.

"1923." *Opportunity* (Jan. 1923): 3.

Nugent, Bruce. [Richard Bruce Nugent.] "Lighting *FIRE!!*" 1982. *Fire!!.* N.p.

———. "Sahdji." Locke, ed., *The New Negro,* 113–14.

———. [Richard Bruce.] "Smoke, Lilies and Jade." *Fire!!* 33–39.

———. [RBN.] Untitled. (Two drawings of women.) *Fire!!* 4, 24.

Olasky, Marvin. *Central Ideas in the Development of Journalism: A Narrative History.* Hillsdale, N.J.: Lawrence Erlbaum Associates, 1991.

Olney, James. "'I Was Born': Slave Narratives, Their Status as Autobiography and as Literature." *The Slave's Narrative.* Ed. Charles T. Davis and Henry Louis Gates, Jr. Oxford: Oxford University Press, 1985. 148–75.

"On Writing About Negroes." *Opportunity* (Aug. 1925): 227–28.

"One Negro Boy's Record." *Opportunity* (June 1923): 27.

Opportunity. New York: National Urban League. Jan. 1923–.

"An Opportunity for Negro Writers." *Opportunity* (Sept. 1924): 258.

"Opportunity Literary Contest." *Opportunity* (Aug. 1924): 228.

"Our Young Negro Artists." *Opportunity* (Jan. 1923): 16–18.

"Out of the Shadow." *Opportunity* (May 1925): 131.

Overton, B. W. "The Cincinnati 'Y.'" *Opportunity* (Feb. 1923): 14.

Ovington, Mary White. "Early Years of the NAACP and the Urban League." *Black and White Sat Down Together: Reminiscences of an NAACP Founder.* Ed. Ralph E. Luker. New York: Feminist Press at City University of New York, 1995. 66–71.

———. [M. W. O.] "Mary Dunlap Maclean." *The Crisis* (Aug. 1912): 184–85.

———. *The Walls Came Tumbling Down.* New York: Arno Press and The New York Times, 1969.

Painter, Nell Irvin. "Representing Truth: Sojourner Truth's Knowing and Becoming Known." *Journal of American History* 81.2 (Sept. 1994): 461–92.

———. *Soujourner Truth: A Life, A Symbol.* New York: Norton, 1996.

———. *Standing at Armageddon: The United States, 1877–1919.* New York: Norton, 1987.

Parris, Guichard, and Lester Brooks. *Blacks in the City: A History of the National Urban League.* Boston: Little, Brown and Company: 1971.

Pearson, Ralph L. "Combatting Racism with Art: Charles S. Johnson and the Harlem Renaissance." *American Studies* 18.1 (1977): 123–34.

Perkins, Huel D. "Wallace Thurman: Renaissance 'Renegade'?" *Black World* (Feb. 1976): 29–35.

Perloff, Marjorie. *The Futurist Moment: Avant-Garde, Avant Guerre, and the Language of Rupture.* Chicago: University of Chicago Press, 1986.

Petesch, Donald A. *A Spy in the Enemy's Country: The Emergence of Modern Black Literature.* Iowa City: University of Iowa Press, 1989.

Powell, Richard J. "Re/Birth of a Nation." *Rhapsodies in Black* 14–33.

Preston, Dickson J. *Young Frederick Douglass: The Maryland Years.* Baltimore: Johns Hopkins University Press, 1980.

Quarles, Benjamin. *Frederick Douglass.* 1948. Studies in American Negro Life. Ed. August Meier. New York: Atheneum, 1968.

Raaberg, Gwen. "Beyond Fragmentation: Collage as Feminist Strategy in the Arts." *Mosaic* 31.3 (Sept. 1998). *Expanded Academic ASAP.* InfoTrac. Wichita State University Libraries, Wichita, Kan. 5 Feb. 2002. http://web5.infotrac.galegroup.com/.

Rampersad, Arnold. *The Art and Imagination of W. E. B. Du Bois.* Cambridge, Mass.: Harvard University Press, 1976.

———. "Introduction." Locke, ed., *The New Negro,* 1992. ix–xxiii.

———. "Langston Hughes: The Man, the Writer, and His Continuing Influence." *Langston Hughes: The Man, His Art, and His Continuing Influence.* Critical Studies in Black Life and Culture. Ed. C. James Trotman. New York: Garland, 1995. 21–34.

Reiss, Winold. "Ancestral: a Type Study." Locke, ed., *The New Negro,* page facing 242.

———. "Aztec Indian from Tepozotlan, Mexico." Stewart 1.

———. "The Brown Madonna." Locke, ed., *The New Negro,* frontispiece.

———. "Four Portraits of Negro Women." Locke, ed., "Harlem," 685–88.

———. "Harlem Types." Locke, ed., "Harlem," 651–54.

———. Untitled. (Portrait of Alain Locke.) Locke, ed., *The New Negro,* page facing 6.

Rhapsodies in Black: Art of the Harlem Renaissance. London: Hayward Gallery; London: Institute of International Visual Arts; Berkeley: University of California Press, 1997.

Richardson, Willis. "Compromise: A Folk Play." Locke, ed., *The New Negro,* 168–95.

———. "The Hope of a Negro Drama." *The Crisis* (Nov. 1919): 338–39.

Richepin, Jean. "The Treasure of the Poor." Trans. Jessie Fauset. Illustrated by Laura Wheeler. *The Crisis* (Dec. 1917): 63–65.

Riis, Jacob A. *How the Other Half Lives: Studies among the Tenements of New York.* 1890. Ed. David Leviatin. The Bedford Series in History and Culture. Boston: Bedford Books—St. Martin's Press, 1996.

Robbins, Richard. *Sidelines Activist: Charles S. Johnson and the Struggle for Civil Rights.* Jackson: University Press of Mississippi, 1996.

Rogers, J. A. "Jazz at Home." Locke, ed., "Harlem," 665–67, 712. Rpt. in Locke, ed., *The New Negro,* 216–24.

Rosenblum, Naomi. *A World History of Photography.* 3rd ed. New York: Abbeville Press, 1997.

Rounds, Helen. "Reform Journalism, Exposés, and Crusading." Sloan and Parcell, eds., 219–28.

Rudwick, Elliott M. "W. E. B. Du Bois in the Role of *Crisis* Editor." *Journal of Negro History* 43.3 (July 1958): 214–40.

———. *W. E. B. Du Bois: Propagandist of Negro Protest.* New York: Atheneum, 1978.

Ruether, Rosemary Radford. "Mary in U.S. Catholic Culture." *National Catholic Reporter* 31.15 (10 February 1995). *Expanded Academic ASAP.* InfoTrac. Wichita

State University Libraries, Wichita, Kan. 11 Dec. 1998. http://web3.searchbank. com/infotrac/.

Schomburg, Arthur A. "The Negro Digs Up His Past." Locke, ed., "Harlem," 670–72. Rpt. in Locke, ed., *The New Negro,* 231–37.

Schuyler, George. *Black No More.* 1931. New York: Macmillan, 1971.

Schwarz, A. B. *Gay Voices of the Harlem Renaissance.* Bloomington: Indiana University Press, 2003.

Scott, Esther Fulks. "Negroes as Actors in Serious Plays." *Opportunity* (Apr. 1923): 20–23.

Scruggs, Charles. "Alain Locke and Walter White: Their Struggle for Control of the Harlem Renaissance." *Black American Literature Forum* 14 (1980): 91–99.

———. *The Sage in Harlem: H. L. Mencken and the Black Writers of the 1920s.* Baltimore: Johns Hopkins University Press, 1984.

Sekula, Allan. "The Body and the Archive." *The Contest of Meaning: Critical Histories of Photography.* Ed. Richard Bolton. 1989. Cambridge, Mass.: MIT Press, 1999. 343–89.

Silvera, Edward. "Finality." *Fire!!* 18.

———. "Jungle Taste." *Fire!!* 18.

Simmons, Charles A. *The African American Press: A History of News Coverage during National Crises, with Special Reference to Four Black Newspapers, 1827–1965.* Jefferson, N.C.: McFarland, 1998.

Singh, Amritjit, William S. Shiver, and Stanley Brodwin, eds. *The Harlem Renaissance: Revaluations.* New York: Garland, 1989.

Sloan, W. David, and Lisa Mullikin Parcell, eds. *American Journalism: History, Principles, Practices.* Jefferson, N.C.: McFarland, 2002.

Smith, Charles Michael. "Bruce Nugent: Bohemian of the Harlem Renaissance." *In the Life: A Black Gay Anthology.* Ed. Joseph Beam. Boston: Alyson, 1986. 209–20.

Spencer, Anne. "Lady, Lady." Locke, ed., *The New Negro,* 148.

Spencer, Jon Michael. *New Negroes and Their Music: The Success of the Harlem Renaissance.* Knoxville: University of Tennessee Press, 1997.

Stange, Maren. *Symbols of Ideal Life: Social Documentary Photography in America, 1890–1950.* New York: Cambridge University Press, 1989.

Stewart, Jeffrey C. *To Color America: Portraits by Winold Reiss.* Washington, D.C.: Smithsonian Institution Press for the National Portrait Gallery, 1989.

Strother, T. Ella. "The Race-Advocacy Function of the Black Press." *Black American Literature Forum* 12.3 (Autumn 1978): 92–99.

Sullivan, Robert. "The Mystery of Mary." *Life* (19 Dec. 1996). *Expanded Academic ASAP.* InfoTrac. Wichita State University Libraries, Wichita, Kan. 11 Dec. 1998. http://web3.searchbank.com/infotrac/.

Tambling, Jeremy. "Dangerous Crossings: Dickens, Digression, and Montage." *Yearbook of English Studies* 26 (1996): 43–53.

Taylor, Graham Romeyn. "Race Relations and Public Opinion." *Opportunity* (July 1923): 197–200.

Teitelbaum, Matthew, ed. *Montage and Modern Life, 1919–1942.* Cambridge, Mass.: MIT Press and Boston: The Institute of Contemporary Art, 1992.

Thurman, Wallace. "Cordelia the Crude." *Fire!!* 5–6.

————. "Editorial." Thurman, ed., 73–74.

————. "Fire Burns: A Department of Comment." *Fire!!* 47–48.

————. *Infants of the Spring.* 1932. Boston: Northeastern University Press, 1992.

————. "Negro Artists and the Negro." *New Republic* (31 Aug. 1927): 37–39.

————. "Nephews of Uncle Remus." *Independent* (24 Sept. 1927): 296–98.

————. "A Stranger at the Gates." Rev. of *Nigger Heaven,* by Carl Van Vechten. *The Messenger* (Sept. 1926): 279.

————. "A Thrush at Eve With an Atavistic Wound." Rev. of *Flight,* by Walter White. *The Messenger* (May 1926): 154.

————, ed. *Harlem: A Forum of Negro Life* 1.1 (Nov. 1928). Rpt. in *Black Writers Interpret the Harlem Renaissance.* Ed. Cary D. Wintz. New York: Garland, 1996. 51–102.

Toomer, Jean. *Cane.* 1923. New York: Norton, 1988.

Trachtenberg, Alan. *Reading American Photographs: Images as History, Mathew Brady to Walker Evans.* 1989. New York: Hill and Wang—Farrar, Straus and Giroux, 1996.

"Two Artists." *Opportunity* (Oct. 1926): 314–15.

Urry, John. *The Tourist Gaze: Leisure and Travel in Contemporary Societies.* Theory, Culture and Society. Ed. Mike Featherstone. London: Sage, 1990.

Van Biema, David. "Mary, so Contrary: Two New Books Re-examine the Virgin Mother, a Popular Favorite with a Checkered Doctrinal Past." *Time* (23 Dec. 1996). *Expanded Academic ASAP.* InfoTrac. Wichita State University Libraries, Wichita, Kan. 11 Dec. 1998. http://web3.searchbank.com/infotrac/.

Van Notten, Eleonore. *Wallace Thurman's Harlem Renaissance.* Costerus New Series 93. Ed. C. C. Barfoot, Hans Bertens, Theo D'haen, and Erik Kooper. Amsterdam: Rodopi, 1994.

"The Waco Horror." *The Crisis* (July 1916). Supplement: 1–8.

Walden, Daniel. "'The Canker Galls . . . ,' or, The Short Promising Life of Wallace Thurman." *The Harlem Renaissance Re-examined.* Ed. Victor A. Kramer. Georgia State Literary Studies 2. Ed. Victor A. Kramer. New York: AMS, 1987. 200–11.

Wall, Cheryl A. *Women of the Harlem Renaissance.* Bloomington: Indiana University Press, 1995.

Walrond, Eric. "The Palm Porch." Locke, ed., *The New Negro,* 115–26.

Washington, Booker T., N. B. Wood, and Fannie Barrier Harris. *A New Negro for a New Century.* Chicago, 1900. Miami: Mnemosyne, 1969.

Washington, Johnny. *Alain Locke and Philosophy: A Quest for Cultural Pluralism.* Contributions in Afro-American and African Studies 94. New York: Greenwood, 1986.

Watson, Steven. *The Harlem Renaissance: Hub of African-American Culture, 1920–1930.* Circles of the Twentieth Century. New York: Pantheon Books, 1995.

"W. E. B. Du Bois." *The Messenger* (July 1918): 27–28. Rpt. Mar. 1919.

"We Begin a New Year." *Opportunity* (Jan. 1925): 2.

Weingrod, Carmi. "Collage, Montage, Assemblage." *American Artist* 58 (Apr. 1994). *Expanded Academic ASAP.* InfoTrac. Wichita State University Libraries, Wichita, Kan. 8 July 2003. http://web7.infotrac.galegroup.com/.

Weiss, Nancy J. *The National Urban League, 1910–1940.* New York: Oxford University Press, 1974.

West, Dorothy. "Elephant's Dance: A Memoir of Wallace Thurman." *Black World* 20.1 (Nov. 1970): 77–85.

Wettlaufer, Alexandra K. "Ruskin and Laforgue: Visual-Verbal Dialectics and the Poetics/Politics of Montage." *Comparative Literature Studies* 32.4 (1995): 514–35.

Wheatley, Phillis. *Poems on Various Subjects, Religious and Moral.* 1773. *The Collected Works of Phillis Wheatley.* Ed. John C. Shields. The Schomburg Library of Nineteenth Century Black Women Writers. Ed. Henry Louis Gates, Jr. New York: Oxford University Press, 1988. 1–127.

White, Walter. "The Burning of Jim McIlherron: An NAACP Investigation." *The Crisis* (May 1918): 16–20.

———. "Color Lines." Locke, ed., "Harlem," 680–82. Rpt. as "The Paradox of Color" in Locke, ed., *The New Negro,* 361–68.

"Why We Are." *Opportunity* (Feb. 1923): 3.

Wilson, Simon. *Beardsley.* 1976. Enlarged ed. Oxford: Phaidon, 1983.

Wintz, Cary D. *Black Culture and the Harlem Renaissance.* 1988. College Station: Texas A&M University Press, 1996.

Without Sanctuary: Lynching Photography in America. Santa Fe, N.Mex.: Twin Palms, 2000.

Wolseley, Roland E. *The Black Press, U. S. A.* 2nd ed. Ames: Iowa State University Press, 1990.

Wright, Julia M. "'The Order of Time': Nationalism and Literary Anthologies, 1774–1831." *Papers on Language and Literature* 33.4 (Fall 1997): 339–65.

Wright, Richard. *Native Son.* New York: Harper & Row, 1940.

Wright, Shirley Haynes. "A Study of the Fiction of Wallace Thurman." Diss. East Texas State University, 1983. *DAI* 44.11 (May 1984): 3385–A.

Yellin, Jean Fagan. "An Index of Literary Materials in *The Crisis,* 1910–1934: Articles, Belles Lettres, and Book Reviews." *CLA Journal* 14 (1971): 452–65; 15 (1971): 197–234.

INDEX

ANNE ELIZABETH CARROLL is Associate Professor of
English at Wichita State University.